Exploring the Religions of our World

Nancy Clemmons, SNJM

ave maria press · notre dame, indiana

Nihil Obstat:
Reverend Michael Heintz
Censor liborum

Imprimatur:
Most Reverend John M. D'Arcy
Bishop of Fort Wayne-South Bend

Given at Fort Wayne, IN on 10 December 2007.

The *Nihil Obstat* and *Imprimatur* are official declarations that a book or pamphlet is free of doctrinal or moral error. No implication is contained therein that those who have granted the *Nihil Obstat* and *Imprimatur* agree with its contents, opinions, or statements expressed. The *Nihil Obstat* applies specifically to those parts of the text that are concerned with a presentation of Christianity and Catholicism.

Passages from Jewish Holy Scriptures are taken from *The Holy Scriptures According to the Masoretic Text* (2 vols.), Philadelphia: The Jewish Publications Society of America, 1955.

Christian Scripture passages are taken from *The New American Bible with Revised New Testament*, copyright © 1988 by the Confraternity of Christian Doctrine, Washington, D.C. All rights reserved.

English translation of the *Catechism of the Catholic Church* for the United States of America copyright © 1994, United States Catholic Conference, Inc.— Libreria Editrice Vaticana. Used with permission.

Founded in 1865, Ave Maria Press is a ministry of the Indiana Province of Holy Cross.

www.avemariapress.com

ISBN-10 1-59471-125-9   ISBN-13 978-1-59471-125-1

Project Editor: Michael Amodei.

Cover, Text design and Photo Research: Katherine Robinson Coleman.

Photography credits: page 416.

Printed and bound in the United States of America.

Contents

Engaging Minds, Hearts, and Hands for Faith

An education that is complete is one in which the hands and heart are engaged as much as the mind. We want to let our students try their learning in the world and so make prayers of their education.

Fr. Basil Moreau,
Founder of the Congregation of Holy Cross

This text encourages you to study several world religions and other Christian denominations with "high regard for the manner of life and conduct, the precepts and doctrine." Although different from our own, they offer a glimpse at God's truth that enlightens all men and women. This task is encouraged through:

surveying the origins, teachings and practices of other religions for a greater understanding of the differences with Catholicism as well as opportunities for sharing.

entering into fraternal discussions with prudence and charity with members of other religions.

following Christ's mandate to preach the Gospel to the "ends of the earth" in both words and actions.

Beginning the Journey

1

● Setting the Stage

We literally live in a global village. All around us are images, sounds, and even smells of people with racial, ethnic, cultural, and religious backgrounds other than our own. We see it in our shopping malls, along our market streets, on the information superhighway, on the television, at the movies, in our schools, and, perhaps, even in our homes. We hear it on our streets, in our buses, at the stadium, and on our radios. As a high school student, you live in a somewhat protected environment with adult guardians to help guide you. Once you leave high school, however, you are on your own as you encounter the world as an adult. One of the major roles of high school is to prepare its students to live as responsible, thinking, productive, loving, active Catholic adults in a very diverse global village.

Religious diversity abounds in our world. It is most prevalent in large cities. Just look at London, Sydney, Montreal, Toronto, Paris, Frankfurt, Johannesburg, Bombay, Singapore, New York, Los Angeles, San Francisco, and Chicago. The religious diversity is more the richer because one may find not only Buddhists in many of these mentioned cities, but

Buddhists from such diverse places as Japan, India, and Vietnam. Not only can Christians be found in all these places, but they may be Roman Catholics, Chaldean Catholics, Russian Orthodox, Church of England, German Lutherans, and Southern Baptists.

This is not just another religion textbook. This book is about religion itself. In other religion classes, you learned about one particular religious tradition. In studying Christianity and specifically Catholicism, you most likely took classes on such topics as Jesus of Nazareth, the Hebrew Scriptures, the New Testament, Sacraments, Morality, Justice and Peace, and Church History. A class on the world's religions is different. Rather than an in-depth study of one religious tradition, this class is an overview of religious traditions other than, yet including, Catholicism. This book challenges Catholic students to proclaim in word and deed Jesus Christ as the way, the truth, and the light and, through the inspiration of the Holy Spirit, dialogue with and learn from other religious traditions.

You are probably familiar with the term "world religions." It refers to those religious traditions that are worldwide such as

Buddhism, Christianity, and Islam. Adherents to world religions can be found on most continents, that is, in the northern, southern, eastern, and western parts of the globe. In this class, you will study worldwide religious traditions. In addition, you will study religious traditions that have great significance, but are not as widespread. For example, you will study Hinduism. While 95 percent of Hindus live on the subcontinent of India, the other 5 percent live in other parts of the globe. Among other things, Hinduism's significance can be seen in its great number of adherents as well as the fact that it is foundational in the rise of Buddhism.

➤ Of what religious diversity are you aware in your geographic region?

➤ Before reading further, how would you define religion?

What Is Religion?

Though we glibly use the word religion, the vast majority of scriptures used by the various religions, including the Bible, do not even have the word "religion" in them. Until modern times, religion was not separated from the rest of life. In birth and death, work and play, relationships with people, and connections with nature, what we now call religion was once—and for many cultures still is—all wrapped up in the fabric of life.

Even now a definition of religion is elusive. It is derived from the Latin word *religio*, meaning "to bind." Under the name of religion, a person or community "bound" itself to something that was worthy of reverence or respect. Generally, certain obligations came along with this willingness to have strong ties with that which was over and beyond them. Asking people to define religion, we hear phrases like "worshipping God," "living a moral life," or "one's belief system." Religion is not just one thing. Imagining the many aspects of the world's religions, the spectrum of religious expression is boundless.

Why Study the World's Religions?

You may wonder, "If religion cannot be defined and if religious expression is boundless, why study the various religions?" This is a fair question. Until very recently, the study of religion was a peculiarly Western discipline. At first glance, it may seem impossible to get a handle on what has already been described above as elusive. On the other hand, there are some patterns or elements that could be included in a systematic study of religion. Reasons to study the world's religions include the following:

- To gain a clearer understanding of one's own faith, which in turn enables a person to be more committed to and thus grow in his or her own religious tradition.

- To assist a person in being more open and accepting of people who, on the surface, seem very different.

- To dispel fears and misunderstandings relating to persons of other religious traditions.

- To gain a better insight into human beings by understanding their religious activities.

- To gain a better understanding of the history of humankind's various civilizations, since religion is almost always an important factor.

- To gain a better understanding of the various cultures around the globe today.

- To learn from some of the world's great sources of wisdom.

> **Which of the listed reasons best describe why you are studying the world's religions?**

A Different Religion Class

As you no doubt have already experienced, religion classes are different from any other class. Putting it succinctly, a religion class calls upon learning in both the head and the heart. More than any other class, religion classes call upon one to deal with facts and experiences. Like other subjects, religion does deal with the rational. Unlike other subjects, topics such as life and death, good and evil, love and hate, joy and sorrow, and questions like where we came from, why we are here, and where we are going are integral to religion classes. What is unique about studying the world's religions as compared to studying one's own religion is that each religious tradition addresses and interprets these, and other experiences, differently.

Studying with a New Attitude

As students of the world's religions, we are asked not to pass judgment upon the various religious traditions. As the documents of the Second Vatican Council state:

> The Catholic Church rejects nothing which is true and holy in these religions. She looks with sincere respect upon those ways of conduct and of life, those rules and teaching which, though differing in many particulars from what she holds and sets forth, nevertheless often reflect a ray of that Truth which enlightens all. (*Nostra Aetate, 2*)

We are asked to suspend judgment as to the truth claims of a religious tradition and accept the tradition on its own terms. Not only does Catholicism have something to teach other religious traditions, but all of the religions that we will study have something to teach us. We are asked to engender an attitude of *empathy*. The word "empathy" means to identify and understand the situation of another. In other words, as we study some of the world's religions, we are asked—to paraphrase a Native American proverb—to "walk a mile in the moccasins of another."

We are not asked to accept what others believe and practice. Rather, we are asked to be humble, open, and respectful. As Pope Benedict XVI once wrote, "Equality, which is a presupposition of interreligious dialogue, refers to the equal personal dignity of the parties in dialogue . . ." (*Dominus Jesus, #22*). Pope John Paul II also emphasized this attitude in his encyclical *Redemptoris Missio*:

> Those engaged in this dialogue must be consistent with their own religious traditions and convictions, and be open to understanding those of the other party without pretense or closed-mindedness, but with truth, humility

and frankness, knowing that dialogue can enrich each side. There must be no abandonment of principles or false irenicism, but instead a witness given and received for mutual advancement on the road of religious inquiry and experience, and at the same time for the elimination of prejudice, intolerance and misunderstandings. Dialogue leads to inner purification and conversion which, if pursued with docility to the Holy Spirit, will be spiritually fruitful. (56)

When our journey is completed, we are able to return with more insight into our Catholic faith, which "proclaims and must ever proclaim Christ, 'the way, the truth and the life' (John 14:6), in whom we find the fullness of religious life, and in whom God has reconciled all things to himself" (cf. 2 Cor 5:18–19).[1]

Setting the Context of Catholics in Dialogue

Before becoming Pope John XXIII, Angelo Roncalli was a Vatican diplomat to Turkey and Greece. There he was in contact with Greek Orthodox Christians and Muslims. During World War II, Roncalli helped thousands of Jews escape death under the Nazis. As Pope John, he continued to work toward Christian unity. In his first encyclical, *Ad Cathedram Petri*, Pope John XXIII referred to Protestants as "separated brethren" rather than heretics. After centuries of strained relations between Catholics and Anglicans and Catholics and Eastern Orthodox, the pope received the Archbishop of Canterbury, Geoffrey Fisher, at the Vatican and sent a delegation to greet the Patriarch of Constantinople, Athanagoras I.

Pope John was interested not only in improving relations between Catholics and other Christians. With his deep affection and respect for the Jewish people, Pope John XXIII had the

egregiously offensive language of praying
for the "perfidious Jews" removed from
the Good Friday **liturgy**. Rejection of the
Jews was later soundly denounced during
the Second Vatican Council (*Notra Aetate*
4; *cf. CCC*, 839).

liturgy

A definite set of forms for public religious worship, the official public worship of the Church. The Seven Sacraments, especially the Eucharist, are the primary forms of liturgical celebrations.

These gestures of respect for persons
of other religious traditions may seem
minor today, but in the early 1960s, they
were tremendously significant. Before the
pontificate of Pope John XXIII, Catholics
were not allowed to step foot in a Protestant church other than
to attend a funeral. As late as 1960, one could still hear and read
Catholic leaders calling Protestants "heretics," Eastern
Orthodox Christians "schismatics," Muslims "infidels," and
Jews "Christ killers."

It was Pope John XXIII's vision that the Catholic Church
not set itself *against* the world, but engage in dialogue *with* the
world. Dialoguing with people of various religious traditions
was part of that vision. With the promulgation of the Second
Vatican Council in October 1962, Pope John wanted it to be a
truly Ecumenical Council. To that end, not only were there
over 2,200 bishops from across the world in attendance at
the opening session, but a number of leaders from other religious traditions were invited as observers of the Council. In
attendance were Protestant, Anglican, Eastern Orthodox, and
Jewish leaders. Pope John XXIII died after the convening of
only one of the four sessions of the Second Vatican Council.
His successor, Pope Paul VI, and the bishops of the Council
continued in the direction of Pope John XXIII's vision.

Benefits of the Council

Three of the sixteen documents that came out of the
Second Vatican Council set an impetus for Catholics to dialogue with other Christians and non-Christians alike. The
Declaration on Human Freedom (*Dignitatis Humanae*) addresses the right of the individual to social and civil freedom with

regard to religious matters. The Decree on Ecumenism (*Unitates Redintegratio*) speaks to the Catholic Church's relationship with other Christians, while the relations with non-Christian religious traditions is spoken to in the Declaration on the Relation of the Church to Non-Christian Religions (*Nostra Aetate*).

The words of these documents are extremely important in setting Catholics on a path to respect and dialogue with persons not of their religious persuasion. The pontificates of Popes Paul VI and John Paul II put the words and spirit of these documents into action by following and expanding on the example of Pope John XXIII.

ecumenism

The movement, inspired and led by the Holy Spirit, that seeks the union of all Christian faiths and eventually the unity of all peoples throughout the world.

For example, Pope Paul VI was very interested in **ecumenism** and religious freedom. He not only met with the Patriarch of Constantinople, Athanagoras I, but they issued a joint resolution at the end of the Council in December 1965, regretting the mutual excommunication of 1054. Pope Paul met with two Archbishops of Canterbury, Michael Ramsey and Donald Cogan. With the latter, they issued a joint declaration to seek unity.

Pope John Paul II was the most traveled pope in history. On his visits, he made it a point to sit down and talk with the various religious leaders of the region. In 1986 and again in 2002 he invited religious leaders from all over the world to Assisi, Italy, for a World Day of Prayer for Peace. John Paul II was the first pope since St. Peter, as far as history can tell, to visit a synagogue. He was the first pope to visit a mosque as he did in Damascus, Syria. He supported serious theological dialogue with Lutherans resulting in a document called the *Joint Declaration on the Doctrine of Justification*. Serious about healing the wounds between Catholicism and Eastern Orthodox churches, Pope John Paul II worked mightily for that cause. The success of Pope John Paul II's outreach to members of religious communities all over the world can be seen by the number and diversity of religious leaders who attended his funeral at the Vatican in April 2005.

Ecumenical Dialogue Is a Duty of All Catholics

As people baptized in Christ Jesus, all Catholics are called to evangelize the world (*CCC*, 849). In the most common usage of the word, **evangelization** is understood as desiring to convert others to Catholic Christianity. Yet, we live in a world of great religious diversity, full of people with their own strong religious convic-tions. How can Catholics engage in dia-

evangelization

From the root word for "gospel," the "sharing of the Good News."

logue with persons of other religious traditions without the expectation that one must try to convert them? The Catholic Church is very clear that there is no con-flict in dialogue and proclamation. In dia-logue, Catholics are evangelizing by **witnessing** to their faith without the need of trying to get people to change their reli-gious allegiance.

witnessing

Giving testimony of one's religious faith to another.

God, who is the Father of all, offers the gift of salvation to all the nations. Through the grace of the Holy Spirit, who is also at work outside the visible limits of the Church, people in every part of the world seek to adore God in an authentic way.

The scriptures of other religions point to a future of com-munion with God, of purification and salvation, and they encourage people to seek the truth and defend the values of life, holiness, justice, peace, and freedom. When Christians engage in interreligious dialogue, they bring with them their faith in Jesus Christ, the only Savior of the world. This same faith teaches them to recognize the authentic religious experiences of others and to listen to them in a spirit of humility, in order to discover and appreciate every ray of truth from wherever it comes. (See *John Paul II, General Audience*, November 29, 2000.)

People from other religious traditions, too, can be recipients of God's grace (*CCC*,847). Jesus Christ is the Savior of all peo-ple. He established the Church as the ordinary means of salva-tion because the Church possesses the fullness of the means of salvation (*CCC*, 846). In July 2007 Pope Benedict XVI issued a statement that reiterated the primacy of the Catholic Church because of its apostolic succession by which it can offer the "means of salvation." While this statement attracted some negative reaction in the secular media, a spokesperson for the Vatican emphasized that the Church was "not backtracking on ecumenical commitment." The Church teaches that people of other religious traditions can be saved by Christ outside the ordinary means of salvation:

> Those who, through no fault of their own, do not know the Gospel of Christ or his Church, but who nevertheless seek God with a sincere heart, and moved by grace, try in their actions to do his will as they know it through the dictates of their conscience—those too may achieve eternal salvation. (*CCC*, 847)

Since evangelization is the mission of the Church and dialogue with other religious traditions is part of that mission, how can one go about fulfilling one's obligation? There are many avenues of dialogue, but one must never forget that the Holy Spirit is present with us in this task. As we evangelize according to the gifts given by God, so we participate in dialogue with others according to our gifts.

Dialogue can be through words, actions, or both. For example, youth groups from various religious traditions getting together to care for people who have been displaced because of man-made or natural disasters is a type of dialogue. Meeting socially and sharing experiences from the positions of each's respective religious tradition is a dialogue. Classroom sharing on experiences such as prayer, God, how families celebrate a religious festival, or what symbols in their religious tradition are most meaningful to them is a dialogue in which each of you can participate right now. You are not asked to be a specialist in each one's religious tradition in order to participate in interreligious dialogue. You only have to share your faith experiences and listen intently while others share theirs.

Of course, participating in this class is a form of dialogue with other religious traditions.

> **What images and thoughts come to you when you hear the word "evangelize"?**

Some Common Elements or Patterns of Religions

Since asking the question "What is religion?" finds our attempts in defining the term "religion" elusive, our study of some of the world's religions will address a slightly different issue. We will look at "what a religion is" rather than "what is religion." In addressing "what a religion is" we can then see that there are some common elements or patterns that can be broadly categorized as aspects of a religious tradition. These aspects or dimensions are not compartmentalized but overlap.

> Before reading the next section, answer the following questions: Why was humankind created? Why are we here? What is the ultimate goal of humankind? What is the origin of Catholicism?

Sacred Stories and Sacred Scriptures

Most religious traditions have stories that tell how the world came to be, how humans, plants, and animals were created and why, and where we are going. Some of these sacred stories, particularly creation stories, are commonly called **myths**. They are not false stories but truth stories—they are intended to convey sacred truths. For some religious traditions, these sacred stories are part of sacred history. Certain core historical events—for example, the birth of Muhammad, the Exodus of the Jews, or the death of Jesus—have become part of that religion's sacred history.

myths

Traditional or ancient stories that help to provide a worldview of a people by explaining their creation, customs, or ideals.

These events are known as empirical history, that is, history verifiable or provable from other sources. Generally, these stories were first passed on orally. Later, some sacred stories became part of the collective memory of the adherents of a religious tradition and often defined them as a community.

The history of a particular religious community often involves myths, sacred history, and empirical history. For example, the story of the Jews includes creation stories, the sacred history of the patriarchs, prophets, and a nomadic tribe, and the centuries of empirical history up to the establishment of the State of Israel in the twentieth century.

We know so many sacred stories because they move from the oral telling of the story through the ages to the writing of the sacred stories into some form that renders them sacred scripture. The Upanishads, the Bhagavad Gita, the Qur'an, and the Bible are all considered not just any writings, but sacred writings. For some religions, their sacred scriptures are considered inspired by God or the gods while others consider their sacred scriptures as the exact word of God or the gods. There are other writings that contain sacred stories that do not have the authority of sacred scripture. For Muslims, there are stories about Muhammad collected into the *Hadith*. For Christians, there are the many lives of the saints. For Jews, there are the many stories told by spiritual leaders known as rebbes of Eastern Europe. Whether sacred stories are codified into sacred scripture or not, they help bring together and unite, preserve, and perpetuate a community of people who have similar beliefs and values. One of the major ways sacred stories are passed on is through ritual.

➤ **What public and personal roles does Scripture play in Christianity?**

Beliefs and Practices

➤ **Comment on this statement: "What you pray is what you believe."**

Though not all religious traditions have a formal set of beliefs, there are certain truths held by each that separate one religious tradition from another. Buddhism and Christianity have well-formulated doctrines. The Four Noble Truths and the Noble Eight-Fold Path are clearly delineated Buddhist doctrines. The Apostles' Creed is a formal statement of Christian beliefs. Though the *Sh'ma* is the one formal doctrine of Judaism and the *Shahadah* is the one formal doctrine of Islam, this does not mean that Judaism and Islam have nothing to say about human nature, sin, and how to relate to widows and orphans. Often individuals or groups communicate their beliefs through how they act or how they explain their actions when faced with such issues rather than through formal doctrinal statements. The beliefs of the faithful of the various religious traditions are acted out in the vertical and the horizontal. The vertical is how adherents relate to the divine, while the horizontal is how adherents relate to both believers and non-believers.

Practices are part of every religious tradition. Some practices may be as simple as a child's bedtime prayers or as formal as the Eastern Orthodox Divine Liturgy. Practices can be personal or communal. Prayer, meditation, and ritual washing can be personal practices, while the sacrifice of animals, going on pilgrimage, or participating in a sacred meal can be communal practices. The more formal the ritual, the more likely the practice is based on at least one sacred story. For example, in the Book of Exodus, God exhorts Jews to remember and recount his saving power in the Exodus of their spiritual ancestors from the slavery of Egypt to the freedom of the Promised Land. Thus arose the annual Jewish celebration of Pesach, or Passover, held every spring.

Observing a person's behavior is a way of detecting his or her beliefs. For example, witnessing our Muslim neighbors praying several times a day tells us that prayer is very important to Muslims. Noticing that many Protestant churches have a pulpit front and center tells us that preaching is important to Protestant Christians.

Each religious tradition has some sort of moral code—written or unwritten—that guides adherents in the conduct expected. It is through proper beliefs and behaviors that one is considered a good Buddhist or a good Hindu. However, some religious traditions place more emphasis on behavior than beliefs while other religious traditions place more emphasis on beliefs than behavior. For many religious traditions, these behaviors also determine how one will spend the next life or eternal life. For a number of religious traditions, the moral code is found in, or at least based upon, their sacred stories and sacred scriptures.

> **Which of your personal behaviors most clearly reflects your religious beliefs?**

Sacred Time

Though most religious traditions consider all time sacred, there are particular times when certain actions or attitudes give greater focus to the sacred. In a sense, participating in a sacred ritual seems to transport an individual or community from ordinary time to sacred time. In another sense, participating in a sacred ritual reminds the participants that all time is sacred. In still another sense, sacred time is timeless. It draws the past and the future to the present so that the adherents can live and cele-brate the now. Whether these times occur daily, weekly, month-ly, yearly or even every seven years, observers are able to document "that time is sacred to them."

Though times for personal devotions often are at the discre-tion of the individual, communal observances are more formal. Muslims have Friday, Jews have Saturday, and Christians have Sunday as their day for weekly observances. Muslims have Ramadan, Jews have Yom Kippur, and most Christians have Lent as annual times of fasting for spiritual renewal and growth. Festivals mark times of celebration for the respective religious traditions. Buddhists celebrate Bodhi Day, Sikhs cele-brate Gobind Singh's birthday, and Hindus celebrate Diwali.

Festivals and religious observances give members of a religious tradition a sense of belonging and are opportunities for personal recommitment and renewal.

Rites of passage are also sacred times. In particular, rites of birth, coming of age, marriage, and death are observed as sacred times in many religious traditions.

> **What times are sacred to you? What do you do to mark those times as sacred?**

Sacred Places and Sacred Spaces

Generally, sacred time is observed and celebrated anywhere. However, sacred time often takes place in a sacred space or at a sacred place. Places where the religious tradition began or where the founder traveled often become sacred places. Hence, Mecca and Medina are sacred places for Muslims. Christians call the State of Israel the Holy Land. Others call places in nature, such as mountains and rivers, sacred places. The Jordan River for Christians and the Ganges River for Hindus come to mind. Mount Sinai is a sacred place to Jews, while Mount Fuji is a sacred place for Shintos. Shrines, temples, churches, mosques, and synagogues are all sacred spaces. Other places can be temporary sacred spaces. For instance, a gym or a large tent can be converted temporarily into sacred space.

Ganges River

> **What places and/or spaces are sacred to you? What makes these places/spaces sacred? How does it feel to move from ordinary places/spaces to sacred places/spaces?**

Other Elements or Patterns

As you study some of the world's religions, the above common elements or patterns found in the various religious traditions will be employed in each chapter. It is like inviting a panel of people from the various religious traditions to speak about their religion. Each speaker is given the same allotted time and each is asked to confine remarks about their respective religious traditions to the following: a brief historical overview, sacred stories and sacred scripture, basic beliefs and practices, sacred time, and sacred places and sacred spaces. Expanding the dialouge, a final section in each chapter views the religion through the lens of Catholicism.

This does not mean there are not other aspects common to religious traditions. In particular, adherents of religious traditions have sacred symbols and objects they use in their various rituals. Some sacred symbols and objects are considered by people both in and out of the religious tradition as beautiful works of art such as the icons of Orthodox Christianity, the architecture of Islam, and the statuary of Hinduism.

Some aspects common, in some way, to all religious traditions are implicit in the chapter description of the various religious traditions. For example, some religious traditions have laws that adherents are to follow. Muslims have the Shar'ia and Jews have the Torah. Some religious traditions have more institutional structure than others. Roman Catholicism has much more institutional structure than Reconstruction Judaism. The various religious traditions have holy people, be they saints, gurus, starets, or mystics, whose lives embody the ideal or point to the divine in their respective religious tradition. Though the holy person, laws, institutional structure, or symbols and objects aspects are not often explicit in the explanation of the religious tradition, they are present and important in any journey in the study of the world's religions.

Finally, we will begin our study of the world's religions with Judaism in Chapter 2, followed by Christianity in Chapter 3. This order is not meant to suggest that these are the two oldest of the world's religions. They are not. However, as a Catholic Christian, the Judeo-Christian religious tradition is the one most familiar to you. This is the purpose for beginning with these religions. By the time you are ready to study the other religions, you will be versed in the pattern of each chapter through the survey of elements that are more familiar to you.

■ Chapter 1 Summary

- ■ Religious diversity abounds in our world, so one of the major tasks of a Catholic is to determine how to remain and grow as a Catholic among such diversity.

- ■ There is a difference between the terms "world religions" and "world's religions."

- ■ Empathy is the attitude one wants to cultivate in studying the world's religions.

- ■ Though difficult to define, the term "religion" traditionally means "to bind."

- ■ Dialogue is the duty of all Catholics, for interreligious dialogue is part of the Catholic Church's mission of evangelization.

- ■ In describing a religious tradition, there are some common elements or patterns to consider including sacred stories and sacred scriptures, beliefs and practices, sacred time, and sacred places and spaces.

■ Chapter 1 Review Questions

1. Briefly describe the religious diversity in our world today.

2. Why use the term "world's religions" rather than "world religions" in studying various religious traditions?

3. In what language did the word "religion" originate? Why do you think it is such a difficult term to define?

4. What attitude is asked of us in studying some of the world's religions? Explain.

5. What makes a class about the world's religions different from other religion classes?

6. What are some reasons for studying the world's religions?

7. Relate some of the ways in which Popes John XXIII, Paul VI, and John Paul II broke ground in the Catholic Church's relationship with other religious traditions.

8. Why is interreligious dialogue a duty of all Catholics? In what ways can a Catholic fulfill this duty?

9. What are some of the common elements or patterns we will employ in our study of some of the world's religions?

Research & Activities

- Use four English dictionaries—a collegiate or concise dictionary, a very large dictionary, a multi-volume dictionary, and a web-based dictionary—to look up the word "religion." After writing down *all* the definitions you find, write your own definition of the word.

- List the common elements or patterns found in religious traditions. Using Catholicism as an example, write down what you know already about each.

- Read and report on statements from Pope Benedict XVI (written either prior to or during his pontificate) that support the Catholic call to ecumenism.

Prayer

This prayer of St. Francis is one that adherents to most religions of the world would be comfortable praying.

Peace Prayer of St. Francis of Assisi

Lord, make me an instrument of your peace;

Where there is hatred, let me sow love;

Where there is injury, pardon;

Where there is doubt, faith;

Where there is despair, hope;

Where there is darkness, light;

And where there is sadness, joy.

Grant that I may not so much seek

To be consoled as to console;

To be understood as to understand;

To be loved as to love;

For it is in giving that we receive;

It is in pardoning that we are pardoned;

And it is in dying that we are born to eternal life.

Judaism

2

A Living Religion

Many Christians think of Judaism as the religion described in the Old Testament. Christians also understand Judaism as the religion practiced by Jesus when he was living on earth. Or, they may think of Judaism as the religion that is still waiting for God's chosen one after not recognizing Jesus as the Messiah. Unfortunately, some Christians have held Jews or Jewish leaders responsible for the crucifixion of Jesus. (The Catholic Church has recently condemned this mistaken view.) Christians are correct in defining Judaism as the religion of the Hebrew Bible, the religion of Jesus, and a religion still longing for God's chosen one. However, these understandings, though true, do not describe the essence of Judaism.

This chapter points out further elements that define Judaism as a living religion. You will look at ways in which Jews express their beliefs through personal and communal prayer, the study of the Torah, and lives lived in holiness before God. Judaism is not based on a set of abstract doctrines. Ideally, what a Jew believes is reflected in how a Jew acts. The actions of a Jew reveal what it means to be part of a historical religious tradition and what the operating values are in a Jew's life. The proclamation of one God, the reverence and study of the Torah, the recognition of Israel as both a nation and a people, and the setting aside of sacred places and times all combine to reveal the religious expression of Judaism.

Before attempting to define Judaism the religion, it is important to first look at what it means to be a Jewish person. To say Judaism is the *religion* of the Jews is not to say that all Jews practice Judaism. Being a Jew has both an ethnic and a religious connotation. Defining who is a Jew is rather difficult for non-Jews to understand. Whereas a Christian is a follower of Christ and a Muslim is an adherent to Islam, a Jew may or may not practice Judaism. Therein lies the confusion. There are *ethnic* Jews and *religious* Jews. A religious Jew practices Judaism. An ethnic Jew

may or may not practice Judaism. A religious Jew may also be an ethnic Jew, but it is just as likely for a religious Jew to be from another ethnic group. Both ethnic Jews and religious Jews are found on virtually every continent. For the purposes of understanding Judaism, the rest of this chapter will focus on an understanding of religious Jews.

BCE (Before Common Era)

ca. 1800	Abraham enters Promised Land
ca. 1250	Moses, Exodus, and reception of the Law
ca. 1200	Re-entry into Promised Land
ca. 1050	Davidic Kingdom
ca. 1000	Written Torah begins
ca. 950	Construction of first Temple in Jerusalem
586	Babylonian exile and destruction of first Temple
537	Return from Babylonian exile
ca. 500	Construction of second Temple begins
331	Jerusalem conquered by Alexander the Great
168	Antiochus IV demands that Jews cease with their rituals in the Temle
165	Maccabean revolt
150	Septuagint compiled

CE (Common Era)

ca. 10	Hillel and Shammai
70	Destruction of second Temple by Romans
ca. 600	Completion of two Talmuds
1000	Golden Age of Judaism commences in Spain
1492	Jews first expelled from Iberian Peninsula
1897	Beginning of Zionist movement
1933	Beginning of Holocaust
1948	Establishment of the State of Israel
1967	The Six-Day War
1993	Oslo Peace Accord between Israelis and Palestinians brokered Israel and Holy See sign fundamental agreement in Jerusalem

1. A Brief History of Judaism

Judaism is the religion of the Jews. It is the religious expression of a people whose history spans thousands of years. Judaism can be dated from the time of Moses, though the seeds of Judaism can be traced to the time of Abraham. From its formation in the Sinai desert, triumphs and tragedies, ambiguities and misunderstandings, laughter and tears have written the history of Judaism and the Jewish people. Though a minority group throughout much of their history, Jews have contributed substantially to the history of the world, particularly the Western world.

Biblical Period

A history of Judaism finds the Jewish people on the move or controlled by foreign governments much of the time. The

Abraham and his family

biblical period often begins with Abraham (ca. 1800 BCE) and concludes with the death of Alexander the Great (323 BCE). Jews believe God called Abraham to leave his country and sojourn to a foreign land. With great faith and obedience to God's will, Abraham and his wife, Sarah, left Ur in Mesopotamia and moved to the land of Canaan along the Fertile Crescent. There, despite many obstacles, God's promise that Abraham and Sarah would have a son and that Abraham would be the "father of all nations" was fulfilled. In Canaan the *habiru*, or Hebrews, formed nomadic tribes. These nomadic tribes gradually settled into an agricultural system.

Generations later, many Hebrew people moved to prosperous Egypt to avoid a major drought in Canaan. Though at first welcomed, they soon found themselves slaves under the power-ful Egyptian government. As slaves, the Hebrew people were a small part of an immense army of people that helped build the majestic cities of Egypt. In approximately 1250 BCE Moses freed the Hebrew people from Egyptian bondage and led them back to Canaan, known to the Hebrew people as the Promised Land. In the forty years they took to return to Canaan, the Hebrew people became a covenantal community, owing their allegiance to one God only. Moses died on the outskirts of Canaan, leaving Joshua to lead the Hebrew people back into the land "flowing with milk and honey." However, after living four hundred years in Egypt, the Hebrews found it necessary to con-quer the inhabitants of Canaan before they could resettle.

Once settled again in Canaan, the Hebrew people became a confederation of tribes and began to establish a powerful kingdom around 1050 BCE under the leadership of Kings Saul, David, and Solomon. A Temple was built in Jerusalem under the patronage of David's son Solomon. Thus, Jerusalem became both the political and religious center of the Hebrew people and remained so for almost one thousand years. As the people became more powerful, they saw less need for the God who once freed them. Prophets such as Samuel and Nathan became more prominent, exhorting the Hebrew people to fol-low the ways of the one God rather than the ways of the neigh-boring Canaanite gods. During this time, the oral tradition of the Hebrew people began to be transcribed into what became known as the *Torah*, a word meaning "law" or "instruction."

After the death of Solomon, the kingdom was divided: the kingdom of Israel to the north with ten tribes and the kingdom of Judah to the south with two tribes. As the kingdoms weakened due to the sin of **idolatry**, Israel and Judah became more vulnerable to outside threats. Israel fell to the Assyrians around 722 BCE, exiling most of the northern kingdom. By 586 BCE, the Babylonians conquered the

idolatry

Giving worship to something or someone other than the one, true God.

Judeans, ravaging their land, destroying their Temple, and send-ing the majority of people to Babylon. Exiled to a foreign land away from the center of their religion where God was worshipped and sacrifices were offered, the captives found a way to strengthen their cultural and religious identity. As prophets had predicted the fall of Judah, so they predicted its rise. Approximately fifty years later, the Persians conquered the Babylonians and allowed Judeans to return to their land. Some chose to stay in Babylon, while others returned to a country that, though destroyed by war, was nevertheless holy because God had given it to them. They would restore the land and rebuild the Temple.

Now living in the land of Judah, the Hebrew people became known as Jews. During this time, the compilation of the Torah was completed. Prophets were becoming less numerous, but their writings kept their words alive for generations to come. In addition, wisdom literature was emerging. Writings such as Psalms, Proverbs, Job, Ruth, Esther, and Chronicles later came to be included in the Hebrew Scriptures.

> **What event marks a defining moment in the history of your family?**

Rabbinic Period

A second major historical period of Judaic history is the *Rabbinic Period*. Also known as *Classical Judaism*, this historical period began in 323 BCE, the year Alexander the Great died. The closing of the period may be dated 625 CE, the year Jerusalem fell to the Islamic army coming out of the Arabian Peninsula. By the end of this era, many Jews found themselves living in a world that was both Christian and Muslim.

Through foreign occupation and conquest over a number of centuries, the Jews found themselves driven from their homeland. This growing number of Jews not living in Judea—as the area around southern Palestine came to be called—was known as the *Diaspora*, for they were dispersed from their land. Late in the fourth century BCE, Alexander the Great was victorious over much of the known world, including Judea. Soon after, the Greek ruler Antiochus IV prohibited the practice of Judaism in Judea and took over the Temple. The Jewish family of the

Maccabees led a revolt against the Greeks in 168 BCE, regaining possession of the Temple in 165 BCE.

The original conquests of Alexander the Great had lasting repercussions and resulted in the **Hellenization** of much of the known world. Judea was no exception. Jews accepted the Hellenistic influences in varying degrees. In Egypt, the city of Alexandria became a thriving Jewish center. Philo of Alexandria was a very prominent Jewish philosopher living around the time of Jesus. Philo was comfortable with integrating Jewish theology and Greek philosophy. The rise of the synagogue and the establishment of centers for Jewish learning were features of this period. The Hebrew Bible was translated into Greek in the third century BCE. It became known as the *Septuagint*, a word meaning "seventy." According to tradition, seventy translators, working independently of one another, came up with exactly the same translated text from the Hebrew translation of the scriptures. It is very likely that some of the New Testament authors were familiar with this Greek translation of the Bible.

Hellenization

The adoption of Greek ways and speech as happened in the case of Jews living in the Diaspora.

Qumran Caves, where the Dead Sea Scrolls were found.

The Rabbinic Period saw tremendous Jewish sectarian development into a variety of competing groups. The three largest groups were the Sadducees, the Pharisees, and the Essenes. The Sadducees were Jews who defined themselves as biological descendants of Zadok, the last high priest before the Babylonian exile. The Sadducees held a strict position in the interpretation of the Torah. Oppositely, the Pharisees held a looser interpretation of the Torah, using oral tradition and popular customs in their interpretation of the Law of Moses. The Pharisees also accepted the doctrine of resurrection while the Sadducees did not. While Sadducees and Pharisees are mentioned in the New Testament, the existence of

Dead Sea Scrolls

Between 1947 and 1956 thousands of fragments of biblical and early Jewish documents were discovered in eleven caves near the site of Khirbet Qumran (previous page) on the shores of the Dead Sea. These important texts have revolutionized our understanding of the way the Bible was transmitted and have illuminated the general cultural and religious background of ancient Palestine, out of which both Rabbinic Judaism and Christianity arose.

rabbi

Hebrew for "My Master" or "My Teacher." A rabbi became known as someone who was authorized to teach and judge in matters of Jewish law.

the Essene community was unknown until 1948. In that year, a young boy found clay jars filled with writing fragments from the Essene community in caves near Qumran. These writings, which became known as the **Dead Sea Scrolls**, indicated the monastic nature of the Essenes and their scrupulosity for the Law.

Greek rule in Judea ended in 63 BCE when the Roman army conquered the region. Romans occupied Judea during much of the Rabbinic Period. In 70 CE, Roman soldiers stormed Jerusalem and destroyed the Temple. At that time, Jews had the choice of disappearing into history or reinterpreting their religious practice without the Temple. They chose the latter. The Sadducee and Pharisee sects disappeared, and **rabbis** gained new prominence. To this day, rabbis are the spiritual leaders in Judaism.

The rabbis began a process of systematically transforming the Temple rituals for practice outside the Temple. Dozens of rabbinical schools sprang up, and with them dozens of different interpretations of how Jews should worship and live their lives. During the time of Jesus, the schools of rabbis Shammai and Hillel were the most notable. A famous story is told about these two men:

A heathen once came to Shammai and said, "I will become a proselyte on the condition that you teach me the entire Torah while I stand on one foot." Shammai chased him away with a builder's measuring stick. When he appeared before Hillel with the same request, Hillel said, "Whatever is hateful to you, do not do to your neighbor. That is the entire Torah. The rest is commentary; go and learn it." (*Mehilta Bahodesh*)

Over the next few centuries, Torah commentaries were finally compiled, codified, and written into two works called the Babylonian Talmud and the Jerusalem (or Palestinian) Talmud. Along with the Torah, the **Talmud** inspires and guides Jews in their religious life.

Also by the end of the first century CE, there was a growing tension between Jews who believed Jesus was the Messiah and Jews who did not. Some Jews were looking

Talmud

Two long collections of Jewish religious literature that are commentaries on the Mishnah, the Hebrew code of laws that emerged about 200 CE.

for the Messiah to be a warrior-king like King David, who would bring an army against their enemies and restore the land of Israel to justice under Jewish sovereignty, enabling the Jews of the Diaspora to return to their homeland. Jesus was not an earthly king, nor did an age of justice return. Both groups used the same Hebrew Bible, but some radically different interpretations emerged. A growing number of Gentiles were becoming followers of Jesus. With the greater number of Gentiles, there was more erosion of Jewish identity among the followers of Jesus. A separation was inevitable. The severance between traditional Jews and Jewish Christians is ambiguous, but by the middle of the second century, distinctions were relatively clear. However, Judaism made an indelible mark upon Christianity that remains with it to this day.

Well into the second century, the emperor Hadrian wanted to establish a Roman city where Jerusalem once thrived. He was interested in establishing a city-state constructing a shrine to the god Jupiter on the site of the Temple Mount. A number of Jews were outraged by such a defilement of a holy place. In 130, Simon bar Kociba, nicknamed bar "Kochba," or "son of the star," led a revolt against the Romans. Hadrian sent in whole legions of soldiers, swiftly putting down all Jewish revolt. He constructed his desired city, built the shrine to Jupiter, changed the name of the land from Judea to Palestine, and banned Jews from ever returning to Jerusalem.

The Jews of the Diaspora fared far better. They were part of the Roman Empire. Not only had they been influenced by Greek culture and civilization, they were now influenced by Roman culture and civilization. Though very different from most other groups of people in the Roman Empire because of their moral standards and their belief in only one God, Romans allowed Jews to live their lives as they wished. In fact, their beliefs and ethics attracted people scattered throughout the Roman Empire to convert to Judaism, to the displeasure of some despotic, decadent Roman rulers. So, also, the number of Christians continually grew.

Like all empires, Rome reached its glory and moved into a long, slow decline politically, economically, and militarily. At the end of the third century, the Emperor Diocletian separated the Empire into eastern and western portions, appointing a leader for each. Of course, powerful men do not like to share power, and Constantine emerged as the victor of the power struggle at the beginning of the fourth century. On the eve of his victory, Constantine believed he had a vision of the cross and that he was to conquer through the power of the cross.

When Constantine became emperor, he desired a worldwide religion for his worldwide empire, and that religion was Christianity. One reason Christianity had been able to blossom was that many of its missionaries went to these Jewish centers in the various cities of the Diaspora. Many Jews were Roman citizens and shared in the privileges of that citizenry. But when Christianity became the official religion of the Roman Empire at the end of the fourth century, Judaism was less prominent and its adherents were treated as inferior. However, by the beginning of the fifth century, the Roman Empire in the west was no more. Its strength resided in the east with the Byzantine Empire, while the west broke into smaller states such as that of the Franks. The leader of Christianity in the west, the pope, or bishop of Rome, once merely a spiritual leader, emerged also as a temporal leader in the once great and now dispirited Rome.

Roman Emperor
Constantine

How can you apply Hillel's teaching of the Torah to your own life?

Medieval Period

During the Medieval Period (638–1783 CE), the Diaspora was moving farther away from Palestine. Jews began to live in places they had never lived before: western, central, and eastern Europe; Asia; the Arabian Peninsula; and portions of North Africa. There was a resurgence of science, mathematics, philosophy and commentaries on the Bible and Talmud. Rabbi Shlomo ben Itsak, a French Jew who became known as "Rashi," wrote commentaries on the Bible and Talmud that most Jews learned at a very young age. Through the development of Jewish philosophy, there were attempts to harmonize reason with faith. The most famous Jewish philosopher was Moses Maimonides. He argued that there was no contradiction between the philosophy of Aristotle and the Jewish religion.

The Medieval Period was also marked by Jewish persecution. At the beginning of the seventh century, another **monotheistic** religion, Islam, came out of the Arabian Peninsula and was in competition with both Judaism and Christianity. Under Muslim rule, Jews were a "protected people" as long as they paid the tax for that protection. They were able to worship as they wished as long as their synagogues were not taller than mosques, and they could conduct their own courts. However, Jews were clearly treated as second-class citizens and there were times when this protection did not hold, and Muslims persecuted the Jews. Just four years after the death of Islam's founder, Muhammad, Muslims invaded Jerusalem, taking it away from the Byzantines. This was a mixed blessing for Jews. The Muslims constructed a beautiful shrine called the Dome of the Rock on the spot where the **Holy of Holies** of the Second Temple once stood. While Jews were outraged over the defilement of such a sacred place, they were not sorry to see the persecuting Byzantine Christians ousted.

monotheistic

Subscribing to the doctrine or belief that there is only one God.

Holy of Holies

The sanctuary inside the tabernacle in the Temple of Jerusalem where the Ark of the Covenant was kept.

While Jews in Jerusalem faced persecutions, the Jews of Babylon were able to flourish under Persian rule. They built great schools and synagogues. In the middle of the eighth century, the Muslims moved their capital from Damascus to Baghdad, very near the Jewish center of Babylonia. Muslims took on the daunting task of reintroducing ancient Greek writings to the medieval world. Jews helped translate the writings from Greek to Arabic for Muslims and from Arabic to Latin for Christians of the West.

From Baghdad, Islamic culture and civilization flourished and Jews were very much a part of the expansion. A large class of Jewish merchants arose. At this point, Muslims and Christians were at odds with each other, and Jews proved to be good mediators between them. Trade between Christians and Muslims happened, but indirectly through the mediation of the Jews, opening up trade routes between east and west. As Muslim empires and trade routes expanded during the Medieval Period, so groups of Jews stretched beyond the borders of the Middle East. While the center of Islam was in Baghdad rather than Damascus, a remnant of Muslims moved early in the eighth century from Damascus to Cordoba, Spain.

It was in Spain where Jews thrived the most during the Medieval Period. Along with Muslims, Jews excelled in such works as science, medicine, philosophy, metal crafts, and trade. Jews of the Mediterranean region became known as *Sephardim*, from a Hebrew word for "Spain." In the twelfth century, however, the Muslim Berbers came to power in Spain and ousted Jews from the country. Among those who had to flee was the family of Moses ben Maimon, known to Jews by his acronym RAMBAM and known in the West as Maimonides. Refugees from their beloved Cordoba, they finally ended up in Egypt. Maimonides wrote in Arabic, since that was his language in Spain. He was a rabbi who earned his living as a physician and worked at the court of the Muslim sultan Saladin in Cairo. He is most famous for his theological and philosophical writings. Along with some Muslim counterparts who were influenced by Greek philosophers such as Aristotle, Maimonides argued that there was no contradiction between Greek philosophy and the teachings of Judaism.

The later years of the Medieval Period brought other persecutions to the Jews. French and German Christian Crusaders marching to Jerusalem to regain the Holy Land from the Muslims burned and destroyed almost all the Jewish communities along the Rhine River, murdering thousands of Jews. Other Jews, along with Muslims and Eastern Christians, were killed when the battle reached Jerusalem in 1099.

It was during this time that Jews in some areas of Europe were forced to wear some sort of clothing and live in areas of a town that would distinguish them from non-Jews. Distinguishing Jews from other members of society and denying them ownership of land was meant to humiliate them. The only way out of such degradation was to convert to Christianity.

Bronze cross worn by eleventh century Crusaders.

The economic system was moving from a barter system to a cash system. In moving to a cash system, the borrowing of money became increasingly important, so Jews became moneylenders. This led to some abuses, such as those who did not or could not pay back the loan accused the Jewish lender of some crime, thus freeing them from their fiscal obligation. However, an economy could not thrive without its moneylenders, so persecutions over this issue were not a steady event.

At the end of the thirteenth century, *pogroms*—officially encouraged massacres and expulsions—started against Jews in England. Yet, in Poland, King Boleslav invited Jews to come to his country. There they would be employed in various areas of finance and administration. Because of the protection of the monarchy, Jews were able to thrive in Poland until the tide turned in the seventeenth century. In Poland, and later other parts of Europe, Jews became known as *Ashkenazim*, from the Hebrew word for "German," and they developed their own language, called Yiddish. In the fourteenth century, France, Germany, and Austria were added to the list of countries that expelled Jews. In addition, Jews were commonly blamed for the Black Plague, a devastation that killed around one third of the population of Europe in the fourteenth century, but Church leaders came to the aid of Jews in this incident.

A meeting between Christopher Columbus, King Ferdinand, and Queen Isabella.

Jews living in Spain did not receive the same support from the Church in the fifteenth century. In that century, the reigning monarchs of Spain, King Ferdinand and Queen Isabella had been fighting an uphill battle, against the Muslims, especially, to reclaim Spain as a purely Christian country. This *Reconquesta*, or "re-conquering," required that all inhabitants who were not Christian convert to Christianity or leave the country. A number of Jews did convert to Christianity and were known as *conversos*. However, a number of these conversions were in name only, and some Jews continued their religious practices secretly. Of course, this was unacceptable to the Spanish monarchs. The infamous Spanish Inquisition was instituted specifically to weed out conversos who continued their Jewish practices. No other group considered heretical was targeted initially by the Inquisition, though it did spread eventually to other groups. Also, even if someone did admit to continuing secretly in some Jewish practices, they were still put to death. In 1492, Jews who had never converted to Christianity were expelled from Spain by Ferdinand and Isabella, who were procuring funding for Christopher Columbus' first voyage.

By the end of the fifteenth century, Jews were mostly absent from the Spanish landscape. The majority of Jews went to Portugal, Italy, the Netherlands, and Turkey. Jews in Turkey fared the best, helping to expand the Islamic Ottoman Empire. The Protestant Reformation of the sixteenth century was no kinder to Jews. Protestant reformer Martin Luther of Germany wrote the book *Concerning the Jews and Their Lies*, which advocated the destruction of everything Jewish—including their homes, synagogues, books, and property—and forbade the Jews themselves from being anywhere near a Christian town.

The various persecutions of Jews in Europe during the Medieval Period left the majority of Jews in grim poverty.

Many Jews were driven from cities into the countryside. Unable to own land, they were serfs and servants to mostly Christian landowners. Both poverty and discrimination left Jews in religious poverty as well. It was a struggle for many to practice Judaism or even to muster the strength to pray to God. Into this religious vacuum of the late seventeenth century arose Rabbi Israel ben Eliezer, nicknamed the Ba'al Shem Tov, or "Master of the Good Name." The Ba'al Shem Tov emphasized the presence of God in all aspects of Jewish life. Amid the darkness of life that befell so many Jews, particularly in Eastern Europe, the message of Rabbi Israel ben Eliezer brought God, joy, and life itself into Jewish communities in a new way. His message spread into a new movement within Judaism called **Hasidism**, from the Hebrew meaning "pious." Forms of Hasidism, with each groups leader call a *rebbe*, are found in Orthodox Judaism today.

Hasidism

From the Hebrew meaning "pious," a movement within Judaism founded in eighteenth-century Poland where pious devotion to God is as important as study of Torah.

Modern Period

The Age of Enlightenment, a philosophical movement of the eighteenth century that emphasized the use of reason to analyze previously accepted doctrines and tradition, ushered in the Modern Period (1783 CE–present). Closely associated with this movement was a philosophy of Jewish enlightenment that was meant to emancipate Jews from their social and legal situation. No longer the chattel or property of prelates or feudal monarchs, Jews were achieving equality before the law alongside their Christian fellow citizens of Germany, France, the Netherlands, and Britain.

Czarist Russia, however, was a different story. The nineteenth century was especially brutal with its hundreds of government-sponsored pogroms, expulsions, and deportations of Jews across the country. Czar Alexander III promulgated what became know as the May Laws against Jews. The government produced a clearly forged document called *The Protocols of the*

Learned Elders of Zion, purportedly written by Jewish leaders. This false document outlined a Jewish conspiracy to take over the world. The government wanted to make Jews a scapegoat for their corruption and economic failings. Many Russian people obliged.

In Western Europe, there was an explosion of sectarian groups in the Jewish tradition. In Germany and later in the United States, *Reform Judaism* emerged, advocating full integration into the culture where one lived. In the United States, the rise of *Conservative Judaism* counteracted Reform Judaism, modifying Jewish tradition in a limited manner. Thus, *Orthodox Judaism* was also a reactionary movement in response to Reform Judaism. Orthodox Judaism is the most traditional wing of Judaism, insisting its members strictly follow the Torah. In the 1930s, *Reconstructionist Judaism* emerged from Conservative Judaism, advocating Judaism as a culture, not only a religion. Reconstructionist Jews do not believe in an all-powerful God, nor do they accept the Torah as divinely inspired.

Zionism

From the name Zion (the historic land of Israel), it is the movement with origins in the nineteenth century that sought to restore a Jewish homeland in Palestine in response to anti-Semitism.

The end of the nineteenth century saw the beginning of Jewish nationalism, known as **Zionism**. The Zionist movement sought a return by Jews to the Jewish homeland, Palestine. The worldwide community was more responsive to the goals of Zionism after the murder of about six million Jews at the hands of the Nazi Germans in the Holocaust of the 1930s and 1940s. In response to the Holocaust, the United Nations returned Palestine to the Jews in 1948. The new nation called itself the State of Israel. Yet the city of Jerusalem was still divided between the countries of Jordan and Israel. The holy places of Christians, Muslims, and Jews were under the jurisdiction of a Muslim country, Jordan. In 1967, the State of Israel recaptured all of Jerusalem in a succession of strikes against neighboring Arab countries that became known as the Six-Day War. One of the results of the Six-Day War was that the ancient holy places in Jerusalem were opened to all visitors. Returning Palestine to the Jews has caused tremendous upset in much of the Middle East. Bringing peace to that part of the world requires a delicate balance that as yet has not been found.

> What traits of national character and values are needed to sustain a community through centuries of persecution, deportations, and foreign occupation?

■ Section 1 Summary

■ The Biblical Period found the Jews living in occupied Palestine or exiled to a foreign land.

■ The Rabbinic Period was a time of emerging institutional structures in Judaism.

■ During the Medieval Period Jews contributed much to the emerging western culture. This time was also marked by Jewish persecutions.

■ The Modern Period reflects one of the most devastating times and one of the most triumphant times in the history of Judaism. The Holocaust resulted in the murder of about six million Jews. Following this, the United Nations approved the return of Palestine to the Jews.

■ Section 1 Review Questions

1. What did the Hebrews become in the forty years it took to return to Canaan from Egypt?

2. After the death of Solomon, why did the kingdom become more vulnerable to outside attacks?

3. What is the Diaspora?

4. According to the Rabbi Hillel, what is the summation of the Torah?

5. Who was Moses Maimonides, and what did he argue for?

6. Define *Hasidism*.

7. Name and briefly differentiate the four types of Judaism that are present in the Modern Period.

A Jewish Legacy

American author Mark Twain wrote on the mark the Jewish people have left on the world in an 1899 article in *Harper's Magazine*:

If statistics are right, the Jews constitute but one percent of the human race. It suggests a nebulous dim puff of stardust lost in the blaze of the Milky Way. Properly, the Jew ought hardly to be heard of, but he is heard of, has always been heard of. He is as prominent on the planet as any other people, and his commercial importance is extravagantly out of proportion to the smallness of his bulk. His contributions to the world's list of great names in literature, science, art, music, finance, medicine, and abstruse learning are also away out of proportion to the weakness of his numbers. He has made a marvelous fight in this world, in all the ages; and had done it with his hands tied behind him. He could be vain of himself, and be excused for it.

The Egyptian, the Babylonian, and the Persian rose, filled the planet with sound and splendor, then faded to dream-stuff and passed away; the Greek and the Roman followed; and made a vast noise, and they are gone; other people have sprung up and held their torch high for a time, but it burned out, and they sit in twilight now, or have vanished. The Jew saw them all, beat them all, and is now what he always was, exhibiting no decadence, no infirmities of age, no weakening of his parts, no slowing of his energies, no dulling of his alert and aggressive mind. All things are mortal but the Jew; all other forces pass, but he remains. What is the secret of his immortality?

(from "Concerning The Jews," by Mark Twain, *Harper's Magazine*, 1899)

2. Sacred Stories and Sacred Scriptures

There are several sources of sacred Jewish writing. Each of these centers around the Torah, which is the first five books that make up the Hebrew Bible. These sacred writings not only offer Jewish beliefs about God, but they are also commentaries that instruct Jews on how they should live in relationship with God and one another while offering insights into specific situations.

Tanakh

Central to all of Jewish life is the Bible. For Jews, the Bible is what Christians call the Old Testament or the Hebrew Bible. Jews tend to call the Bible the *Tanakh*, an acronym for three divisions of the Hebrew Bible. The first component of the Hebrew Bible is the *Torah*, or the first five books comprising Genesis, Exodus, Leviticus, Numbers, and Deuteronomy. The second component of the Hebrew Bible is the *Nevi'im*, or prophets. This includes the three Major Prophets, Isaiah, Jeremiah, and Ezekiel, as well as the twelve Minor Prophets, such as Hosea and Amos. The third component of the Hebrew Bible is *Ketuvim*, or writings. This section includes such writings as Job, Psalms, and Proverbs.

Of the three divisions of the Hebrew Bible, Torah is the most important (see pages 49–50). For traditional Jews, it is not only known as Torah, but as the *Five Books of Moses*, for they believe Moses was the author. For traditional Jews, Torah is the source of the 613 laws they must follow to be good Jews. These 613 laws are divided into two types: 248 positive laws and 365 negative laws. However, not all these laws can be observed in our modern era. Laws pertaining to the Temple or to criminal proceedings can no longer be observed because both the Temple and the ancient style of government no longer exist.

As the holiest "books" of Judaism, Torah used in synagogue services is no mere printed book. Torah is produced as a scroll. The Five Books of Moses are handwritten in Hebrew on a series of parchments. The parchments are then hand sewn together and sewn onto two wooden rollers, dressed and decorated. A portion of Torah is read every Sabbath and completed in a one-year cycle with the year beginning right after the Sukkot festival.

Actually, Jews believe God gave Moses two Torahs at Mount Sinai that cannot be separated from one another—the Written Torah, described above, and an Oral Torah. The Oral Torah is the explanation and interpretation of the Written Torah. For example, the Written Torah mandates no work on the Sabbath, but does not define work. The Oral Torah was written down eventually, codified and arranged by Yehudah HaNasi (Judah the Prince) around 200 CE. Called the *Mishnah*, or "teaching," the laws were organized into six sections: agriculture and the Land of Israel, holidays, family life, relations with other people, sacrifices and dietary laws, and ritual purity.

Talmud

After the destruction of the Second Temple, two centers of rabbinic Judaism emerged in the following centuries. One center was in the Roman province of Judea, but outside Jerusalem. That rabbinic center was made up largely of refugees from the Jerusalem area. The second major rabbinic center was in Babylonia where the descendants of the Jews who were taken into Babylonian Exile five centuries earlier composed a number of thriving Jewish communities. Rabbinic scholars from both of these centers studied the Mishnah and wrote commentaries and discussions that later became two very different *Talmuds* or "learnings." One was called the Palestinian or Jerusalem Talmud while the other was called the Babylonian Talmud. Almost from the start the Babylonian Talmud was, and still is, considered the more authoritative of the two.

Midrash

The type of biblical interpretation found in rabbinic literature, especially the Talmuds. Midrash assumes that the Scriptures provide answers for every situation and every question in life.

Midrash

Midrash is a way of interpreting the biblical text. Sometimes the interpretation included the use of imagination and seeing how far the text could go. Often it is a story that explains a biblical text. It is like filling in the blanks or historical fiction. Midrash is not unique to the Jews. There is also Christian Midrash. For example, the book *Ben Hur* and its later motion picture could be called Christian Midrash. If someone wrote about St. Peter's wife, that could be Christian Midrash. The term Midrash comes from its Hebrew meaning "to examine" or "to seek out." Jewish sages after the return of the exiled from Babylon began to "seek out" the real meaning of a biblical passage. The passage may have some missing information or seem contradictory or be in the form of a metaphor. Their interpretations were in various literary genres. They could be in the form of a parable, a homily, or a narrative of some sort. Midrash is not a particular book, but much can be found in the Talmud. Midrash has never really ceased. The contemporary book *Does God Have a Big Toe?: Stories About Stories in the Bible* is midrashic in nature.

■ Section 2 Summary

■ The Tanak is an acronym for what comprises the Hebrew Bible.

■ The Mishnah is a commentary on the Torah.

■ The Talmud is a commentary on the Mishnah. There are two major versions of the Talmud.

■ Midrash is a literary genre used in interpreting scripture.

■ Section Review Questions

1. What are the three divisions of the Tanak?
2. What is the Talmud?
3. What is the difference between the Oral Torah and the Written Torah?
4. What is Midrash?

3. Beliefs and Practices

If Judaism could be summed up in three words, those words would be God, Torah, and Israel. God gave the Torah to Israel. In this case, Israel is not to be thought of as the political State of Israel with national boundaries, but as a people chosen by God with a specific purpose.

God

Who is this God who chose a small group of people to be a "light to the nations"? The opening words of the Sh'ma, a statement recited daily by devout Jews, offers an answer: "Hear, O Israel, the Lord our God, the Lord is One" (Deuteronomy 6:4). For Jews, God exists, God is one, God is Creator, and God is good. Judaism is a monotheistic religion, that is, Jews believe in one, supreme God.

Unlike Christians, Jews do not have a set of formal doctrines that articulate their beliefs. Yet, whatever branch of Judaism, they all believe in one God. Not only does God exist, but God is also the creator of all things. The opening line of the Bible reads, "In the beginning, God created . . ." (Genesis 1:1). God created, and thus, God is good. Because God is good, God desires goodness from all creation. Scripture again is helpful in clarifying Jewish understanding of the responsibility of humankind:

> So now, O Israel, what does the LORD your God require of you? Only to fear the LORD your God, to walk in all his ways, to love him, to serve the LORD your God with all your heart and with all your soul, and to keep the commandments of the LORD your God and his decrees that I am commanding you today, for your own wellbeing. (Deuteronomy 10:12–13)

How have you personally experienced God as good? God as Creator? God as one?

Torah

The central source for how to live as a Jew is the Torah. The Torah is literally God's self-revelation to the Jewish people. It is the most sacred of objects. Yet, there is at once a formality and an intimacy in relating to Torah. Both reverence and familiarity are operational. When not in use, the scrolls are kept in a specially made place within the synagogue, called an **Ark**. There are special prayers before and after reading the holy book. When the scrolls are taken out of their place of honor, they are carried around the synagogue by the rabbi for people to reverence by a touch, kiss, or even a proximate dance.

Ark

A repository traditionally in or against the wall of a synagogue for the scrolls of the Torah.

The presence of Torah is a joyous occasion, for where there is Torah, Jews believe there is God, in an ordinary, yet extraordinary way.

In studying Torah, a Jew finds it penetrating in every aspect of his or her life. Though Torah may mean "law" or "teaching," there is nothing sterile about it. The study of Torah is more a spiritual exercise than an intellectual one. In Torah, one encounters God and his will for one's life: "How I love your teaching [Torah], Lord! I study it all day long" (Psalm 119:97). Keeping Torah is keeping the Law. However, the "law" in this sense is the "law" of God, that is, the commandments of God. When Christians think of Jewish law, they imagine it as contained in the Ten Commandments. Actually, to Orthodox Jews, the Torah contains 613 commandments that are particular ways in which the Torah is made real in the world. As the Jewish sages explain, there are 613 words in the Decalogue, so implicit within the Ten Commandments are 613 commandments.

These commandments are called **mitzvot**. God issues mitzvot not to give commands, but to offer guidance for what will make people truly happy. Keeping

mitzvot

A commandment of the Jewish law.

Torah does not bring bondage, but freedom. What has taken place in the history of Judaism is the interpretation and application of these commandments through a variety of new situations that Moses and the ancient Israelites could not have anticipated. For example, in reference to the third command-ment to keep the Shabbat holy, Jews desist from "forty minus one" categories of labor. From these categories, rabbis interpret various kinds of bodies of knowledge in order to make a specif-ic commandment or injunction for a specific situation applica-ble. This process of interpretation is known as *halakhah*, the total body of Jewish law. For example, according to Jewish law, kindling a fire is prohibited on Shabbat. A Jew may place tape over the light mechanism in a refrigerator, not because it is one of the 613 commandments, but because it is related to Torah law prohibiting the kindling of a fire on the Sabbath.

> ➤ **Do you find the application of Jewish law dealing with the refrigerator light scrupulous or not? Explain.**

Israel

Jews are often described as God's Chosen People. (Many religious traditions have the belief that their members are cho-sen or elected.) Another word for "chosen" is "holy." When Jews talk about being God's Chosen People, they are really talk-ing about being "holy" or "separate."

The Jews' call to holiness originated with the call of Abram (later named Abraham) in Genesis 12:1–3. In that biblical pas-sage, Abram was called by God to leave Ur, the land of his father, and follow God. In return for his breaking with idolatry and his show of faith in the one God, Abraham was gifted with progeny and land. In addition, God blessed those who blessed Abraham and his descendants and cursed those who did not.

covenant

A binding and solemn agreement between human beings or between God and his people, holding each to a particular course of action.

Being chosen by God brings with it both privilege and responsibility. Being "chosen" is not passive, but active. Jews are Jews only insofar as they *respond to being chosen*, that is, insofar as they are holy. The privilege of being a member of God's Chosen People is that God has made a special **covenant** with the Jewish people to be their God. The responsibility of being a member of the Chosen People is that Jews must "choose" to accept God's commandments and live lives that are holy and right-eous, lives that are examples to the rest of humanity. This cho-sen nature of the Jews is passed from one generation to the next: "I have given you as a covenant to the people, a light to the nations" (Isaiah 42:6).

halakhic

What are ways in which Jews act as Chosen People? A traditional Jew is an "observer of the commandments" and participates in the various **halakhic** obliga-tions. For Jews, all life is holy. Setting aside special times at special places is just part of ongoing religious expression for Jews.

From the Hebrew meaning "way," Jewish law that covers all aspects of the life of an individual and of the community.

➤ What do you feel chosen or destined to do in your life?

■ Section 3 Summary

- ■ The essence of Judaism can be summed up in three words: God, Torah, and Israel.
- ■ Judaism is a monotheistic religion, focusing on one God only.
- ■ The Torah is literally God's self-revelation to the Jewish people. It is the most sacred of objects.
- ■ For Jews, being a "Chosen People" has both privilege and responsibility.

■ Section 3 Review Questions

1. What do Jews believe about God?
2. What do Christians understand the Torah to be?
3. How are both reverence and familiarity operational with the Torah?

4. When did the call to be a Chosen People originate with the Jews?

5. What does it mean to say that Jews are God's Chosen People?

4. Sacred Times

For Jews, all life is holy. Further, sacred time is cyclical to the Jews. From the earliest waking hours of the day through the long hours of the night, from infancy to old age, all life is holy. Hence, all life is to be devoted to God, including a person's very thoughts, actions, memory, and talents. To mark the sacredness of life, Jews take special moments annually during the life of a person to remember and to celebrate. To understand sacred times, a better grasp of the Jewish calendar is needed.

Most people operate under several different kinds of calendars. There is the academic calendar that starts in the fall and ends in late spring. There is the civil calendar that begins on January 1. A personal income tax calendar follows the civil calendar, but many non-profit organizations have a fiscal year that begins July 1. Many Christians use a liturgical calendar that begins with the first Sunday of Advent, occurring in late November or early December.

So, too, the Jews have a special, sacred calendar. For Jews, God is the God of history. Hence, it made sense to the Jewish sages to begin the Jewish calendar at the beginning of history, that is, at the creation of the world. Using only the Torah, the sages figured out when the world was created and began its annual calendar. Hence, the beginning of the second millennium on the Roman calendar, January 1, 2001, was Tevet 6, 5761, on the Jewish calendar (meaning 5,761 years since God created the earth).

While our civil calendar is a solar calendar in which a day begins and ends at midnight, the Jewish calendar is a lunar calendar with a day beginning and ending at sunset. Also, the Jewish calendar has 354 days and begins in the fall on Rosh Hashanah, the Jewish New Year. In addition, the Jewish calendar is eleven days shorter than the civil calendar. The Jews found it necessary to adjust this eleven-day discrepancy so that a holiday that is celebrated in the fall as commanded in the Bible will not eventually end up in the spring. The eleven-day discrepancy between the solar and lunar calendars is reconciled in two ways. First, a month is added seven times in nineteen years. Second, one day is added or subtracted each year to two different months. The next section names the two main cycles of the Jewish calendar and describes the festivals and holy days that occur in each. It also discusses the crown jewel of Jewish sacred time, *Shabbat*.

Festivals and Holy Days

The major Jewish festivals are divided into two main cycles: the *Tishri* cycle in the fall and the *Nisan* cycle in the spring. Tishri is named for the first month of the cycle (occurring in September or October) and contains, besides Rosh Hashanah, the festivals of *Yom Kippur* and *Sukkot*. Nisan is the first month of the spring cycle. The name "Nisan" comes from the Sumerian word for "first fruits." The Nisan cycle contains two festivals, *Pesach* and *Shavuot*. Rosh Hashanah and Pesach are similar in that both are memorial festivals. Rosh Hashanah memorializes the creation of the world while Pesach memorializes the creation of the Jews as a people. Sukkot and Shavout are both harvest festivals.

In comparison to the other feasts, two relatively minor festivals are celebrated during the Jewish year. *Hanukkah* and *Purim* are festivals that celebrate freedom from the wrath of foreign rulers.

Rosh Hashanah and Yom Kippur

The period in the Tishri cycle between Rosh Hashanah (Jewish New Year) and Yom Kippur—which means "Day of Atonement"—is known as the "days of awe." This ten-day penitential period is the high holy time for Jews during which the creation of the world is ritually commemorated.

Rosh Hashanah is celebrated on the first day of the Jewish month of *Tishri* (September or October on the Roman calendar). Besides marking the creation of humanity, Rosh Hashanah is also the day that Jews believe God judges each individual for his or her actions of the previous year. Yom Kippur, generally accepted as the holiest day of the year for Jews, is a day of prayer, fasting, and repentance. Jews ask forgiveness for both communal and personal sins. In asking for forgiveness, Jews go directly to the person they offended, if possible.

During the "days of awe" between Rosh Hashanah and Yom Kippur, Jews strive for repentance, or more accurately, a turning back to the proper way of living. This is known as *tishuvah*. God's judgment on whether tishuvah took place is sealed in a symbolic Book of Life at the end of Yom Kippur.

The central ritual in the celebrations of Rosh Hashanah and Yom Kippur is the blowing of the *shofar*, or ram's horn. A ram's horn is used rather than a calf's horn because the latter conjures up the image of the idolatrous golden calf from the Israelites' time in the desert. Also, the bent nature of the ram's horn signifies that Jews must bend their hearts toward God.

➤ What would be a first step if you were to seek repentance for the purpose of reorienting your life?

Sukkot

Sukkot is another festival during the Tishri cycle. It is also known as the Feast of Tabernacles or the Feast of Booths. (Sukkot means "booths.") Sukkot begins five days after Yom Kippur and lasts for eight days. Sukkot commemorates the time when the Jews were in the desert for forty years and later, when in Israel, they had to protect themselves from the elements during harvest. To do so they built covered huts, or booths. With this protection from the weather, Jews also came to understand that God alone was their great protector. Sukkot also marks the end of the fruit harvest season, especially the harvest for grapes used for making wine.

Pesach

Pesach retells the story of the Exodus. It is the first major feast of the Nisan cycle. Pesach is more commonly known as Passover, celebrating the Hebrews' freedom from Egyptian slavery when the angel of death "passed over" the houses of the Hebrews that were marked with blood from a lamb. The story of the first Passover is told in the Book of Exodus:

> Then Moses called for all the elders of Israel and said unto them: "Draw out, and take you lambs according to your families, and kill the passover lamb. And ye shall take a bunch of hyssop, and dip it in the blood that is in the basin, and strike the lintel and the two side-posts with the blood that is in the basin; and none of you shall go out of the door of his house until the morning. For the Lord will pass through to smite the Egyptians; and when He seeth the blood upon the lintel, and the two side-posts, the Lord will pass over the door, and will not suffer the destroyer to come in unto your houses to smite you. And ye shall observe this thing for an ordinance to thee and to thy sons forever. And it shall come to pass, when ye come to the land which the Lord will give you, according as He hath promised, that ye shall keep this service. And it shall come to pass, when your children shall say unto you: What mean ye by this service? that ye shall say: It is the sacrifice of the Lord's passover, for that He passed over the houses of the children of Israel in Egypt, when He smote the Egyptians, and delivered our houses." And the people bowed the head and worshipped. (Exodus 12:21–27)

Today each Jew celebrates being personally freed by God. They believe that if God had not freed them, they would still be slaves. Jews see themselves as enslaved in each generation and freed by God in each generation. This means that Jews from every generation symbolically go forth from Egypt toward the Promised Land.

➤ **What is something in your life to which you are symbolically or literally a slave?**

Shavuot

Shavuot means "week" in Hebrew. Shavuot is celebrated fifty days after the first day of Pesach, so some see Shavuot as the conclusion to Passover. Shavuot was originally a harvest festival celebrating the firstfruits of the wheat harvest. Centuries later, Jews associated Shavuot with the giving of the Torah to Moses on Mount Sinai.

Today, some Jews also combine the celebration of Shavuot and the reception of the Torah with Jewish confirmation. In a confirmation ceremony, Conservative and Reformed Jewish teenagers publicly state their acceptance of Judaism.

Hanukkah

Hanukkah ("festival of lights") celebrates one of the great military victories in Jewish history. Nevertheless, Hanukkah is not a major Jewish holiday. In fact, Hanukkah was not celebrated much at all until Jewish parents felt it was important to counteract the strong influence of Christmas on non-Christian members of American society. Since Hanukkah is also a winter celebration and, like Christmas, has light as one of its symbols, Jews' placing a greater emphasis on the celebration of Hanukkah was a natural counterpart to the Christmas season.

Hanukkah celebrates the victory of the Jews led by Judas the Maccabean over the Syrian Greeks led by Antiochus IV. Besides mandating Hellenism in Judea, Antiochus denied Jews the freedom to practice their religion. Worst of all, Antiochus captured the Temple and converted it into a pagan temple. In 165 BCE, the Jews recaptured the Temple, cleansed it from pagan impurities, and rededicated it to God.

Hanukkah is an eight-day celebration. Its main ritual is the lighting of one additional candle of a Hanukkah **menorah** each evening. This commemorates a tradition that after the Maccabeans had recaptured the Temple, there was enough oil for the relighting of the Temple Menorah for just one day. However, the miracle was that the candle stayed lit for eight days, hence the lighting of one candle for each day of Hanukkah.

menorah

A candelabra with seven or nine lights that is used in Jewish worship.

Purim

Purim translates to "feast of lots." Purim celebrates the victory of Jews living in Persia in the fifth century BCE over Haman, the prime minister of Persia. The feast of lots refers to the lots Haman randomly cast to determine which day he would slaughter the Jews. The Jewish Queen Esther heard about the plot and was able to convince King Ahasueros of Persia to desist with the plan. Instead, Haman and his family were executed on the gallows prepared for the Jews. This story is recounted in the Book of Esther.

Shabbat

While the festivals described in the previous section occur annually, Shabbat, the Jewish Sabbath, is a weekly event. Shabbat is celebrated from sunset Friday until sunset Saturday. Keeping the Sabbath holy is the fourth commandment (according to Jewish count) given by God to Moses on Mount Sinai. It is a reminder to the Jews that God rested from work on the seventh day, and so, too, must they. As the scripture text reads:

> Remember the sabbath day, to keep it holy. Six days shalt thou labor, and do all thy work; but the seventh day is a sabbath unto the Lord thy God, in it thou shalt not do any manner of work, thou, nor thy son, nor thy daughter, nor thy man-servant, nor thy maid-servant, nor thy cattle, nor thy stranger that is within thy gates; for in six days the Lord made heaven and earth, the sea,

and all that in them is, and rested on the seventh day;
wherefore the Lord blessed the sabbath day and hallowed it. (Exodus 20:8–11)

~~Friday evening is the Shabbat dinner, a family ritual that ushers in the Sabbath.~~ On this holiest day of the week, observing Jews refrain from work, attend synagogue services, and study the Torah. A common greeting for the Sabbath is "Shabbat Shalom," that is, "Sabbath peace."

~~The Sabbath dinner table includes a white tablecloth, two candles, wine, and a braided loaf of bread called hallah.~~

Sabbath begins eighteen minutes before sunset with the lighting of the Sabbath candles. A prayer of blessing over the candles is generally recited by the woman of the house:

Blessed are you, Lord our God, King of the Universe, who has blessed us with your commandments and commanded us to light the Sabbath candles.

The blessing over the wine and bread is:

Blessed are you, Lord our God, King of the Universe, who creates the fruit of the vine.

Blessed are you, Lord our God, King of the Universe, who brings forth bread from the earth.

Havdalah

A religious ceremony that symbolically ends the Shabbat, usually recited over kosher wine or kosher grape juice.

~~After these blessings, the meal begins. The Sabbath candles are not extinguished. They are allowed to burn themselves out.~~

Sabbath ends at sunset Saturday. A brief ceremony called **Havdalah** concludes this sacred time. A braided candle is lit and held in the hand so one can see its reflection of light on the fingertips. Again, wine accompanies this closing ceremony as a symbol of thanksgiving and joy. A box of aromatic spices is lit, carrying the aroma of the Sabbath into the week.

> ➤ **For you, what does it mean to keep a day "holy"?**

Life Cycle Celebrations

For Jews, life cycle celebrations focus on transitional moments in their personal lives. Until recently, most of these ceremonies were male-oriented with no female counterpart. For example, *Bar Mitzvah* (literally "Son of the Commandment") is the coming of age ceremony for a thirteen-year-old boy, recognizing that the boy has become an adult and is responsible for his religious and moral training. The counterpart ceremony for girls, the *Bat Mitzvah*, was created in the twentieth century. Other ways Jews mark important times in life include the following:

Birth

Circumcision, the cutting away of the foreskin of the penis, usually takes place eight days after birth. This practice dates from the time of Abraham (see Genesis 17:10–11) when God commanded Abraham to circumcise all his male descendants as a sign of the covenant between God and his people. Circumcision gives a permanent mark to Jews as a way to differentiate them from other people.

The ceremony for an infant girl involves the giving of her name. She is brought to the synagogue where she is welcomed into the congregation. The full Hebrew name of the child is revealed for the first time by the rabbi.

Coming of Age

A Jewish child becomes a mature individual, responsible for keeping the Torah. Religious majority is associated with the age of thirteen for boys and twelve for girls. When the individual is minimally competent in prayer and the Torah, he or she is called to read publicly from the Torah.

Marriage

The three major elements of the marriage ritual include the chuppah (wedding canopy), the blessings, and the breaking of the glass. The huppah is a canopy held up by four poles representing the future home of the bride and groom. There are usually vegetative symbols embroidered on the canopy, representing the notion that the bride and groom are in the Garden of Eden and are the first man and woman. The symbolism of the breaking of the glass is linked to the destruction of the Temple in Jerusalem in 70 CE.

Death

For Jews, funerals take place as soon as possible, often within twenty-four hours of the death. At the burial, blessings are made, prayers are said, and psalms are read aloud.

■ Section 4 Summary

■ For Jews, all life is holy. A person's every thought, action, memory, and talent is to be devoted to God.

■ Two main cycles in the Jewish calendar are the creation cycles of Tishri and Nisan.

■ Yom Kippur, the Day of Atonement, is the holiest day of the year for Jews.

- Sukkot and Shavuot were originally harvest festivals that eventually gained deeper religious significance in the Jewish people's relationship to God.
- Shabbat, the Jewish Sabbath, is a weekly event that is celebrated from sunset Friday until sunset Saturday. Keeping the Sabbath holy is the fourth commandment God gave to Moses on Mount Sinai.

■ Section 4 Review Questions

1. What are the two main cycles on the Jewish calendar?
2. How is the Jewish calendar different from the Roman or civil calendar?
3. What happens on Yom Kippur?
4. Cite the similarities between Rosh Hashanah and Pesach.
5. What are the "days of awe," and what is their significance?
6. Why did a relatively minor feast, Hanukkah, take on more significance, especially in America?
7. Explain what takes place on Shabbat.

5. Sacred Places and Sacred Spaces

Judaism is unique in that most religious festivals and life cycle rituals are performed in the synagogue with a corresponding ritual in the home. *Synagogue* comes from a Greek word that means "place of assembly" outside of one's homeland. The sacredness of synagogue and home for Jews is featured in this section. Also, a significant geographical area of the world has always been sacred to Jews. The very land of Israel—more than its political entity—along with its holy city Jerusalem remain significant to the spiritual life of Jews worldwide.

Synagogue

The Temple in Jerusalem was the center of Jewish worship for centuries. The Temple was where the ritual sacrifice of animals, the main expression of worshipping God, took place.

With the scattering of the Jews in the Diaspora and the eventual destruction of the Temple in 70 CE, a number of alternatives were established over the centuries to replace the institution of the Temple and its rituals. Some Jews maintained that the deeds of righteous people were equivalent to the sacrificial order of the Temple. Others equated personal prayer with Temple sacrifices. The three daily periods of prayer replaced the three daily animal sacrifices. Also, the synagogues became the place where Jews could worship God communally. Originally, while captives in Babylon, the exiles met in private homes for worship. These were the forerunners of synagogues. Over the centuries, the functions of the synagogue and number of synagogues multiplied.

A synagogue became multidimensional. It was a House of Prayer (where Jews address God), a House of Study (where Jews study the Torah), and a House of Assembly (where Jews meet socially). These three names suggest the three separate, yet interrelated functions of the synagogue.

bimah

The elevated platform in a Jewish synagogue where the person reading aloud from the Torah stands during the service.

Synagogues are now typically built to replicate Zion in the shape of a square with the **bimah** in the center representing Mount Zion. There is a gathering space for men, women, and children and a central chamber for the reading of the Torah and for prayer. The Torah is kept in an Ark on the wall that faces Jerusalem. The people face the east, not only facing the Ark, but also facing Jerusalem.

➤ How would your religious tradition survive if its place of worship was taken away?

Home

The home of a Jew is distinguishable because it is transformed into sacred space. A traditional Jewish home attaches a **mezuzah** on at least one exterior doorpost of the house. In the west in some Jewish homes, one wall is designated the *mizrakh*, or eastern wall. This wall is sometimes marked with a special picture or embroidery, showing the direction one must face for prayer.

A **kosher** home is one that has special dishes for eating and cooking that separate meat from dairy products. Since a traditional Jewish table is not only a place for building familial relationships but also a place for ritual, food must be kosher or "proper." Pork and shellfish are forbidden. Other meats must be slaughtered in a kosher manner. The combination of meat and dairy products is forbidden. On Shabbat, a "Sabbath-like" atmosphere prevails in the home. The house must be especially clean, and a Shabbat cloth must be on the table along with the Shabbat candlesticks.

➤ What outward signs designate your house as holy?

mezuzah

Meaning "doorpost," a small parchment containing Jewish scripture, usually the Sh'ma, that is placed in a case on or near the right doorframe at the home of an observant Jew.

kosher

From the Hebrew word kaser, *meaning "proper." Commonly, it refers to food permitted by Jewish dietary laws. Jews observe kosher laws to remind themselves that they are to be a holy and separate people.*

Land of Israel

Israel, also known as Canaan, the Promised Land, Judea, Palestine, and the State of Israel, is of great significance to the Jewish people. The land promised by God to Abraham and his descendants is "flowing with milk and honey." It is holy ground.

Over their more than three millennia history, Jews have had to leave the land because of famine, exile, deportation, and the like. However, there were always a few who remained. Wherever Jews were in the world, they never forgot the Promised Land. Many of the mitzvot are connected with the land of Israel. Hence, some Jews believe that they must live in Israel to fulfill God's will and that the many centuries Jews have had to live in the Diaspora was a sense of being exiled from the land. There are even some Jews who believe that Israel is so sacred that the presence of any groups there that are not Jewish defiles the land.

Jerusalem

Jerusalem is a holy city for each of the three religions that traces its roots to Abraham: Judaism, Christianity and Islam. For Jews, however, Jerusalem is the holiest city; there is no other. It is in Jerusalem where the foundations of Mount Moriah—the spiritual center of the universe—once stood. It was on Mount Moriah where Abraham intended to sacrifice his son Isaac. It was there that Jacob had his dream about the ladder: "When Jacob awoke from his sleep, he exclaimed, 'Truly, the Lord is in this spot, although I did not know it!' In solemn wonder he cried out: 'How awesome is this shrine! This is nothing else but an abode of God, and that is the gateway to heaven!'" (Genesis 28:16–17).

King David captured the city of Jerusalem from the Jebusites and called it the City of David. Solomon's Temple was also built on Mount Moriah, though centuries later it was destroyed by the Babylonians. After returning from the Babylonian Exile, a Second Temple was built on the same place, also known as the Temple Mount.

Hence, for Jews, God is most present in Jerusalem. Jews face Jerusalem daily in prayer. At the end of Pesach, Jews pray,

"Next year in Jerusalem!" Orthodox Jews believe a Messiah will come and rebuild Jerusalem to its former glory and usher in a time when "they shall beat their swords into plowshares." At Jewish weddings, a glass is broken in commemoration of the destruction of the Temple. Jews worked hard to keep the land of Israel and Jerusalem in its collective memory. Jews fought hard to take back Jerusalem in the Six-Day War in June of 1967. As they prayed when they were in Babylonian captivity:

> If I forget you, Jerusalem, may my right hand wither. May my tongue stick to my palate if I do not remember you, If I do not exalt Jerusalem beyond all my delights. (Psalm 137:5–6)

■ Section 5 Summary

■ After the destruction of the Temple in 70 CE, the synagogue replaced the Temple as the central place of worship for Jews.

■ The synagogue has three main functions: House of Prayer, House of Study, and House of Assembly.

■ A traditional Jewish home is a place where both fellowship and ritual take place.

■ For Jews, Israel and its historic city Jerusalem are their holiest places.

■ Section 5 Review Questions

1. What does the word *synagogue* mean?
2. What takes place in a synagogue?
3. What makes a home kosher?
4. What is the significance of the Land of Israel and the city of Jerusalem for Jews?

6. Judaism through a Catholic Lens

The relationship between Catholics and Jews is unique indeed. Catholicism is rooted in Judaism historically, scripturally, liturgically, and theologically. No two religious traditions have so much in common. We both believe in one God (*CCC*, 228). We share Abraham as our father in faith, the first to believe in the one God (*CCC*, 72). We believe God has made multiple

covenants with the Jewish people—with Noah, with Abraham, with Moses, with David—and that God has broken no covenant (*CCC*, 71). We know God has broken no promises. We affirm God's revelation on Mount Sinai to Moses, then to the Jewish people, and then to all humankind (*CCC*, 72). We accept the Ten Commandments as a minimum guide for moral living (*CCC*, 1980). We pray the same psalms. We believe that God has spoken to us through the prophets. We accept the Hebrew Bible as the Word of God, and it is contained in the Old Testament. We know

that at the end of time we will see that history has meaning, that there will be a final judgment, and that the world will be redeemed (*CCC*, 1060). Yet, those things that are common to both religious traditions are also the sources of our differences. Both the similarities and differences are discussed in the following sections.

Messiah

The most noted difference between Catholics and Jews is in the person of Jesus. Both agree Jesus was a historical figure. Jesus was born of a Jewish woman named Mary, raised in a traditional Jewish home in the Jewish homeland, was a charismatic itinerant preacher and wonder-worker, and died a criminal, crucified by Romans around 30 CE (AD). Here the commonalities end and the differences begin.

Jews still expect a Messiah or messianic age to come. Jews believe that the Messiah ("the anointed one") will be a wise person who will reestablish the House of David and that he will bring about the messianic era when the "lion shall lie down with the lamb and swords shall be turned into plowshares." Catholics believe the Messiah has already come in the person of Jesus of Nazareth. While Jews at the time of Jesus were looking for a Messiah who would be a warrior-king, a political figure, from the House of David, Jesus of Nazareth was a spiritual rather than a political figure. The coming of the Messiah is the inauguration of God's reign on earth. It is a spiritual, moral reign rather than an earthly reign, for Christ's kingdom is not of this world. The Gospel of Luke cites Jesus reading in the synagogue from the scroll of the prophet Isaiah:

> "The Spirit of the Lord is upon me, because he has anointed me to bring glad tidings to the poor. He has sent me to proclaim liberty to captives and recovery of sight to the blind, to let the oppressed go free, and to proclaim a year acceptable to the Lord." Rolling up the scroll, he handed it back to the attendant and sat down, and the eyes of all in the synagogue looked intently at him. He said to them, "Today this scripture passage is fulfilled in your hearing." (Luke 4:18–21)

At the end of time, it will be revealed that Jesus was indeed the long-awaited Jewish Messiah and Redeemer for the entire world. For Christians, the end of time will be the Second Coming of the Messiah, while for Jews it will be the first coming.

Incarnation

Jesus is something else besides the Messiah, the Anointed One of God (*CCC*, 453). Jesus is God. "The Word became flesh and made his dwelling among us, and we saw his glory, the glory as of the Father's only Son, full of grace and truth" (John 1:14).

God became one of us in Jesus. At conception, the divine person of the Son took upon himself a complete human nature. (*CCC*, 479). Jesus is not part human and part divine. Rather, Jesus is truly God and truly human (*CCC*, 480). God became one of us in Jesus to bring about our salvation, to reconcile us to God. This is the doctrine of the Incarnation.

Jews expect the coming Messiah to be a human being, anointed by God, but not divine. Jews see no reason for a mediator between them and God. Each person has the power within to reconcile, to make right, with God.

However, the doctrine of the Incarnation is not totally foreign to Jews. Both Jews and Christians believe the Word of God was present at creation, for God spoke, and it came to be. While for Christians the Word became Incarnate in the person of Jesus, for Jews, the Word became Incarnate in a book. These are not the same or even similar doctrines. Rather, they both say that God is present to us through something concrete. For Christians, the tangible is Jesus, who is truly God and truly human. For Jews, the tangible is the Torah. It, too, has a divine and a human nature. The words of Torah make God present in the midst of the human reader.

Scripture

To Catholics, God's inspired word in Scripture is contained in more than the Hebrew Bible. All Christians accept also the New Testament as revealed scripture. While Jews accept the New Testament as documents written, for the most part, by first-century Jews, they do not accept the New Testament as revealed by God. Christians commonly believe that the Old Testament is the same as the Hebrew Bible, though that is not exactly true. The Catholic Church included seven books (1 and 2 Maccabees, Judith, Tobit, Baruch, Sirach, and Wisdom), which were mostly written in Greek after 300 BCE, not included in the Hebrew Bible). These seven books are referred to as deuterocanonical—"second canon"—to show that they are not accepted in the Jewish canon.

The word "testament" means "covenant." So, while Christians could say that their scriptures are made up of the Old Covenant and New Covenant, as noted above, God made multiple covenants with the Jewish people, the most important of which is the covenant on Mount Sinai. God does not break covenants. God's covenants are eternal. Jesus did not enter human history to render the Old Covenant void.

Liturgy

There are striking similarities between the annual Passover meal of the Jews and the daily Eucharistic celebration of Catholics, also known as the Mass or the Lord's Supper. In each there are readings from scripture, the offering, blessing, and fracturing of unleavened bread, as well as the offering, blessing, and consuming of wine. Even the beginning of the blessings can be similar. Jews pray, "Blessed are you, King of the universe," and Catholics pray, "Blessed are you, God of all creation."

Holy Thursday and Passover

There is a connection also between Holy Thursday and Passover. The Gospels of Matthew, Mark, and Luke report that the Last Supper was a Passover meal. The Passover is in commemoration of the Jewish exodus from Egypt. In this historical event, Jewish slaves in Egypt were brought to freedom through the leadership of Moses. After many attempts to get the pharaoh to release the slaves through the use of plagues, it was the last plague that caused the release. In the last plague, the first-born son would be slain. To avoid the killing of the first-born son, the Jews were to slaughter an unblemished lamb and mark the post and lintel of their dwelling with the blood of the lamb. The angel of death would "pass over" any dwelling that was marked with blood. The death of first-born sons was too much for the pharaoh, and he let the Jews go free. Christians see Jesus as the Lamb of God who was slain and whose blood released believers from the slavery of sin to freedom in Christ Jesus.

Pentecost and Shavuot

The Christian feast of Pentecost and the Jewish fest of Shavuot are related. In fact, Shavuot is known also as Pentecost. While Shavuot means "weeks," referring to seven weeks after Passover, the name Pentecost refers to fifty days after Passover. Shavuot began as a spring harvest feast, but it is better known as a celebration of when God gave the Torah and the Mosaic Law to the Jews through Moses. This momentous occasion on Mount Sinai is when the Jews became a covenantal people. When the first followers of Jesus were celebrating Shavuot/Pentecost in Jerusalem, the Holy Spirit came upon them. They, too, became a people. Pentecost is sometimes known as the "birthday of the Church." In accepting Jesus, the Mosaic Law was not nullified, but fulfilled.

Challenges of Dialogue

Catholics and Jews have had both a rich and troubled history together. The difficulties between the two have left some Jews wary of Catholic intentions about being equal partners in dialogue. Jews have faced discrimination, violence, expulsions, deportations, and death at the hands of people claiming to be Christian. This includes the burning of their synagogues and sacred texts. Sometimes Jews were put in situations in which it was difficult to maintain their human dignity. They were called "Christ-killers." They were told that they had their poor lot in life because they did not accept Jesus and if they did accept Jesus, all would be well. Some were forced into conversion. Some chose to convert, but were accused of secretly practicing Judaism.

Many of these negative experiences were perpetrated by mob violence rather than from spiritual or temporal leaders of the Church. For example, when the first Crusaders plundered Jewish communities in the Rhineland, there are stories of when Jews went to the bishop of the region for help. They not only received help, but sometimes the bishop was killed for helping the Jews.

In the Second Vatican Council document *Nostra Aetate*, the Church set a course for righting these wrongs toward Jews. Even before the Second Vatican Council began, Pope John XXIII cut out the Latin word *perfidis*, or "perfidious," from the prayer for the Jews during the Good Friday service. Contempt for the Jews was to be no more. On the contrary, the Jews were, and remain, God's Chosen People. God never severed the covenant made on Mount Sinai. There is no collective

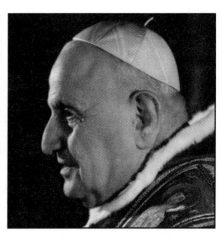

Pope John XXIII

guilt of Jews for the death of Jesus (*CCC*, 597). Roman soldiers crucified Jesus at the instigation of some, not all, Jewish leaders. Jews do not need to become Catholic to be saved. Jews who adhere to their covenant with God are in line with God's plans for them (*CCC*, 839). The Catholic Church no longer has an organized missionary program to convert Jews.

Yet, we sometimes are unaware of lingering anti-Semitism. Dialogue with each other often sensitizes us to the poor language used about the other. For example, in the beautiful Advent hymn "O Come, O Come Emmanuel," or "*Veni, Veni Emmanuel*" in Latin, we sing in the first verse:

O come, O come Emmanuel,
And ransom captive Israel;
That mourns in lonely exile here,
Until the Son of God appear.

We still are saying the Jewish people are in exile from their God. Both Catholics and Jews pray the same psalms, and we know that this is far from the truth. Just look at another verse of the song:

O come, Desire of nations, bind
In one the hearts of all mankind;

Bid Thou our sad divisions cease,
And be Thyself our King of Peace.

This verse speaks of the hope that all desire.

Our past requires us to engage in dialogue with people who adhere to the Jewish religious tradition. With our difficult past, meaningful dialogue is not always easy. Jews find it difficult to hear Jesus as the source of salvation. Many Jews are uncomfortable with the Christian symbol of the cross, for it evokes many painful memories. Catholics find it painful to hear that Jews cannot accept Jesus. The cross is a sign of God's unconditional love for humankind. So while Jews find the cross a sign of human hatred, Catholics find the cross a sign of divine love.

Because of the painful history of forced conversion, especially during the Medieval Period, Jews find it difficult for Catholics to talk about evangelization or missionary activity. Catholics must acknowledge the difficulty Jews have with evangelizing activity and assure Jews that conversion to Catholicism is not the sole purpose of its missionary activity. Evangelization is part of our religious identity as Catholics. Giving witness to Jesus, sharing the Good News about Jesus, is a consequence of our faith. Witnessing and attempts at conversion are two very different things. Jews and Catholics have one missionary activity they can share. Catholics and Jews, as well as Muslims, can all share in the missionary activity of calling all people to conversion from idolatry to faith in the one, true God.

Shoah

Hebrew for "calamity," it refers to the mass murder of Jews by the Nazis during World War II.

There are two major areas of dialogue for Catholics and Jews to pursue at this time in their history together. One is the **Shoah** and the other is contemporary life issues. Shoah is a modern Hebrew word for Holocaust. It means "catastrophe" or "devastation." For Jews, Shoah is an experience of the extermination of millions of their own people in "civilized" Europe at the hands of the Nazis. Shoah can be a very emotionally charged topic, but meaningful sharing sometimes goes beyond being merely nice or polite. As the Passover and the Paschal Mystery are not just events that happened in the past but are at all times profound and powerful, so, too, is the Shoah. As the Passover is part of the collective memory for Jews and the Paschal Mystery is part of the collective memory for Catholics, so, too, the Shoah must become part of our collective memories. We must never forget, lest it happen again somewhere, some time, to some other group of people. In their own ways, Catholics and Jews must

World War II prison camp at Auschwitz in Poland

pass on the memory of the Shoah to future generations. Though it is painful on both sides for very different reasons, we must never lose courage in confronting historical truth, for therein lies a source for reconciliation and healing.

Finally, English-speaking Catholics and Jews live in a materialistic, consumeristic, secular, individualistic world. It is a world where the human person is treated as an object. Human dignity is not important—only how useful a person is to another. It is a society in which greed is a virtue. Another good topic for dialogue for Jews and Catholics is how this dark side of human nature, the contempt for God's creation, can be dispelled and light and hope can reign. Maintaining the beauty of the earth, healthy families and communities, justice and peace, equality for all, and many other topics fall under those by which Catholics and Jews can affirm their faith in God.

■ Section 6 Summary

- ■ There are striking similarities between Catholic and Jewish history, scripture, liturgy, and theology. In these same areas we can find the greatest differences between the two religious traditions.

- ■ Some Jews are wary of any serious dialogue with Catholics. A long history of contempt, forced conversions, and persecution is hard to forget.

■ Two major areas of dialogue between Catholics and Jews are the Shoah and contemporary issues of life.

■ Section 6 Review Questions

1. List four areas in which Jews and Catholics are in agreement.

2. What is the difference between what Catholics believe about Jesus and what Jews believe about Jesus?

3. What are some similarities between the Mass and Passover, Holy Thursday and Passover, and Shavuot and Pentecost?

4. What are some other topics that can further Jewish-Catholic dialogue in a positive way? Explain why.

● Conclusion

From a sociologist's point of view, Jews should have disappeared off the face of the earth at the time of the Babylonian Exile. Sociologists point out that such a small group of people that are continually exiled, expelled, enslaved, and exterminated would not seem to be able to continue. Either assimilation or annihilation or both would have claimed this small community. A plausible answer to sociologists is that they underestimate God, the Torah, and Israel as powerful sources of life for Jews. The single-minded belief of Jews in one God, the Torah as a living document, and Israel as both a Promised Land and a Chosen People have sustained Jews against incalculable odds. This threefold essence is the heart of Judaism. It is in the pure intent of the heart that the God of the Jews is most interested.

As part of the revision of the new *Roman Missal*, Pope John Paul II had the prayer for the Jews during the Good Friday service completely rewritten. We end this chapter by praying for "the Jewish people, first to hear the word of God, that they may continue to grow in the love of his name and in faithfulness to his covenant."

■ Chapter 2 Summary

■ Jewish history spans more than three thousand years. Much of that time, Jews were ruled by foreign governments.

■ The Oral Torah and the Written Torah are the most sacred writings to Jews.

■ Judaism is the religious expression of the Jews.

■ The essence of Judaism is God, the Torah, and Israel.

■ Jewish beliefs are expressed through actions, not doctrines.

■ Jewish festivals and holy days memorialize and celebrate the religious history of Judaism.

■ Both the home and the synagogue are places for Jewish ritual worship.

■ Jerusalem is the most sacred place to Jews.

■ Because Catholicism is rooted in Judaism, there are striking similarities and profound differences between these two religious traditions.

■ Meaningful dialogue between Jews and Catholics can be difficult, but rewarding.

■ Chapter 2 Review Questions

1. What is the significance of Mount Sinai?
2. Compare and contrast the experience of Jews in Babylon during the sixth century BCE with the Jews of Babylon during the sixth century CE.
3. Why would Jews say the year 70 CE was one of the worst in Jewish history?
4. Why did the synagogue gain in importance during the Rabbinic Period?
5. Define *Diaspora*.
6. What was the general experience of Jews in Spain under Muslim rule?

7. Who was Moses Maimonides?

8. Define *converso*.

9. Define *Hasidism*.

10. Why can it be said that the Age of Enlightenment in Europe was an age of emancipation for Jews?

11. Why do Jews call the Hebrew Bible Tanak? Why do they not call the Hebrew Bible the Old Testament?

12. What is the Mishnah?

13. What is the Talmud? What is considered the most authoritative version of the Talmud?

14. Define *Sh'ma*.

15. How is the Torah reverenced? What does it represent?

16. What are the two meanings of the term "Israel" to Jews?

17. Define *halakah*. Give an example.

18. What are major characteristics of Orthodox, Conservative, Reform, and Reconstructionist Judaism?

19. Define *Ashkenazim* and *Sephardim*.

20. Briefly describe the significance of the time between Rosh Hashanah and Yom Kippur, including each of those holy days.

21. What festivals are in the Tishri cycle? In the Nisan cycle?

22. How is Passover related to both the Mass and to Holy Thursday?

23. What is the significance of Hanukkah?

24. How do Jews mark major times in the life cycle: birth, coming of age, marriage, and death?

25. How is a Jewish home made sacred?

26. Why are some Jews wary to engage in meaningful dialogue with Catholics?

27. Who is Jesus according to the Jewish faith? *apostate*

28. What is the Shoah?

29. What are some of the Jewish roots of Catholicism? Give examples.

■ Research & Activities

■ The words "Hebrew," "Jew," and "Israelite" are commonly interchangeable with regard to the Jewish people. Write an essay on the difference between these terms.

■ Interview a Jewish teen or adult. Ask the person to offer his or her personal perspective on the main themes of Judaism offered in this chapter: history, belief, sacred time, and sacred place.

■ Research how Orthodox, Conservative, Reform, and Reconstructionist Jews celebrate one of the following: Rosh Hashanah Shavuot, Yom Kippur, Hanukkah Sukkot, Purim, Shabbat, birth, Bar/Bat Mitzvah, or marriage. Include both the synagogue and home observances when applicable. Note the similarities and differences.

■ Read and write a book report on one of the following novels by Chaim Potok: *The Chosen, The Promise,* or *My Name is Asher Lev.*

■ Research the "Dreyfus Affair" of 1894.

■ Research Hasidism and its presence in your country.

■ Choose a passage in the Hebrew Bible and write a 250-word Midrash related to it.

■ Look through the Gospels and find examples where Jesus has discussions with the various Jewish leaders. What are some of the topics discussed?

■ Find examples in the New Testament that could be considered Midrash with regard to the Hebrew Scriptures.

■ Write an essay on why Jews and Catholics need one another.

■ Give a class presentation on the Western Wall.

Give a class presentation on the following Jewish symbols: yarmulke, tallit, tefillin, menorah, and Star of David.

Prayer

Traditionally, Jews recite this prayer—Aleinu—at the end of synagogue services. The prayer is believed to have been recited by Joshua after the death of Moses and prior to the entrance to the Promised Land.

It is our duty to praise the Master of all,

to acclaim the greatness of the One who forms all creation.

For God did not make us like the nations of other lands,

and did not make us the same as other families of the Earth.

God did not place us in the same situations as others,

and our destiny is not the same as anyone else's.

And we bend our knees, and bow down, and give thanks,

before the King, the King of Kings,

the Holy One, Blessed is God.

The One who spread out the heavens, and made the foundations of the Earth,

and whose precious dwelling is in the heavens above.

and whose powerful Presence is in the highest heights.

The Lord is our God, there is none else.

Our God is truth, and nothing else compares.

As it is written in Your Torah:

"And you shall know today, and take to heart,

that Adonai is the only God,

in the heavens above and on Earth below.

There is no other."

Christianity

Followers of the Nazarene

The history of Christianity is rich and diverse. From its inception approximately two thousand years ago as a small Jewish **sect** to its present state as one of the world's largest religious traditions, Christian history is full of saints and sin- ners, expansion and division, music, art, and wars.

sect

A religious group that separates from the larger religious denomination.

The diversity of Christian denominations can be witnessed on Sunday morning television. As you surf the channels, you cannot help but see the differences. There are evangelists exhorting people to "receive Jesus into their hearts." There are gospel choirs singing in full voice. You may see a Christian preacher in a Jewish prayer shawl and yarmulke or scull cap. Usually a Catholic Mass is televised, or in some places, a Catholic nun in full habit explains a Catholic teaching. Don't forget the Dutch Reform preacher delivering the Word from a "crystal" cathedral or a Southern Baptist preacher exhorting the faithful in an arena.

denominations

a religious organiza-
tion whose congrega-
tions are united in their
adherence to its beliefs
and practices.

This chapter examines the various branches of Christianity, beginning with a brief overview of the history of Christianity from its beginnings as part of Judaism to its expansion and splintering into various **denominations.** For all Christians, Jesus of Nazareth is the central figure of their faith. As recorded in the Christian Bible, it is through his life, death, and resurrection that Christians find both meaning in life and instruction in how to live. Major Christian feasts commemorate important events in the life of Jesus and the lives of his followers. These holy days are celebrated at both church and home, though the physical church building is considered the more sacred place.

doctrines

Principles, beliefs, and
teachings of a religion.

Church is defined as both a people and a location, and Christians define themselves by what they believe. Christianity has many **doctrines**—traditions and beliefs vary widely from denomination to denomination. Yet there is a core of beliefs that almost every

Christian can accept. For example, Christians believe that Jesus is Lord of all and has risen from the dead. Christians also believe and follow the two great commandments of love, which translate to giving full love and commitment to God and neighbor.

What is the most unique Christian television program you have ever watched?

Christianity   83

BC	(Before Christ)
4	Jesus of Nazareth is born
AD	(*Anno Domini*; "In the year of our Lord")
30	Jesus is crucified and raised from the dead
50s	Epistles written by Paul of Tarsus
90s	Last gospel written
ca. 250	Rise of monasticism
313	Edict of Milan
325	Council of Nicea I
451	Council of Chalcedon
500s	Reform of monasticism
978	Vladamir I brings Christianity to Russia
1054	Great Schism
1099	First Crusade captures Jerusalem from Muslims
1204	Crusaders ravage Constantinople
1517	Luther's Ninety-five Theses posted on church door
1534	Act of Supremacy in England
1563	Council of Trent closes
1701	John Wesley and Methodist movement
1948	World Council of Churches
1965	Second Vatican Council closes
1978	Pope John Paul II elected Pope
2005	Pope Benedict XVI elected Pope

1. A Brief History of Christianity

What we know about the beginning of Christianity and its early years is largely through sources written by followers of Jesus of Nazareth. These writings include both faith statements and historical facts. Biblical scholarship in the last 150 years has helped to define the actual actions and words of Jesus and the developing traditions about Jesus, even as both are included in four books of the New Testament known as *Gospels* ("good news").

Jesus of Nazareth

The history of Christianity begins with Jesus of Nazareth. Stories of the birth of Jesus are recorded in the Gospels according to Matthew and Luke. A point of agreement in the two accounts is that the birth of Jesus was in ful-fillment of Jewish prophecy found in the Hebrew Bible. According to both gospels, Mary, the virgin mother of Jesus, conceived him by the power of the Holy Spirit. Jesus was born around 4 BC, shortly before Herod the Great died. This date is calculated based on information in Luke 2:2 that Quirinius was governor of Syria and that Roman emperor Caesar Augustus had ordered a census in Palestine, in the town of Bethlehem in the Roman-occupied province of Judea. There is little known about the childhood of Jesus other than that his family settled in Nazareth in the province of Galilee. Joseph, from the lineage of King David, was a carpenter, so it is likely Jesus took up the same trade.

The public ministry of Jesus was inaugurated by his baptism in the Jordan River by a Jewish baptizer named John. John's was a baptism of repentance and preparation for the coming of the long awaited Jewish *Messiah* ("Anointed One"). After a period of temptations, Jesus returned to the region of Galilee, where he became known as a storyteller and miracle worker. His message included themes of repentance and reconciliation, as well as love and justice. In particular, Jesus taught that the Kingdom of God was at hand. The "kingdom," as Jesus described it, was not an earthly, political kingdom. Rather, it was a kingdom of justice where the poor would not go empty-handed and the oppressed would be freed. Even more astonishing, prostitutes and tax collectors would enter the kingdom before the righteous. The kingdom was one that was both present with Jesus' words and yet still to come in the future. Jesus' unusual actions in the name of the kingdom included physical healing, casting out demons, taming nature, and raising the dead to life.

Eventually, as Jesus' followers multiplied, the Jewish leaders and Roman authorities became alarmed. Jewish leaders accused Jesus of **blasphemy**. He was brought before the Roman procurator Pontius Pilate as an insurrectionist. Pilate condemned Jesus to death, and he was crucified publicly on a cross.

Yet, Jesus' story did not end there. Three days later, his followers found an empty tomb. Several of his followers, including Mary Magdalene and Jesus' **Apostles**, were visited by the Risen Jesus in the days and weeks that followed. This was more than resuscitation: Jesus transcended mortality. With their experiences of the Risen Jesus, the lives of Jesus' followers were changed. Those who had abandoned Jesus on the cross were now willing to die horrible deaths for their convictions. Jesus' resurrection helped the early Christians understand his divinity and his mission.

➤ If Christians did not believe Jesus is risen from the dead, what significance do you believe the religion would have today?

blasphemy

Any word or deed that defames that which is considered sacred by a group of people. In Christianity, it is any thought, word, or act that expresses hatred for God, Christ, the Church, saints, or other holy things.

Apostles

Meaning "one who has been sent," originally it referred to the Twelve whom Jesus chose to help him in his earthly ministry. The successors of the Twelve Apostles are the bishops of the Catholic Church.

The Early Church

After a period of forty days, some of Jesus' disciples witnessed his return to heaven. Subsequently they returned to Jerusalem for the Jewish spring harvest festival of Shavuot. As the disciples hid in an upper room for fear that the same people who arrested and crucified Jesus would come for them, they experienced a phenomenon that they determined to be the coming of the Holy Spirit. At this, the disciples lost all fear and went out into the streets of Jerusalem to preach to the Jews. In their native languages, Jews from the Diaspora heard about Jesus for the first time. A number of Jews became followers of Jesus on that day, which is known as Pentecost because it is fifty days after the resurrection of Jesus. Pentecost has become known as the "birthday of the Church."

God made a new covenant through Jesus Christ. In that covenant, the Church became the New Israel. Jerusalem became the first center of Christianity. From there, missionaries went to other places in Palestine, including the region of Samaria. They quickly moved beyond Palestine to other cities with Jewish populations such as Antioch, Alexandria, and Rome. In Antioch, the followers of Jesus first became known as "Christians." In their minds, they were not starting a new religion. Rather, the coming of Jesus was the fulfillment of God's promise to send a Messiah to the Jews.

➤ **What does it mean to say "Jesus was not a Christian"?**

Gentile

A person who is not of Jewish origin.

council

The gathering of all bishops of the world in their exercise of authority over the universal Church. A council is usually called by the pope.

The spread of Christianity drew opposition from both Jews and Romans. Preaching about a Jewish Messiah in a synagogue evoked a spectrum of responses—from acceptance, to polite disagreement, to outright hostility. Paul of Tarsus was originally a Pharisaic Jew who persecuted Christians. After a conversion experience, Paul helped found Christian communities in Asia Minor and Greece. He wrote letters called *epistles* to the fledgling communities to encourage their new life in Christ. Internal dissensions were also prevalent. Christians had to decide which Jewish laws **Gentile** converts would need to follow. Eventually it was decided at a **council** in Jerusalem that Gentile Christians would not have to follow all of the Mosaic Law. In fact, the council made the following decision:

It is the decision of the Holy Spirit and of us not to place on you any burden beyond these necessities, namely, to abstain from meat sacrificed to idols, from blood, from meats of strangled animals, and from unlawful marriage. If you keep free of these, you will be doing what is right. Farewell. (Acts 15:28–29)

➤ *Anti-Semitism* **means discrimination against Jews. Anti-Semitism involving Christians had its roots in the early Church. How so?**

As Christianity spread, it quickly became more a Gentile religion than a Jewish one, though Jewish scriptures and forms of worship were maintained. As more Gentiles became Christian, it became less likely for Jews to convert to Christianity. By the second century, distinctions between Judaism and Christianity were clear.

Roman leaders decreed Christianity illegal throughout much of its first three centuries. With such laws, many Christians were targets of various forms of persecution. The city of Rome was the most notorious in its persecution of Christians. Many Christians welcomed their fate, for their persecutions were an opportunity to suffer as Jesus had. Those who died for their faith were called

marytr

A witness to the truth of faith, in which the person endures even death to be faithful to his or her beliefs.

martyrs. Some notable early Christian martyrs are Ignatius of Antioch, Polycarp of Smyrna, and Felicitas and Perpetua. The burial places of martyrs became destinations of Christian pilgrimages in the second and third centuries.

Things changed for Christians when the Roman Emperor Constantine proclaimed official toleration of all religions in his Edict of Milan (AD 313), including Christianity. Constantine was baptized a Christian on his deathbed. Christianity was made the official religion of the Roman Empire at the end of the fourth century.

Legalized Christianity

As the persecutions ceased, Christians organized themselves with bishops—successors of the Apostles—as leaders. Questions of Christian identity arose. Unlike Jews, who were defined as Jews at birth or by conversion, Christian self-definition was not as clear. A central issue was to express a unified understanding of Jesus, the God Jesus called Father, and the Holy Spirit he sent. Another issue involved the relationship between Jesus' divinity and his humanity.

A number of Church councils convened (for the most part at the order of the emperor of Constantinople) between 325 and 451 to address the questions of the nature of God and the nature of Jesus. With regard to Jesus' relationship with the Father and the Holy Spirit, the Nicene Creed was composed at the Council of Nicaea (325) and at the Council of Constantinople (381). The Nicene Creed spells out what is believed about the nature of God. The doctrine of the Trinity states that God is Three Persons in one substance: Father, Son, and Holy Spirit. With regard to the nature of Jesus, the Council of Ephesus (431) declared that Mary was indeed the human mother of Jesus as well as the Mother of God, while the Council of Chalcedon (451) declared Jesus to be fully human and fully divine. Belief in these doctrines came to define a person as a true Christian.

As Christianity became more accepted, some men and women withdrew into the Egyptian desert for an austere life of prayer and solitude. The word *monk* comes from the word *mono*, meaning "one." Athanasius, an important figure at the Council of Nicea, wrote a biography of St. Antony of Egypt (362). This book was widely read in both Greek and Latin. Antony later became known as the "father of monasticism." Less austere, but no less dedicated, St. Benedict, the founder of Monte Cassino, a monastery in Italy, wrote a "rule" for his monks that became a foundation for monasticism throughout the centuries. Benedict's rule emphasizes a balanced life of prayer, work, and study.

➤ Of prayer, work, and study, which has the most prominence in your life? Which has the least prominence?

Growing Divisions

Constantine's decision to move the capital of the Roman Empire to Byzantium (renamed Constantinople) in Asia Minor in 330 resulted in two political centers. This decision exacerbated the already existing differences between the Greek-speaking east and the Latin-speaking west. Christianity was not immune to this division. The Church became more easily separated into the Roman Church in the West and the Eastern Church in the Byzantine Empire. Differences in language, culture, music, art, architecture, government, and ritual became increasingly distinct between the eastern and western wings of the Church.

Constantine

patriarchates

The Council of Chalcedon established five major centers of Christianity. These **patriarchates** were Constantinople, Antioch, Alexandria, and Jerusalem in the east and Rome in the west. Each center developed autonomously. The leaders of these Christian centers, called "patriarchs," made up a loose confederation of equals. As the Roman Empire decreased in power, the patriarch or bishop of Rome increased in his esteem. Believing Rome to be the burial place of Peter, the person on whom Jesus would build his Church, the bishop

Any of the bishops of the ancient or Eastern Orthodox sees of Constantinople, Alexandria, Antioch, and Jerusalem or the ancient and Western see of Rome with authority over other bishops.

of Rome claimed primacy over the other patriarchates. The eastern patriarchs agreed *respect* should be given to the bishop of Rome, but they disagreed that the bishop of Rome should have *primacy* over them. In fact, the patriarch of Constantinople

pope

From the Latin word for "papa," the pope is the Bishop of Rome and has primacy over the other bishops in the Catholic Church.

believed his city was the New Rome because it was the seat of the Emperor (though he did not believe he had more authority than the other patriarchs did).

As the Roman Empire collapsed in the fifth century, the Germanic tribes moved into Europe in great numbers. With no strong political leader, the bishop of Rome (called the **pope**) took on some of the temporal leadership. A large number of conversions to Christianity took place within these tribes. Often the conversion of the tribal leader meant the conversion of the entire tribe, as with the Frank leader, Clovis. The more conversions, the stronger the Western Church became as an institution. On Christmas Day in the year 800, Pope Leo III crowned Charlemagne emperor of the newly established Holy Roman Empire.

In the seventh and eighth centuries, Muslims, adherents of the new religion called Islam, began conquering the Byzantine Empire. Egypt, Syria, and Palestine were captured. Thus, three of the four eastern patriarchates—Alexandria, Antioch, and Jerusalem—were controlled by Muslims.

By the Middle Ages the tension between the Eastern and Western Church reached its boiling point. While the claim of primacy by the bishop of Rome, the crowning of Charlemagne as Emperor in the west, and the missionary efforts of the east into Slavic lands were major issues, other differences compounded the problem. For example, the use of leavened bread for Eucharist in the east and unleavened bread for Eucharist in the west, the ordination of married men in the east, and differences in Lenten observances. In addition, at the Council of Toledo, western bishops added a line ("the Holy Spirit . . . who proceeded from the Father *and the Son*") to the Nicene Creed without consulting eastern patriarchs. Not happy with the addition and excluded from the discussion, eastern patriarchs found the statement heretical. Known as the *filioque* ("and the son") controversy, this was the final straw. In 1054, a mutual excommunication between Rome and Constantinople took place. Even if that did not seal the split, the destruction of Constantinople by western Christian Crusaders in 1204 did. These events led to what is known as the *Great Schism*.

Though the emperors at the Council of Lyons (1274) and the Council of Florence (1438–39) made attempts at reconciliation, Eastern Church authorities rejected the attempts. The patriarchs, who considered each other, including the pope, as equals, could not accept the claim of papal superiority. Eastern Christianity became known as Orthodox Christianity, meaning they maintain apostolic teaching in a "right" or "straight" manner. The Christians of the east believed their form of Christianity came *straight* from Jesus and the Apostles.

> ➤ Of all the causes leading to division between East and West, which to you seems most serious? Why?

Seeds of Reformation

In both the east and west, Church-state relationships were not always amicable. In the west, a controversy grew over who could appoint local bishops. Kings felt they had the power to do so, but Church leaders disagreed. The controversy, known as the *Investiture Controversy*, became so great that King Henry IV and Pope Gregory VII clashed. The pope excommunicated the king. Eventually, the king gave in to the sovereignty of the pope as long as the king had the right to approve of the pope's choices for bishops.

The Church and state were more likely to cooperate when they had a common enemy. One example of this was when the Muslims captured Jerusalem. To counter the Muslim insurgence, the **Crusades** were launched from Europe. However, after three centuries of Crusades, Christians were unable to permanently restore Jerusalem to their possession.

The Western Church—commonly called the Roman Catholic Church—of the twelfth and thirteenth centuries had many temporal concerns and exerted great political power, especially through

Crusades
A series of military expeditions by Western Christians in the eleventh through thirteenth centuries designed to take the Holy Land back from the Muslims.

The Stigama of St. Francis

its landholdings. Many bishops and abbots possessed as much power as the local princes did. Attempts were made to reform the Church. St. Francis of Assisi (1182–1226) introduced a new religious order in which its members owned few, if any, possessions. Rather, he and his followers were *mendicants* ("beggars") who encouraged people to imitate Jesus by embracing poverty.

Not all efforts at internal reform worked. In 1309 the French king controlled the election of the pope, and the French pope, Clement V, took up residence at Avignon, France, where the western Church was ruled until 1377. Arguments over who was pope, where the pope should reign, and pockets of corruption within the institutional Church all contributed to the growing dismay with the Roman Catholic Church. These and other factors compromised the integrity of the Church and left the door open for further reform.

Though there were others before him, the German Augustinian priest Martin Luther is generally recognized as the catalyst of the Protestant Reformation. On October 31, 1517, the eve of All Saints, Martin Luther nailed his *Ninety-five Theses* to the door of the church at Wittenburg. His action set off a firestorm between himself and Roman Catholic officials. Luther had come to believe that authority within the Catholic Church should lie solely within the Bible and not Church tradition or the **Magisterium**. He believed salvation had no connection with a person's actions, but only with a person's faith. He also believed in the priesthood of all believers, not just an ordained ministry. With the

Magisterium

The official teaching authority of the Church. The Magisterium is the bishops in communion with the successor of Peter, the Bishop of Rome (Pope).

Bible as his sole source of authority, Luther left the priest-hood, and a denomination of Christianity emerged called Lutheran.

The Protestant movement spread throughout much of northern Europe, Scandinavia, and North America. Luther's reform had a dramatic effect on Christians in Germany. Southern Germans tended to stay with the Catholic Church while northern Germans tended to follow Luther. National churches following the Lutheran tradition soon sprang up in the Scandinavian countries of Norway, Finland, Sweden, and Denmark.

There were other reformers in the sixteenth century besides Luther. The French-born John Calvin and the Swiss-born Ulrich Zwingli began church reforms of their own in Zurich and Geneva, Switzerland, respectively. Along with Luther, however, Calvin and Zwingli retained a number of Catholic liturgical practices.

More radical Protestant groups believed that the reformers had not gone far enough. The Anabaptists and Mennonites abolished most liturgical practices, calling for still simpler forms of worship. They did not accept infant baptism, insisting that baptism into Christ was an adult decision. They were also against the establishment of a state church. A number of Anabaptists and Mennonites, as well as some Puritans, escaped to America because of religious persecution by the more tradi-tional Protestant groups like the Calvinists and Lutherans.

As the Protestant movement grew, King Henry VIII of England was having his own problems with the Catholic Church. Once called the "Defender of the Faith," Henry received a dispensation from the Pope to marry his dead brother's widow, Catherine of Aragon. Henry insisted his heir to the throne be male, but Catherine did not bear a son who lived to maturity, so Henry petitioned Pope Clement VII to rescind his dispensation so Henry could marry the young Anne Boleyn. The pope would not grant the king his wish, so Henry countered by declaring himself head of the Catholic Church in England. Anyone who refused to accept his Act of Supremacy was considered a traitor to the throne. The

Catholic Church in England declared its independence from papal authority and became a national church, known as the Church of England. Most inhabitants of England accepted this change because there was little difference in the doctrine or practice of the faith. The difference came in who was in charge.

Martin Luther

The English Reformation spread to other parts of the British Empire, each becoming national churches, such as the Church of Scotland or the Church of South Africa. The growing confederation of national churches is known today as the Anglican Communion.

Though it is difficult to generalize about the more than two thousand Protestant denominations today, those Protestant groups that began in the sixteenth century do have some broadly held beliefs that were articulated by Martin Luther. For example, most Protestants hold that salvation is by faith alone, defer authority on matters of faith to what is written in the Bible, and accept just two sacraments, Baptism and Communion.

Ulrich Zwigli

Henry VIII

John Calvin

➤ Name some occasions of reform you have witnessed in your own religious community.

The Catholic Reformation

In 1545 the Catholic Church called a council to address the issues promulgated by the Protestant reformers. The decisions made at the Council of Trent (1545–1563) were to have lasting effects within the Roman Catholic Church and with its relationship to Protestantism and Anglicanism for the next four hundred years.

The Council of Trent reiterated Catholic teaching in several doctrinal areas. The council reaffirmed papal supremacy. It said that salvation is marked by faith *and* good works. It named the Mass as a true sacrifice and reaffirmed (from the Forth Latern Council) **transubstantiation** as the doctrine stating how Jesus is truly present in the consecrated bread and wine. It emphasized its teaching that there are seven true sacraments.

transubstantiation
The term used to express how the reality (substance) of bread and wine changes into the reality of Jesus' risen and glorified body and blood in the Eucharist.

The Modern Period

A revolution of ideas known as the Age of Enlightenment in the seventeenth century inaugurated the modern period. For example, *rationalists* stressed the power of human reason. *Empiricists* taught that reality is perceivable only in the five senses. Some Enlightenment views in this period diminished religion by increasing the emphasis in the belief that people could determine their own destiny and had little need for God. There was a growing movement toward democracy and the separation of church and state.

More positively, the modern period witnessed successes in the missionary efforts in North America from Catholicism, Protestanism, and Anglicanism. French Catholics went to North America, Indochina, and Africa. Spanish Catholics went to North America and South America. Portuguese Catholics went to Brazil, Africa, China, and India. Dutch Reformers went to Africa and Indonesia. In the late eighteenth and early nineteenth centuries, various other Protestant groups made headway in Asia, Africa, and especially North America (except for the French Province of Quebec, Canada). Anglicanism spread as the British Empire expanded.

In the east, the czars subordinated the Orthodox Church in Russia. In fact, Czar Peter the Great abolished the Russian patriarchate and had the church administered by the state. Though the patriarchate was reestablished during the Russian Revolution, communism persecuted all forms of religious expression not only in Russia, but wherever communism ruled. It was not until the breakup of the Soviet Union in 1991 that the Orthodox Church in eastern and central Europe and in Russia regained some life.

A bright light within the vast diversity of Christianity is the *ecumenical movement*. This movement attempts to bring about understanding among the various Christian groups. The World Council of Churches based in Geneva was founded in 1948 and presently has more than three hundred members from Orthodox, Anglican, and Protestant denominations. Also, the Second Vatican Council (1962–65) made major strides in recognizing the validity of the existence of the various religions in the world. Such openness was exhibited when members of the Eastern Orthodox churches, Anglican Communion, and some Protestant churches were invited to attend the Council.

➤ **Agree or disagree: The division among Christian groups is a great scandal to Christianity.**

Movements within Protestantism

The words *fundamentalism*, *evangelicalism*, and *pentecostalism* are often interchangeable in popular culture. However, though related, they are distinct movements within Protestantism.

Christian fundamentalism is a movement begun at the beginning of the twentieth century in the United States. The distribution of a series of pamphlets called *The Fundamentals* advocated returning to what was understood as the basics or fundamentals of Christianity. Believing Protestantism was becoming too secularized, especially in the area of science, fundamentalists advocated the infallibility of the Bible on issues of historical and scientific matters. In other words, fundamentalists hold that what is written in the Bible is to be understood in its most literal sense. Hence, the world was created in six days of a seven-day week.

Though related to fundamentalism, evangelicalism is more moderate. It, too, is a movement within Protestantism, based mainly in North America and Northern Europe. The word *evangelical* comes from the Greek word for "good news." Evangelicalism emphasizes a personal faith in Jesus Christ and the Bible as an individual's sole religious authority. In addition, "witnessing," or sharing faith with others, is important in this movement. The evangelical movement is often manifested in such events as tent revivals and crusades like those initiated by Billy Graham.

Billy Graham

Pentecostalism is one form of evangelicalism. It is a movement that emphasizes the "gifts of the Holy Spirit" as recorded at the first Pentecost in the Acts of the Apostles. These gifts may include speaking in tongues, healing, holy joy, and holy tears. Pentecostalism exhibits the widest spectrum of doctrinal beliefs and can be found in all branches of Christianity.

■ Section 1 Summary

- Jesus of Nazareth is the central figure in Christianity.

- Christianity began as a small Jewish sect but later became distinct from Judaism.

- Early Christians were defined by what they believed.

- Many Christians were martyred for their faith; later, monasticism became the most austere life a Christian could choose.

- Eventually the Church was divided into East and West in what is known as the Great Schism.

- The Protestant Reformation was a multifaceted attempt to reform Catholic Christianity.

- The Council of Trent highlighted the Catholic reformation and restated Catholic teaching on several doctrinal issues.

- In the modern period, Christianity encountered the Age of Enlightenment.

- The ecumenical movement was an attempt to unify the Christian churches.

■ Section 1 Review Questions

1. What do Christians believe about Jesus of Nazareth?

2. Why is Pentecost significant to Christians?

3. What was the role of Paul in the spread of Christianity?

4. Explain the significance of the Emperor Constantine in the history of Christianity.

5. Name two important Christian doctrines that were defined at the Church councils between the fourth and fifth centuries.

6. Who was Benedict?

7. Briefly trace the events that led to the division between the Church in the East and the Church in the West.

8. What major doctrines and beliefs do most Protestants share?

9. How did Anglicanism begin?

10. How did rationalism and empiricism affect Christianity during the modern period?

11. What is the ecumenical movement?

12. Define *fundamentalism, evangelicalism,* and *pentecostalism.*

• 2. Sacred Stories and Sacred Scriptures

The Bible (from the Greek word *biblia* meaning "books") is the collection of sacred Christian writings, or Scriptures. The Bible is actually a book of books. The Christian Bible includes the Hebrew Scriptures used by Jews, more commonly known to Christians as the Old Testament. The New Testament includes the gospels, which are the stories of the life of Jesus, as well as epistles or letters of the early Christian communities. In addition, one book is a history of the early Church, while the last book is apocalyptic in nature. All Christians agree on the twenty-seven books of the New Testament. There are some differences between accepted Old Testament books of the Protestant and Catholic Bibles.

There are other important Christian writings that are not in the Scriptures. One explained in this section is *apologetics,* from the Greek for "in defense of." Apologetics is a style of writing that defends and explains the Christian faith.

The Bible

For the first Christians, who were Jews, the Hebrew Bible was recognized already as authoritative. Since we studied the Hebrew Bible last chapter, we will move to the group of Scriptures written by first-century Christians called the New Testament. God inspired the human authors of the sacred books. To quote the Second Vatican Council document *Dei Verbum:*

To compose the sacred books, God chose certain men who, all the while he employed them in this task, made full use of their own faculties and powers so that, though he acted in them and by them, it was as true authors that they consigned to writing whatever he wanted written, and no more. (11)

The New Testament itself is a collection of twenty-seven books written in Greek in the first century. All but one author was Jewish. The author of the Gospel according to Luke and the Acts of the Apostles was a Gentile. There are four distinct literary genres among these twenty-seven books. There are four gospels, one narrative history, twenty-one letters, and one apocalyptic book. The gospels are the pre-eminent books of the New Testament, for they proclaim Jesus as the Son of God through the telling of his life, ministry, death, and resurrection (*CCC*, 139). The *epistles*, or "letters," are what we would consider formal letters written by an individual to Christian communities or to individuals. The Acts of the Apostles narrates a history of the first Christians and their missionary efforts from Jerusalem to Rome. The Revelation to John is the highly symbolic and allegorical account of a vision a man named John had of future earthly disasters and the intervention of God to set up the kingdom of heaven here on earth.

There were a number of other Christian writings that were written as gospels, epistles, or were **apocalyptic** in nature (e.g., the Gospel of Thomas or the Apocalypse of Peter); however, these were written in the second or third centuries and were judged to not meet the criteria of the Christian **canon**. Early Christian leaders set up four criteria for a book to be included in the New Testament. It must be

apocalyptic

A prophetic or symbolic revelation of the end of the world. These were written in a number of Jewish and Christian texts from around the second century BC to the second century AD.

canon

For Catholics, the twenty-seven New Testament books and forty-six Old Testament books that are accepted as inspired books by the Church.

1) apostolic, that is, attributed to an Apostle or one of his companions; 2) ancient; 3) widely read among the faithful; and 4) a source of the truth of God's revelation and not **heresy**.

All branches of Christianity agree on what books are authoritative in the New Testament. They do not agree on what books are authoritative in the Hebrew Bible. All agree on the same thirty-nine books. Catholics include seven more books written during the Second Temple period, making the number of authoritative books in the Hebrew Bible forty-six. Various Eastern Orthodox churches have more than forty-six Old Testament books in their Bibles. Protestants typically consider any books beyond the agreed upon thirty-nine as *apocryphal*, that is, "dubious" or of dubious authority.

While it can be said that there is a general consensus among Christians regarding the content of the Bible, this cannot be said about interpretation. All Christians agree the Bible is the inspired Word of God. Both the Old and New Testaments reveal God's divine plan to humankind. Catholics, Eastern Orthodox, Anglican, and some Protestant groups believe the Bible is the inspired Word of God in human language. They believe that there is no error in any matters regarding salvation, but there may be inaccuracies with regard to secular matters such as history and science. Many more Protestants believe that since God is the author of the Bible, it is the literal Word of God who dictated word-for-word to the various writers over the centuries. For them, the Bible errs neither in spiritual nor secular matters because God does not err.

Christians use the Bible in both public and private settings. Individuals may read the Bible as part of their prayer

heresy

For Christians, an obstinate denial after Baptism to believe a truth that must be believed with divine and Catholic faith, or an obstinate doubt about such truth.

life. The Bible is often used as part of family devotions or study groups. All Christians use the Bible in their worship services. Good homilies and sermons have the potential to bring the power, nourishment, and support of the Word of God to all in its hearing.

➳ Explain this phrase from St. Jerome: "Ignorance of scripture is ignorance of Christ."

Apologetics

The second century saw a rise in Christian writings called *apologetics*. Apologetics is a style of writing that defends and explains the Christian faith. The intended audience is Christians, for contents of apologetic writings are meant to be tools Christians can use to explain and defend their faith in a world they feel does not always understand them. Influenced by Greek philosophical writings, early Christian apologists tended to appeal to the intellect in explaining and defending Christianity to Latin- and Greek-speaking polytheists. One of the first authors of apologetic literature was Irenaeus of Lyon. He wrote *Against Heresies*, a treatise against the teachings of the Gnostics, from the Greek work meaning knowledge. Gnosticism tended toward elitism, for its adherents set themselves up as purer than the Apostles because they possessed the secret spiritual knowledge necessary for salvation.

The best-known apologist of the second century was Justin Martyr. Once calling himself a "disciple of Plato," he converted to Christianity and wrote numerous treatises on Christianity. In his writings, Justin defended Christianity as a legitimate religion and lifestyle in the wider pagan world. He was martyred for the Christian faith around AD 165.

■ Section 2 Summary

■ The Sacred Scripture used by Christians is the Bible.

■ The Bible is the Word of God, revealing to humankind God's divine plan.

- Not all Christians recognize the same books in the Hebrew Bible as authoritative.

- All Christians accept the same twenty-seven books in the New Testament as authoritative.

- While there may be general consensus among the various Christian branches with regard to the content of the Bible, there is wide disagreement in its interpretation.

- Apologetics refers to a style of writing intended for Christians to help them explain and defend their faith.

■ Section 2 Review Questions

1. Name the four literary genres represented in the New Testament.

2. What is the difference among the various Christian branches with regard to the understanding of the Word of God?

3. List two ways in which Christians use the Bible in their lives.

4. What were the intentions of apologetic writings?

3. Beliefs and Practices

For all Christians, Jesus is the central figure. He is the Son of God. The importance of his life, death, and resurrection is not questioned. Christians articulate their beliefs in creeds. The Apostles' Creed, formulated about AD 150, is the most widely used among Christians. The Apostles did not write it, but it does articulate what the Apostles passed on:

> I believe in God, the Father Almighty, creator of heaven and earth. And in Jesus Christ his Son, our Lord, who was conceived by the Holy Spirit, born of the Virgin Mary, suffered under Pontius Pilate, was crucified, died, and was buried. He descended into hell and on the third day he arose again from the dead. He ascended into heaven and sits at the right hand of

God, the Father Almighty. From there he shall come to judge the living and the dead. I believe in the Holy Spirit, the holy catholic church, the communion of saints, the forgiveness of sins, the resurrection of the body, and life everlasting.

The Nicene Creed, formulated by bishops who attended the Council of Nicea in 325, is often recited at a Sunday worship service. It is similar to the Apostles' Creed in that it begins with a statement of belief in God the Father, followed by beliefs about Jesus, the Holy Spirit, and the Church. An explanation of some of the most prominent Christian beliefs and actions follows.

Trinity

Like Jews, Christians believe in only one God. God is the creator of all things, both visible and invisible. In addition, Christians believe God is all knowing, all loving, and all powerful. God is present everywhere and is unchanging. God desires only the best for all creation. However, Christians hold that there are Three Persons in the one God, Father, Son, and Holy Spirit. This doctrine of the Holy Trinity is central to Christian faith.

Jesus

Incarnation

Meaning "enfleshed," for Christians it is the taking on of human nature by God's Son.

Jesus is the second person of the Trinity, making him God. According to the doctrine of the **Incarnation**, God became flesh in the person of Jesus. Christians state this in terms of the two natures of Jesus: Jesus is fully human and fully divine. God became human so that human beings could get closer to God. Jesus was like all humans in everything but sin.

Sin

An understanding of sin helps us understand why Christians need Jesus. Sin is an offense against God. For Christians, Adam and Eve were the first sinners. God commanded them not to eat from the tree of the knowledge of good and evil, but Adam and Eve disobeyed. Thus, the first sin was the sin of disobedience. Christians believe that the sin of Adam and Eve "closed the gates of heaven" and this sin—known as the **Original Sin**—became a part of the human condition.

Original Sin

The condition of sinfulness that all humans share, resulting from Adam's first sin of disobedience.

Original Sin is washed away in Christian Baptism, though the propensity of humans to commit actual sins remains.

Salvation

God chose to redeem humanity through Jesus. Though people sin, they can be reconciled to God. There is nothing more pleasing to God than one who turns away from wrongdoing and returns to God. There is no sin that God cannot forgive. Christians believe that those who truly follow Jesus and his way of living are saved. When they die, they will be fully united with Jesus in heaven.

Christian Living

The Bible offers instruction on Christian living. Christians follow the Ten Commandments contained in the Torah. Answering a question by one of his followers on which is the greatest commandment, Jesus said, "You shall love the Lord your God with all your heart and all your soul and with all your mind. This is the greatest and the first commandment. The second is like it: You shall love your neighbor as yourself" (Matthew 22:38–39).

I THOU SHALT HAVE NO OTHER GODS BEFORE ME
II THOU SHALT NOT MAKE UNTO THEE ANY GRAVEN IMAGE
III THOU SHALT NOT TAKE THE NAME OF THE LORD THY GOD IN VAIN
IV REMEMBER THE SABBATH DAY, TO KEEP IT HOLY
V HONOUR THY FATHER AND THY MOTHER
VI THOU SHALT NOT KILL
VII THOU SHALT NOT COMMIT ADULTERY
VIII THOU SHALT NOT STEAL
IX THOU SHALT NOT BEAR FALSE WITNESS AGAINST THY NEIGHBOUR
X THOU SHALT NOT COVET

Known as the "Great Commandment," it is the foundation of a Christian life, though Christians have interpreted it in very different ways. For example, some Christians believe that to love God, they must destroy what they perceive to be the enemies of God. Others have interpreted loving God as loving what God created, including imperfect human beings. Some have interpreted loving God as abstaining from alcohol, dancing, or card playing.

Nevertheless, it is the Great Commandment to love, and the way Christians practice it has attracted many converts to Christianity. "See how the Christians love one another" has been a familiar refrain.

In the Sermon on the Mount (Matthew 5–7), Jesus offers a new interpretation of the Mosaic Law by using the formula, "You have heard it said . . . but I say to you . . . ." For example:

> You have heard that it was said to your ancestors, "You shall not kill; and whoever kills will be liable to judgment." But I say to you, whoever is angry with his brother will be liable to judgment.

> You have heard that it was said, "You shall not commit adultery." But I say to you, everyone who looks at a woman with lust has already committed adultery with her in his heart.

> It was also said, "Whoever divorces his wife must give her a bill of divorce." But I say to you, whoever divorces his wife (unless the marriage is unlawful) causes her to commit adultery, and whoever marries a divorced woman commits adultery.

> You have heard that it was said, "An eye for an eye and a tooth for a tooth." But I say to you, offer no resistance to one who is evil. When someone strikes you on (your) right cheek, turn the other one to him as well.

> You have heard that it was said, "You shall love your neighbor and hate your enemy." But I say to you, love your enemies, and pray for those who persecute you, that you may be children of your heavenly Father. (Matthew 5:21–45)

Jesus states one of the laws of Moses and then reinterprets it in a more radical, personal manner. Adultery is not committed only by action, but by the thought, whether one acts upon the thought or not. Not only should one not kill, which is prohibited in most societies, but one should not even be angry with another. Hence, Christian living calls people to go beyond the minimum and act as Jesus would act. Jesus not only loved his enemies, but was willing to die an ignominious death on the cross for them. While Jesus was mocked and scourged by his enemies, he offered no resistance.

For Jesus, the interior thought process is just as important as the exterior action. One's bad thoughts are just as sinful as one's bad actions. To live in God as Jesus did, we are to "put on the mind of Christ" (1 Corinthians 2:16). In the concrete, we put on the mind of Christ by such actions as loving our enemies, walking beyond the distance asked, giving them our coats when they are cold, washing their feet, and serving them with love. If all Christians acted as Jesus did, we would again hear our neighbors say, "See how the Christians love one another."

"There is something almost cruel about the Christian's being placed in a world which in every way wants to pressure him to do the opposite of what God bids him to do with fear and trembling in his innermost being. It would be something like the cruelty of parents if they were to threaten and sternly order their child to do thus and so—and then place the child together with the kind of children who would pressure him in every way to do just the opposite."

Søren Kierkegaard (1813–1855)

➤ **What is your reaction to Kierkegaard's statement?**

The Church

Christians are defined as those who believe in the divinity of Jesus. Further, Christians are those who accept the Bible without adding or subtracting writings. The Church is a gathering of those who believe under the guidance of the Holy Spirit that Jesus is God.

Church is the name given to the "convocation" or "assembly" of the people God has called together from every corner of the earth. With the myriad divisions of Christianity, it would seem difficult to speak about one homogeneous group, yet the Catholic Church is the Church established by Christ on the foundation of the Apostles. It possesses the fullness of the means of salvation that Christ has willed: correct and complete confession of faith, full sacramental life, and ordained ministry in apostolic succession.

One can hear in some Protestant churches from time to time expressions like, "Isn't that right, church?" or "Let the church say 'Amen!'" As Jews are considered Israel in a spiritual sense, Christians would consider themselves the New Israel. As Jews are bound by a covenant between God and themselves established with Moses in the desert, Christians are bound by a new covenant established by Jesus. Christianity does not supersede Judaism. Rather, Christians believe the coming of Jesus is the fulfillment of God's promise to the Jews.

■ Section 3 Summary

- ■ The most important Christian doctrines are contained in creedal statements such as the Apostles' Creed.

- ■ The Great Commandment on love is foundational for Christian living.

- ■ "Church" is defined as a gathering of people who proclaim Jesus as God.

■ Section 3 Review Questions

1. According to the Apostles' Creed, what do Christians believe about God?

2. Define these major Christian beliefs in Trinity, Jesus, sin, and salvation.

3. Give examples of two different ways Christians have interpreted the Great Commandment.

4. Define *Church*.

5. What does it mean to say that the Catholic Church possesses the "fullness of the means of salvation"?

● 4. Sacred Times

Like Jews, Christians find that keeping sacred time is important. The Christian calendar is centered on the life, ministry, death, and resurrection of Jesus. These sacred times, whether they are celebrated daily, weekly, or annually, have the power to sanctify life. Christian festivals and holy days vary widely among the denominations. Generally, the more formal the worship service of a denomination, the more festivals and holy days it celebrates.

For all Christians, Sunday is a holy day. As the first Christians were Jewish, they kept Saturday as their weekly day of rest, but also commemorated Sunday as the Lord's Day. Early Christians associated Sunday with the resurrection of Jesus, so they celebrated Sunday as a "little Easter." As the

Christian population became less Jewish and more Gentile, Sunday became the official Christian Sabbath.

All Christians celebrate Christmas and Easter. Many Christians expand their celebration to the Christmas cycle and the Easter cycle. The Christmas cycle includes Advent, Christmas, and Epiphany, while the Easter cycle contains Lent, Easter, and Pentecost. More information on these annual Christian cycles follows.

The Christmas Cycle

Advent

The annual Catholic Christian calendar begins with the first Sunday of Advent, which falls four Sundays before Christmas. It is a season of preparation for the *advent*, or coming, of Jesus. Eastern Orthodox and Eastern Rite Catholic churches celebrate the "Nativity Fast," a similar season of preparation that begins on November 14, forty days before Christmas.

Not only does Advent celebrate the first coming of Jesus more than two thousand years ago, but Advent is also a preparation time for the coming of Jesus into the hearts of people today and a readying for Jesus' Second Coming at the end of time. The season of Advent is in the winter, a time when the light of day gets shorter and shorter until the winter solstice on December 21. In symbolizing that the coming of Jesus is a light in the darkness, many Christians light candles on an Advent wreath. The wreath is decorated with a circle of evergreens and contains four candles. An additional candle is lit on each Sunday of the four weeks in Advent.

Christmas

The Advent season ends on Christmas Day. Christmas celebrates the birth of Jesus. Christmas is the second holiest day in the Christian year. For most Christians, Christmas Day is December 25, but for some Orthodox churches, Christmas is celebrated January 7, the day after Epiphany. Actually, the date of the birth of Jesus is unknown. In the fourth century, Christians began to celebrate the birth of Jesus (the Son of God) to contrast with the pagan winter solstice celebration of the Unconquered Sun, which was celebrated near December 25.

Epiphany

Twelve days after Christmas, using the western Gregorian calendar, is the feast of the Epiphany. The word *epiphany* means "manifestation" or "revelation." In the early days of Christianity, Epiphany was associated with three moments in the life of Jesus where he first revealed some aspect of himself to the world. Those three moments were his birth, his baptism, and his first miracle at the marriage feast of Cana. In the fourth century, the birth of Jesus came to overshadow Jesus' baptism and first miracle as moments of initial revelation. Thus, in the West, Christmas and Epiphany became two separate feasts, while in most Orthodox churches, the more ancient celebration of Epiphany was maintained.

The Easter Cycle

Lent

Easter, the greatest feast in the Christian year, is preceded by forty weekdays of preparation called Lent. The word *lent* comes

from an old English word for "springtime." The forty days of Lent are in remembrance of Jesus spending forty days in the wilderness. Ash Wednesday begins the Lenten season. It is called "Ash" Wednesday because a small cross of ashes is inscribed on the forehead of a person, reminding them that their physical bodies are transitory. During Lent, Christians prepare for the great feast of Easter by praying, doing penance, almsgiving fasting, and abstaining from other pleasures.

The last week of Lent is called Holy Week. This most solemn of weeks begins with Palm Sunday, remembering the occasion when Jesus was welcomed into the city of Jerusalem with palm branches. Holy Thursday, or Maundy Thursday, commemorates the Last Supper Jesus had with his disciples. The word *Maundy* comes from the Latin word meaning "commandment." At the Last Supper, according to the Gospel of John, Jesus gave his disciples the commandment to "love one another as I have loved you." Good Friday commemorates the crucifixion and death of Jesus. Holy Saturday remembers the day when Jesus descended to the abode of the dead. It is observed by a quiet time of prayer until that evening.

> ➤ Why do you think Christians call Good Friday "good"?

Easter

Easter is the holiest day for Christians. Easter celebrates Christ's resurrection from the dead. It is a movable feast related to the Jewish Passover. Most Christians celebrate it annually on the first Sunday after the first full moon of spring.

Catholic, Orthodox, and Anglican churches have an Easter vigil service on Holy Saturday evening. These services recall the darkness of the tomb and Christ's breaking forth from that tomb, bringing light to the world. Many Protestant churches have an Easter sunrise service that begins in darkness and continues as the sun rises, symbolizing that Jesus is the Son who rose from the dead.

Pentecost

Pentecost means "fiftieth day." As described in the Acts of the Apostles, the Holy Spirit descended on the frightened disciples of Jesus like "tongues of fire." This extraordinary experience enabled the disciples to go out into the streets of Jerusalem and proclaim the good news of Jesus. Thousands of Jews were converted on the first Pentecost. For this reason, Pentecost is known as the "birthday of the Church."

➤ **Describe a time you were frightened or afraid to publicly admit to your faith.**

Sacraments

Sacraments are sacred times marked by Christians that are not tied to a particular season. Sacraments are defined as an "outward and effective sign of the Church given by Christ to give grace." The sacraments are signs authorized by Christ that transmit God's grace to the participant, usually through something tangible like water, bread, wine, or oil. Catholics celebrate seven sacraments: Baptism, Confirmation, Eucharist, Penance, Anointing of the Sick, Holy Orders, and Matrimony. Baptism is the only sacrament recognized by all Christians. Most Christians also acknowledge Eucharist (under various names) as a sacrament.

Baptism is the sacrament that initiates the individual into the Christian community. Whether immersed in a river or pool or sprinkled with water, the priest or minister proclaims the words, "I baptize you in the name of the Father, and of the Son, and of the Holy Spirit." Anglican, Catholic, Orthodox, and some more traditional

Protestant groups such as Lutherans and Methodists baptize infants. Other Protestant denominations have "believer's baptism," where a person is only baptized when old enough to proclaim a personal belief in Jesus. The Catholic Church recognizes "one baptism for the forgiveness of sins" and accepts as valid baptisms from most other Christian denominations (for example, when a person converts from a Protestant church to the Roman Catholic Church).

Eucharist (also called the Lord's Supper or Holy Communion) fulfills Jesus' Last Supper command to break bread and share wine in his memory. This sacred meal not only brings the partakers into communion with Jesus; they also are in communion with one another as the "Body of Christ" on earth. Catholics, Orthodox, Anglicans, and some Protestants believe that Jesus is truly present in the blessed bread and wine.

➤ How can the Eucharist bring Christians together? How can the Eucharist pull Christians apart?

Prayer

Prayer is another sacred occasion for Christians. Prayer is a two-way conversation between God and an individual or group. Prayer can be formal or informal, long or short, verbal or silent. Prayer can involve singing. Different postures and various gestures can be used at different times for prayer. A person can pray anytime and anywhere.

The Bible contains a number of prayers. The Book of Psalms is a prayer book within the Bible. The Lord's Prayer, taught to the disciples by Jesus, is the prayer common to all Christians, though the wording may be slightly different:

> Our Father, who art in heaven,
>
> hallowed be Thy name.
>
> Thy kingdom come;
>
> Thy will be done on earth
>
> as it is in heaven.
>
> Give us this day our daily bread,
>
> and forgive us our trespasses
>
> as we forgive those
>
> who trespass against us.
>
> And lead us not into temptation,
>
> but deliver us from evil.
>
> For the kingdom, the power, and the glory
>   are yours
>
> now and forever.
>
> Amen.

➤ According to the Lord's Prayer, what do Christians believe?

■ Section 4 Summary

- ■ Christians commemorate the Sabbath on Sunday, the day of the Lord's resurrection.
- ■ Easter is the holiest day for Christians.
- ■ Most Christians observe the Christmas cycle and the Easter cycle of the Christian calendar.

- The Christmas cycle includes Advent, Christmas, and Epiphany. The Easter cycle includes Lent, Easter, and Pentecost.

- Sacraments are outward signs of inward spiritual grace. Baptism and Eucharist are two sacraments celebrated by most Christians.

- Prayer is a two-way conversation between an individual and God, or a community and God.

■ Section 4 Review Questions

1. Why did the early Christians change their Sabbath from Saturday to Sunday?

2. How is the Christian calendar different from the civil calendar?

3. What are the special events in the Christmas cycle?

4. What are the special events in the Easter cycle?

5. What are two sacraments that most Christians celebrate?

6. Name some of the characteristics of prayer.

● 5. Sacred Places and Sacred Spaces

A physical place called a church is the most sacred place for Christians. A church is where the community comes together

for worship and fellowship. A church is the place where new members are initiated and rites of passage are marked. Besides churches, Christians also hold the place on earth where Jesus lived and walked to be sacred. This area, in modern-day Israel, is known to Christians as the "Holy Land."

Catholic Mission Church in New Mexico

Church

Besides meaning "a gathering of people," a church is also a building. A church is the most sacred place for Christians. The exterior architecture of a church does not always clearly tell the church denomination. For example, a Gothic style church may be, among others, Catholic, Anglican, or Presbyterian. An urban storefront church may be Lutheran, Assembly of God, or Catholic.

The inside of a church is more telling. A church with an altar in the middle and a pulpit on the side would tend to be Catholic, Anglican, Orthodox, or perhaps

Chartres Cathredral

Lutheran. If, in addition, there are statues of Jesus, Mary, and the saints, then the church is likely to be Catholic. If, instead of statues, there are **icons**, it is most likely Orthodox. Protestant churches tend to be simpler in ornamentation, some with just a pulpit in the center of the sanctuary.

icons

Religious images or paintings that are traditional among many Eastern Christians.

All Christian denominations would agree that how God is worshipped is more important than where God is worshipped. In times of war, persecution, or natural disasters, Christians have worshipped in any type of building available, or outside in a meadow, forest, seashore, or desert.

Holy Land

Since Jesus is the central figure in Christianity, where Jesus lived, ministered, died, and rose from the dead is sacred to Christians. Most of the Holy Land is located in the present State of Israel. Bethlehem, where Jesus was born, Nazareth, where Jesus grew up, and the region of Galilee, where Jesus did much of his preaching and healing, are especially sacred. In addition, Jerusalem and areas surrounding it are holy spaces. Jesus preached and healed the sick in that locale. Inside the walls of Jerusalem, Jesus was tried as a criminal. Outside the walls of Jerusalem, Jesus died, was buried, resurrected, and ascended to heaven.

➤ Name a holy place that fills you with the presence of God.

■ Section 5 Summary

■ Exterior church architecture varies widely among Christian denominations.

■ Church interiors provide insight to what is important to that worshipping community.

■ Christians agree that how they worship is more important than where they worship.

■ Places where Jesus carried out his ministry are sacred spaces to Christians. These places in modern Israel are known as the Holy Land.

■ Section 5 Review Questions

1. Describe the various church architecture depicted in the photos on pages 116–117.

2. Why are Protestant churches often less formally decorated than Catholic, Orthodox, or Anglican churches?

3. Name and explain the significance of several sacred places in the Holy Land.

● 6. Other Christian Denominations through a Catholic Lens

The very word *catholic* means "universal" or "for everyone." The Church is catholic in two ways. First, it is catholic because Christ is present in the Church in the fullness of his

body, with the fullness of the means of **Church Fathers**
salvation, the fullness of faith, sacraments, *Church teachers and*
and the ordained ministry that comes *writers of the early*
from the Apostles. The Church is also uni- *centuries whose teach-*
versal because it takes the message of sal- *ings are a witness to*
vation to all people. *the Tradition of the*

A traditional statement of the **Church** *Church.*
Fathers is that "outside the Church there
is no salvation." A positive way to refor-
mulate that statement is that all people are called to this
catholic unity of the Church. However, though the Church is
for everyone, not everyone belongs to the Church in the same
way. There is a certain ordering of people in the Church: full
members are those who are baptized Catholics and who accept
all the tenets of the Church, besides behaving in a loving way.

The Church also knows that other Christians, who for various reasons do not profess the Catholic faith in totality or have
had their unity in the pope severed, are still joined in many ways
with the Church. Others who have not received the good news
of Jesus Christ are also related to the Church in various ways.

The Church desires to recover the gift of unity of all
Christians. This is the charge of ecumenism, which seeks a visible unity of the Christian faith. Ecumenism is the responsibility of all Catholics. Certain things are necessary for Catholics to
promote Christian unity. The person must be committed to:

- a permanent renewal of the Church in greater fideli-
  ty to its vocation;
- a conversion of heart, that is, a commitment to live a
  holier life;
- praying with separated Christians;
- growing in knowledge of other Christians;
- understanding the goals of ecumenism;
- witnessing and learning from dialogue between
  Catholic theologians and theologians of other
  Christian denominations;
- collaborating in service to all people.

The Catholic Church has engaged in official dialogue with quite a number of Christian denominations, including Anglican and Orthodox Christians. Major topics included Baptism, the Eucharist, episcopacy and papacy, and mixed marriages. A starting point in many of the discussions is Sacred Scripture, since all Christians hold up the importance of the Word of God in the life of the Church and world. This particular issue and the dialogue it offers are presented in the following subsections.

The Book of the Church

Catholics (and Anglicans and Eastern Orthodox) understand the Bible as the "Book of the Church." This is a significant difference from other Christian denominations that belong to a "church of the Book." Catholics understand that the inspired text of the Bible contains the fullness of God's revelation and that the Church continues to guide the People of God through its integration and application of truths of Scripture. God continues to guide the successors of the Apostles—the pope and the bishops—in every generation to preserve, expound on, and spread God's word to all. This ongoing teaching is known as the Church's Tradition. Several Christian denominations do not assign equal weight to Scripture and Tradition. For some Christians, the Bible is God's final revelation to the world. Answers to every human question imaginable can be answered in the pages of Scripture.

Historically speaking, the purpose for advocating *sola scriptura* ("scripture alone") was to limit the authority of the Catholic Church to what was in the Bible. For example, Protestant reformers denied the doctrines of papal supremacy and veneration of images because neither was found in the Bible. Rather, the Word of God cannot be restricted to the printed word. The Word had a long, gradual process in oral tradition before it was written down. Reflecting on their experience of the God of history, the Jewish people before the time of Jesus as well as the first followers of Jesus reinterpreted and revised the telling of God's actions among them. As has been noted earlier, the oral tradition of the Apostles existed before the first book of the New Testament was ever written down. The many writings of the early Christians of the first century that later became part of the New Testament were seen as coming out of apostolic tradition. The oral tradition was no less the work of the Holy Spirit than was the written Bible.

Many Christians—Catholics included—have misunderstandings about the role of the Bible in the life of the Church. Listening to evangelists on the radio or watching them on television adds to the confusion. Until recently, personal reading of the Bible was not encouraged by the Church. The Protestant Reformation coincided with the invention of the printing press. During this time, Bibles were being translated into the vernacular so that individuals could read and interpret the Bible for themselves. The Church discouraged personal interpretation of Scripture. This attitude toward the Bible led to many Protestants calling Catholics non-biblical Christians, though Scripture never ceased from being proclaimed during every Mass.

The Second Vatican Council document *Dei Verbum* encouraged Catholics to read, study, and pray the Sacred Scriptures. Ecumenical dialogue has broken down many of the barriers established during the Protestant Reformation. Biblical scholars from all branches of Christianity have cooperated in the study of the Bible as well as publishing joint Bible translations and commentaries.

Understanding Inerrancy

Catholics, Orthodox, Anglicans, and some Protestants understand biblical inerrancy quite differently. Each agrees that there is no error in the Bible with regard to those truths that are necessary for our salvation. For instance, it is necessary for salvation to affirm that God, and no other god or gods, is the creator of the world.

Some Protestants believe the Bible is *completely* inerrant, that is, free from error. They believe the Bible is free from error not only in the areas of faith and morals, but also in history, geography, and science. God's words are very clear to them, so interpretation is not necessary. They try to have Scripture answer questions that were never pondered by the biblical authors. For example, how God created the world or how long it took God to create the world is not a necessary truth for our salvation. Similarly, it is not necessary to know how many angels were at the empty tomb—one in Matthew 28:2 or two in John 20:12. What is important for salvation is faith in the resurrection of Jesus. The Bible is meant to guide us in faith and morals, not in science, geography, or history. The former is necessary for our salvation, while the latter is not.

Interpreting the Bible

The Catholic Church continues to interpret the meaning of God's Word. This interpretation takes place through the inspiration of the Holy Spirit and through Church leadership, the Magisterium. Many Protestants see interpretation as necessary, but encourage private and personal interpretation. This is an area of disagreement.

The self-revelation of God to all humankind is expressed in a very special way. This special revelation is sufficient and thus closed. All God wanted to reveal regarding divine will and divine plan are so revealed, and no other revelation is necessary. Though revelation has ceased, interpretation of God's revelation has not. For example, there is nothing in the Bible that speaks against one human being owning another human being as a slave. Human history, in the light of the Holy Spirit, has shown us the egregious error of such a human institution. Just because it is in the Bible does not mean God approves of human slavery. The Catholic Church believes that such interpretation must take place under the direction of the Church, particularly the Magisterium.

The Word of God is transmitted by human language and human history. The words printed in the Bible are not the property of the author at the time it was written, but they are part of the Church, the People of God. One finds great meaning in a passage when one goes beyond what is written. The written word cannot be left to itself, but must be interpreted with the guidance of the Holy Spirit. It is God still speaking to the Church today, not just when the words were written down.

When disputes with regard to faith and morals arise, it is the duty and obligation of the Magisterium to interpret in the light of its long history of apostolic tradition, the writings of the Greek and Latin Fathers of the Church and the ecumenical councils, and the Bible itself. The Magisterium does not see itself as an entity that opposes personal thinking. Rather, it sees itself as a servant safeguarding Scripture and Tradition from being manipulated.

The official teaching office of the Catholic Church interprets Scripture not from the point of view of what the biblical author may have meant when he wrote it, but what a passage means to the Church community to each generation that follows. Some Bible passages may not seem clear to those reading the Bible millennia removed from what is being written. More than one interpretation may be valid as long as these interpretations are not in conflict with the Church's long tradition.

Taizé

Taizé is a monastic community of about one hundred Protestant and Catholic brothers from more than twenty-five countries and every continent. The community welcomes thousands of visitors each year. Visitors are invited to join with the brothers in their prayer. The mission of the community is reconciliation among the diverse Christian communities. Reconciliation is not an end in itself. Rather, the community encourages those who visit to return home as leavens of reconciliation in their own communities.

Workshop in the ecumenical community of Taizé in France

Three times each day, everyone gathers in the "Church of Reconciliation" for prayer together. The church was built in 1962 and was enlarged in 1990. The "songs of Taizé" are easily recognizable. They are made up of a simple phrase taken up again and again, in many different languages, and they are a way of expressing a basic reality, quickly grasped by the mind and then gradually penetrating the entire person. In the evening, the sung prayer continues far into the night. Meanwhile, brothers remain in the church to listen to those who wish to talk about a personal problem or question.

The Saturday evening prayer is celebrated as a vigil of the Resurrection, a festival of light. On Friday evenings, the icon of the Cross is placed in the center of the Church, and those who wish can come and pray around it in silence as a way of entrusting to God their own burdens and those of others, and so accompanying the Risen Christ who remains close to all who are undergoing trial.

(Adapted from www.taize.fr.)

How many Christian denominations different from your own can you name?

What is one way you have personally experienced the division that exists among Christians of different denominations?

■ Section 6 Summary

■ The traditional purpose of ecumenism is Christian unity.

■ Ecumenism is a uniquely Christian movement.

■ Catholics dialoguing with Christians about Scripture has had a spectrum of responses from collaboration to non-engagement.

■ All Christians agree on the content of the New Testament; but interpretation of its contents varies widely.

■ While most Protestants believe the Bible is the sole authority for faith and morals, Orthodox and Anglicans join Catholics in believing Scripture and Tradition go hand in hand as sources of authority on faith and morals

■ The teaching office of the Catholic Church, the Magisterium, sees itself as obligated to safeguard Scripture and Tradition from being manipulated.

■ Section 6 Review Questions

1. Define ecumenism.

2. What are the two understandings of *inerrancy* described in this section?

3. What is *sola scriptura*?

4. Why does the Catholic Church say that both Scripture and Tradition are sources of authority for Catholics?

5. What is the difference between describing the relationship between the Church and the Bible as "the book of the Church" versus "the Church of the book"?

● Conclusion

A major symbol for Christianity is the cross. The cross without a body is a symbol of the risen Jesus, the Jesus that Christians believe is present in all creation. The cross has both a vertical and a horizontal beam. The place where the beams come together symbolizes the place where the God of heaven is made flesh on earth. In turn, because of the life of Jesus, humans can participate in the divine.

There is something very concrete about Christian beliefs. Christianity is about a God who participates fully in all that God creates. In turn, all creation is lifted up. Those Christian denominations that are sacramental in nature believe the use of ordinary things in their liturgies like bread, water, wine, and oil transform the ordinary into the extraordinary. (For those Christians in whom the Word of God is emphasized, it is held that that word has the power to transform lives.) In any case, it is Christians who state that belief in Jesus transforms lives.

It is ironic, then, that belief in Jesus can evoke so many different understandings. The chapter closed with a description of the Taizé community. Like so many other Christian communities and individuals, Taizé strives for reconciliation among Christians both institutionally and individually. It is the gift of diversity rather than the pain of division that most Christians believe Jesus Christ desires.

■ Chapter 3 Summary

- ■ Jesus of Nazareth is the central figure in Christianity.

- ■ Christianity began as a small Jewish sect and grew to be a predominantly Gentile world religion.

- ■ The first Christians were persecuted by Roman authorities until the Roman emperor Constantine legalized Christianity.

- ■ Monasticism was a response to the growing complacency of Christians.

- ■ A number of Church councils of the fourth and fifth centuries defined the major Christian doctrines.

- ■ Growing divisions between east and west led to a split between the church centered in Rome and the church centered in Constantinople.

- ■ The Protestant Reformation was initiated by Martin Luther, an Augustinian priest.

- ■ The Catholic Reformation was punctuated by the teachings of the Council of Trent.

- ■ The Age of Enlightenment posed a threat to many Christians because of its emphasis on rationalism and empiricism.

■ The ecumenical movement attempts to emphasize the similarities rather than the differences between Christian denominations.

■ The Bible is a "book of books." It is the sole source of authority for some Christians, while some denominations, including Catholics, recognize the authority of both Scripture and Tradition.

■ The Christian Bible draws on its Jewish roots by including the Hebrew Scriptures.

■ The doctrine of the Trinity is the central Christian doctrine. It states that God, though one, is in three persons: Father, Son, and Holy Spirit.

■ In Jesus, God became human. Jesus is both fully human and fully divine.

■ The Great Commandment—loving God and loving neighbor—is foundational for Christian living.

■ Church is generally defined as a gathering of those who under the guidance of the Holy Spirit believe Jesus is God.

■ Easter, the day Jesus rose from the dead, is the preeminent Christian feast.

■ Prayer—a two-way conversation with God—is essential to Christian life. The Lord's Prayer is the one common prayer among Christians.

■ The physical church building is a sacred place for Christians.

■ Christians consider the Holy Land, in the State of Israel, sacred.

■ The ultimate purpose of ecumenism is Christian unity.

■ Christians differ widely with regard to attitude and interpretation of the Bible.

■ Catholics are encouraged to make Bible reading part of their prayer life.

■ Chapter 3 Review Questions

1. Who was Jesus?

2. What are *epistles*?

3. How was the Christian life different after the Edict of Milan?

4. What did the monastic rule of Benedict emphasize?

5. What doctrines were defined at the Council of Nicea and Council of Ephesus?

6. How did the eastern patriarchs regard the bishop of Rome?

7. Explain how Christian conversion of Germanic tribes often occurred.

8. What was the stated purpose of the Crusades?

9. What were some of the beliefs stated by Martin Luther in his *Ninety-five Theses*?

10. What is the derivation of the word *lent*?

11. How did the Council of Trent respond to the reformers?

12. How was religion in the modern period diminished?

13. What is the ecumenical movement? How is it manifested today?

14. What are some of the ways Christians use the Bible?

15. Name the Great Commandment that is the foundation of Christian living.

16. Define *church*.

17. How can the interior design of a church indicate which denomination worships there?

18. Which two sacraments are accepted by most Christians?

19. What are some of the ways that Christians pray?

20. What do all Christians agree about the Bible?

21. What is *sola scriptura*?

22. Why does the Catholic Church teach both Scripture and Tradition are sources of authority with regard to faith and morals?

Research & Activities

- Explain what the fallacy is in the statement, "I'm not Christian; I'm Catholic."

- Research one Christian denomination. Include in your study its history, major beliefs, and forms of worship.

- Interview a religious leader from a denomination other than your own. Ask questions to determine why the religious tradition is important to them, what are their main beliefs, and who are their role models.

- Write a report on church-state relations in your country today.

- Research the papacy in Avignon. Why was it there? Why did it remain there so long? Who were the popes? What did they accomplish? What brought the papacy back to Rome?

- Prepare a presentation on the twentieth-century Catholic apologist G.K. Chesterton.

- Prepare a presentation on Christian apocalyptic literature.

- Research Orthodox and Anglican views on the relationship between Scripture and Tradition. Compare them to the Catholic understanding.

Prayer

God, through your coming to us in Jesus and through using fallible people, you have shown yourself to be a vulnerable God; we thank you that you still trust us to offer service and work for the building of your kingdom. Keep us alert to your will and purpose and open our eyes that we may see the true needs of people around us. Enable us in humility to learn from one another, that we may be united in our mutual accountability and devoted in service for your kingdom. Through Jesus Christ, our Lord. Amen.

(From Pontifical Council for Promoting Christian Unity, 2005)

Islam

4

● Submission Brings Inner Freedom

Islam came on the world scene in the seventh century CE with the preaching of the Arab prophet Muhammad. Like Judaism and Christianity, Islam is an Abrahamic religion. All three religious traditions believe themselves heirs of Abraham and his belief in one God. Also like Judaism and Christianity, Islam is a worldwide religion covering almost every continent and race of people. While there are more Christians in the world than any other religion, Islam is not far behind in its number of adherents. In the twenty-first century, Islam's growth in the number of adherents is one of the fastest in the world.

The Arabic word *Islam* derives from the same root as the Hebrew word *shalom* for "peace." Islam means "surrender" or "submission" and refers to one who surrenders or submits to the will of God. True peace is promised with that surrender. An adherent of Islam is called a *Muslim*, which means literally "one who submits to the will of God."

Islam is a monotheistic religion. In fact, Muslims are so adamant about the oneness of God that some are uncomfortable celebrating the birthday of Muhammad because that celebration may take focus away from God. Muslims use the

Allah

The Arabic word for God.

Arabic word **Allah**, meaning *"The* God," to address God. They believe all creation is Muslim. That is, all that Allah created naturally submits to his divine will. While plants and animals instinctively submit to the will of God, human beings have free will to choose to submit or not. Allah does not force anyone to submit. Muslims insist that submitting to God is not a confining, negative command. Rather, it is a gracious surrendering to the all-compassionate, all-merciful Allah where true freedom lies.

> Which aspects described in the first three paragraphs correspond to what you see and hear about Islam and Muslims in the various forms of media? Which do not? What personal experiences have you had with Muslims?

Because all creation is Muslim at birth, Muslims do not recognize Muhammad as the founder of Islam. According to Muslims, Islam has always existed from the beginning with Adam. Muhammad did not found Islam—he restored it. God's message had been revealed since the time of Adam to the Jews and Christians through the prophets as revealed in the Torah and Gospels. While the people may follow a prophet's correct guidance for a time, eventually their message became corrupted, and God would send another prophet to guide the people back onto the straight path. For Muslims, Abraham, Moses, and Jesus were prophets and genuine Muslims who submitted to the will of God. Their message was the true message, but followers of their guidance did not persist in the right path. God wanted to bring an end to the faith-apostasy-faith cycle and called upon Muhammad to restore God's true message to the world once and for all. Muhammad himself was both a political leader and a spiritual leader. It is incorrect to call Muslims Muhammadans, for they are not followers of Muhammad. Muhammad was God's messenger to all humanity to return to their true calling, that is, to submit to the will of Allah.

Allah is at the center of Islamic life—physical, mental, economic, political, social, and spiritual. This chapter offers a brief historical overview of Islam and Islamic beliefs and how those beliefs are expressed in daily living. Islam is a universal community with members from all walks of life. Membership in the community carries with it certain obligations to God and others.

CE

ca. 570	Birth of Muhammad
610	First revelation from Allah
622	The emigration to Medina
632	Final revelation and death of Muhammad
661	Beginning of Umayyad dynasty at Damascus
680	Martyrdom of Husayn at Karbala
750	Beginning of Abbasid dynasty at Baghdad (until 1258)
909	Beginning of Fatimid dynasty in Egypt (until 1171)
1099	Capture of Jerusalem by Christian
1187	Recapture of Jerusalem by Muslim
1258	Destruction of Baghdad by Mongols
1453	Capture of Christian Constantinople by Ottoman Turks; renamed Istanbul
1502	Beginning of Safavid dynasty in Iran (until 1736)
1517	Beginning of Ottoman caliphate
1526	Founding of Mughal dynasty in India
ca. 1760	Beginnings of the Wahhabi movement in Saudi Arabia
1800s	Era of European colonialism on Muslim land
1918	End of the Ottoman Empire
1947	Partition of India and the creation of Pakistan
1948	State of Israel founded by the United Nations, displacing thousands of mostly Muslim Palestinians
1979	Islamic revolution in Iran
2001	The United States prepares for a military response after September 11 terrorism in the United States is attributed to Muslim extremists

1. A Brief History of Islam

For Muslims, Islam has always existed. Islam began with Adam, the first man. Muhammad is the "Seal of the Prophets," that is, the final messenger of God. He is the last of the prophets who received messages from God to pass on to humanity. He is not, therefore, the founder of Islam according to a Muslim definition.

Muhammad, Messenger of God

The Hijrah: Muhammad fled to Medina to establish Islam, 622 CE.

Muhammad was born in approximately 570 CE in Mecca (Makkah), located in present day Saudi Arabia. His father died before he was born and his mother died when he was six years old. Orphaned, Muhammad was raised first by his grandfather, and then by his uncle, Abu Talib, a caravan merchant. When Muhammad was old enough, he traveled with the caravans. In his travels, Muhammad often met with Jews and Christians and heard their stories. Then Muhammad met Khadija, a widowed businesswoman fifteen years his senior. She employed him, and later they married and had children.

Muhammad was accustomed to going to a cave about once a month for a time of prayer and reflection and to meditate on life's meaning. One evening, in the year 610, he was in the cave and an angel appeared to him. The angel commanded:

Read, in the name of your Lord, who created,
He created man from an embryo,
Read, and your Lord, most Exalted,
Teaches by means of the pen.
He teaches man what he never knew. (Surah 96:1–5)

Since Muhammad was illiterate, he memorized the words commanded him. The messenger was revealed as *Jibril*, or the Angel Gabriel.

According to Jibril, Muhammad was to be the messenger of Allah, the one God. Muhammad had a number of these revelations until his death and shared these revelations with his wife and close friends. His message was not unfamiliar to Jews and Christians: there is only one God, care for the poor and disadvantaged should be a priority, and people will be judged at the time of death based on how they lived. Few people believed Muhammad, for Mecca was a place of many gods. In the center of Mecca was a large, cube-like structure called the **Ka'bah**, which housed more than 360 idols. Asking the people to believe in only one God was too much for most of the people of Mecca. In addition, calling the various tribes of Mecca to be a people under one God was destructive of the diverse tribal social structures.

Ka'bah

The first Islamic shrine that Muslims believe was built by Abraham. Destroyed by pagans, it was reclaimed by Muhammad when he captured Mecca in the seventh century.

Eventually, Muhammad gained a small following. His wife always believed him and was very supportive of him. His two friends, Abu Bakr and 'Uthman, his cousin Ali, son of his uncle Abu Talib, and a former slave named Zaid were also among his first followers. Life became so unbearable for these Muslims at Mecca that they had to move. The move in 622 to present day Medina became known as the **Hijrah**, or "migration." The Hijrah marks the beginning of the Islamic calendar. Hence, the Western calendar date of 622 is 1 AH (After Hijrah) on the Islamic calendar.

Hijrah

A term meaning "migration," it recalls the escape of Muhammad from his enemies in 622 and the establishment of Islam. The Hijrah marks the start of the Islamic calendar.

Initially, things went well for the Muslims in Medina. Muhammad was not only a capable spiritual leader, but his gifts as a political leader were also recognized. As his following grew, so did his opposition. Muslims ended up battling Arabs as well as Jews in Medina. In addition, tribes from Mecca engaged in battles with Muslims of Medina. Strengthened by their many battle victories, Muhammad and thousands of his followers made their way back to Mecca and captured it. He went immediately to the Ka'bah, the shrine where various tribes worshiped their gods. Muhammad purified the Ka'bah by having all the statues removed. He rededicated the Ka'bah to the worship of the one God.

By the time Muhammad died in 632, many Arab tribes were calling themselves Muslim and submitting to the will of Allah.

➤ **What are some similarities between Christianity and Islam?**

The Rightly-Guided Caliphs

The successors of Muhammad were called **caliphs**. The first

caliphs

Islamic leaders regarded as successors of Muhammad for Sunni Muslims.

to succeed Muhammad was Abu Bakr (632–34), one of Muhammad's original disciples. Though caliph for a mere two years, Abu Bakr consolidated the loyalty of the newly Islamized tribes of the Arabian Peninsula to the Muslim leadership and community. Umar, who ruled the longest of the first four caliphs, was chosen as Abu Bakr's successor. At first an enemy of Islam, Umar oversaw the expansion of Islam to Persia, Damascus, and Jerusalem, often through military conquest. Before he died, Umar appointed a committee of

Qur'an

In Muslim belief, God's final revelation, superceding both the Jewish and Christian Bibles. The word means "recite" or "recitation."

six people to choose his successor. The committee chose 'Uthman (644–656). As caliph, 'Uthman was instrumental in the publication and distribution of the **Qur'an** (Koran).

'Uthman's rule was marred by some weaknesses, however, which began a period of strife in Muslim history. Problems developed with the administration in the provinces, and some groups felt that the governors he appointed were not responsive to their needs. 'Uthman was eventually killed by a rival faction within Islam, and Muhammad's cousin 'Ali became the fourth caliph. However, some members of 'Uthman's clan, the Umayyah, could not accept the legitimacy of 'Ali's caliphate because his selection was supported by some who were responsible for 'Uthman's death. 'Ali moved the Islamic capital from Medina to Kufah in present-day Iraq, believing it to be a more central location. In the meantime, 'Uthman's cousin, Mu'awiyah, an Umayyad and governor of Syria, had also been proclaimed caliph. A power struggle ensued. Battles were fought, but no decisive victory was made on either side. Both sides agreed to a non-partisan arbitration, and the decision was made in favor of Mu'awiyah. 'Ali could not accept the decision and continued to try to rule from Kufah, but he lost some of his support. Mu'awiyah ruled from Damascus, Syria, and 'Ali was eventually assassinated. 'Ali's supporters elevated his son Hasan to caliph, but Hasan soon recognized Mu'awiyah as caliph, and most of 'Ali's supporters concurred.

The death of 'Ali opened a rift in the Muslim community that has never completely healed. In 680, not recognizing the legitimacy of the Umayyad caliphate, 'Ali's younger son, Husayn, attempted to make a claim to leadership of the Muslim community. As Husayn, his companions, and his family headed to Kufah from Medina via Mecca, they were massacred at Karbala in Iraq. Later known as the Battle of Karbala, Shi'ah Muslims saw Husayn as a martyr whose death restored Islam to the purity given it by his grandfather, Muhammad. To this day, special events celebrate the martyrdom of Husayn each year.

Though the majority of Muslims, the Sunni, accepted the rule of the Umayyads, they did not always approve. The Shi'ah Muslims, on the other hand, remained loyal to 'Ali and his family. While the Sunni supported a caliphate and called their leaders caliph, the Shiáh supported an *imamate* and called their leaders **Imam.** While the first four caliphs, the Rightly Guided caliphs, are recognized by Sunni Muslims, Shi'ah Muslims see 'Ali as the first Imam. Shi'ah Muslims believe 'Ali was given special authority or inspiration by his cousin Muhammad, and that

Imam

The leader for prayer at a mosque who is chosen for his knowledge of Islam and his personal holiness.

authority and inspiration was to be passed on to certain descendants of 'Ali, who would be given the title Imam. As for Sunnis, the guardianship and promulgation of *shari'ah*, or Islamic law, is the duty of the caliph. To this day, the Sunni and the Shi'ah differ on who is to lead the Muslim community, but there are no fundamental differences in beliefs and practices of Islam.

Classical Period

The Umayyad caliphate was a marked change in the history of Islam. It was a physical move from Medina to Damascus. Also, for the first time, leadership was made up of others besides companions of Muhammad. By the time 'Ali died, the rise of Islam with its military, political, and religious power spread throughout the Arabian Peninsula. Within a century after the death of Muhammad, the Muslim state had expanded into the Byzantine Empire and contributed to the fall of the Persian Empire. It spread further to North Africa, Spain, and

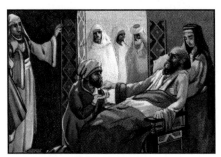

even France until Charles Martel pushed the Muslims out of France in 713 at the Battle of Poitiers. Though Muslims were rulers of these regions, it took the majority of the people living in these countries a long time to become Muslim because conversion to Islam was not accomplished on command or "by the sword." The Umayyads led the caliphate, expanding its empire to the borders of China and India, until 750.

The Death of Muhammad.

The rapid expansion of the Muslim state brought many challenges, especially in an age when communication over long distances was slow. Gradually, Arabic became more widely used as an official language. The requirement to use Arabic in worship and the recitation of the Qur'an was related also to the gradual spread of Islam among the population. With a common language of administration and education, a unified culture began to emerge.

Umayyad rule began to weaken as the expansion of the state slowed. New groups of Muslims asserted their right to a greater voice in society and government. Ruling a large empire required the caliphs to put much energy into the temporal rather than the religious realm. Opposition to their worldliness grew in the beginning of the eighth century. A relative of Muhammad claimed himself to be the rightful caliph. Various opposition groups, including Shi'i, coalesced and then defeated the Umayyads. As Abu al-'Abbas took the caliphate in 750, replacing the Umayyad dynasty with the 'Abbasid dynasty, a remnant of the Umayyad dynasty escaped to Spain and set up a caliphate there. The 'Abbasids established a new capital at Baghdad, and it became one of the largest and most magnificent cities in the world.

Medieval Period

Under 'Abbasid rule, Muslim civilization and culture flourished, so much so that this period of time became known as the Golden Age of Islam. They moved the capital from Damascus to Baghdad and expanded Islam beyond its Arab heritage to a more multicultural one. Baghdad became an important Islamic intellectual center. Scientific, literary, and philosophical works from Greek, Persian, and Indian sources were translated into Arabic at Baghdad's House of Wisdom, a library and archive containing thousands of books. Muslim scholars' exposure to Greek and other traditions led to a great intellectual ferment as Muslim scholars sought to reconcile reason and faith, science and religious teachings.

Muslim scholars wrote important commentaries that later passed as Hebrew and Latin translations into Europe, where, centuries later, Jewish scholars like Moses Maimonides and Christian scholars like Thomas Aquinas wrestled with the same questions and often quoted from the works of Muslim philosophers. Scientific research flourished also in Muslim lands. Many books were written on engineering, geography, astronomy, mathematics, and chemistry. Medicine was an especially important area of contribution, combining the classical traditions of Greek, Persian, Egyptian, and Indian medicine with the advancements of skilled Muslim doctors. Several Muslim works later became standard texts used for centuries in the West, which formed the foundation of medical colleges and teaching hospitals.

Muslim literature flourished in many fields. Wealthy donors funded libraries housing thousands of books in cities across the Muslim world. Poetry was the most respected type of literature. Stories were popular, as well, from teaching tales like fables from Indian and Greek literature to tales that were later collected into the *Thousand and One Nights*, which circulated as popular entertainment among all classes in the cities. Fine arts included elaborate geometric and botanical designs. In addition, *calligraphy*, or artistic writing, was prevalent, especially the artistic writing of Qur'anic verses. Because the artistic representation of human or animal figures was not allowed in Islam, one found beautiful calligraphy of Qur'anic verses decorating mosques throughout the Muslim world.

Example of artistic Muslim writing

One of the most important and long-term contributions of Islamic civilization was the vast network of trade and communication that developed within the expanding Muslim territory. Between the eighth and fifteenth centuries, the gradual but steady expansion of this region linked Africa, Malaysia, India, China, Arabia, and Europe. Trade routes that were supplied by Arab, African, and Asian traders in ancient times became joined by a common language, belief system, and law. Muslims facilitated trade, and trade facilitated the continuing spread of Islam. Along these routes, ideas, products, innovations, technologies, as well as food crops and people, migrated from place to place, paving the way for the global linkages that would be completed by Europeans with the oceanic voyages of the fifteenth and sixteenth centuries.

Politically, however, the 'Abbasids were unable to maintain a unified Muslim rule. Little by little beginning in the ninth century, a province here and there began to proclaim their independence from the central government. Local rulers, military factions, and rival caliphates sprang up. By the twelfth century, there were a number of independent Islamic states. In Egypt, a Shi'i group called the Fatimids, named after Muhammad's daughter and 'Ali's wife, Fatimah, founded the great city of Cairo and its famous al-Azhar University, one of the oldest universities in the world. The remnant Umayyads who had escaped to Spain ruled from Cordoba and were free to develop religious scholarship and an attractive Islamic civilization of their own.

Like Baghdad, Cordoba was a great intellectual center and could boast of magnificent palaces, mosques, and libraries. Rival factions in Islam forced the demise of the Umayyad dynasty in 1037. As strife grew among Muslims, Christian kingdoms within Spain forged ahead with what they called the Reconquest of Spain, which took place between the eleventh and fifteenth centuries. Finally, in 1482, the last great stronghold of the Muslims, the Alhambra in Granada, was captured, and Spain was again a Christian nation. Until the seventeenth century, Muslims were able to stay in Spain, freely worship, own land, work, and even serve in the army. However, as the Spanish Inquisition became more of a threat to Muslims, many left and, by the early seventeenth century, the remaining Muslims were exiled from Spain.

In the meantime, Christian Crusaders from the West captured Jerusalem from the Muslims in 1099, only to be retaken by the Muslims in 1187. Though Christians embarked on a number of other Crusades, none were militarily successful. The Fourth Crusade, in which Christians of the West attacked Christians of the East at their capital in Constantinople in 1204, accomplished for Muslims what they could not do themselves. The attack of Christians upon Christians sealed the Great Schism between the Eastern Church and Western Church and left the once great Byzantine Empire in a weakened state. A success of the Crusades was the opening of trade routes, bringing Muslim trade of goods and ideas to the West.

The Golden Age of Islam came to an end in the thirteenth century. The Mongols had captured China, Russia, and Central

Europe and were headed for the Middle East. They ended the 'Abbasid caliphate with the capture of Baghdad in 1258. They not only laid waste cities wherever they went, but they also destroyed many of the scientific, literary, and scholarly works Muslims had amassed over the centuries. The Mongols were finally defeated in Palestine near Nazareth in 1269 by the Turkish Mamluks who ruled Egypt.

After a period of fragmented rule, the next important regional power that developed was the Ottomans. Muslim rule had expanded at the expense of the Byzantine Empire for centuries, but the city of Constantinople eluded them. The Crusaders' attacks and control of the city in 1204 and the expansion of Turkish rule into Byzantine territory left the city helpless, and it finally fell to the Ottomans in 1453. The peak of the Ottoman Empire was in the sixteenth century under a sultan called Suleiman, the great administrator and military leader of the time. The end of the fifteenth and beginning of the sixteenth centuries was the great move of Europeans into the shipping industry, setting up trade posts along the Indian Ocean, to the disadvantage of Muslim merchants. By the beginning of the seventeenth century, the rise of Europe as an empire and the decline of the Ottoman Empire were apparent. However, this once great giant would not quickly disappear.

Modern Period

The advance of Europe's economic, industrial, military, and political power contributed to internal factors in the long, slow decline of Muslim societies. Much of their territory in Africa and Asia came to imperial rule, especially by the English and French, during the eighteenth and nineteenth centuries.

This decline was accompanied and accelerated by the loss of economic power due to shifting global trade patterns and industrialization. Inexpensive European-manufactured goods flooded Indian, Turkish, Arab, and African markets, starving out the old handicraft industries to which European trade had been apprenticed centuries earlier. Merchants and economic treaties were a foot in the door of Muslim countries for increasing European political inroads. Economic and political disruption, as well as the increasing awareness of the impact of the West, upset the established Muslim social norms and loyalties. Concerted efforts were made both internally and by the imperial powers to undermine traditional and religious institutions.

With European markets came Christian missionaries to the Muslim world. While the missionaries saw their work as reclaiming land that was once Christian back from Muslims, Muslims saw Christians as part of the West, corrupting their lands and society. European dominance during the nineteenth century in the Middle East set up situations of conflict that are still with us in the twenty-first century. Conflicts in Lebanon, Syria, Egypt, Israel/Palestine, and Iraq can all point to European colonization as a source of their struggles. A great deal of ferment took place, leading Muslim leaders and intellectuals to reassess the foundations and traditions in their societies.

The political decline of Islam also brought about its social and moral decline. Though there were a number of Muslim reform movements throughout its history, the eighteenth to the twentieth centuries saw a marked rise in revivalism and reform movements. Islamic reform movements tended to go in two directions. One direction was an attempt to return to what they considered the pristine Islam found at the time of Muhammad and the early Muslim community in Medina. Becoming subjects of colonial powers, the belief was that Islam was corrupted by non-Islamic elements and it needed to be purified by returning to the literal teachings of the Qur'an and the *Sunnah*. Those who did not were believed to not be true Muslims. Some reformers even took up arms against other Muslims who disagreed with them. Popular religious practices such as the honoring of Muslim saints were to cease, for Muhammad would find such a practice idolatrous. Many of these reformers found difficulty with many, if not most, of the Islamic scholars who continually interpreted Islam in light of the changing social, cultural, and scientific realities over the centuries. The effects of these more "fundamental" reforms can be found in such countries as Saudi Arabia and the Sudan.

A second direction for Islamic reform was to reinterpret Islam in the light of the social and historical reality of the day. These reformers believed the social and moral decline in Islam was due not only to European colonialism as it was to the personal, social, and moral decline of the Muslim community, as well as an avoidance of flexibility and adaptability, which had been a hallmark of Islam and had enabled it to be a strong force in such things as science, medicine, and architecture. These reformers believed that Muslims should accept the current political reality and embrace the movement toward the separation of religion and state. Adapting the best the West had to offer as well as maintaining the essentials of Islam would enable Muslims to be strengthened in their faith and Islam to gain the prestige it once had. The effects of these more "adaptation" reformers can be found today in such countries as Malaysia and Egypt.

At the beginning of the twentieth century, the Ottoman Empire was in such disarray that it was known as the "Sick Man of Europe." Reform was attempted but unsuccessful. Siding with the Germans during World War I, the Ottoman Empire was defeated. A nationalist movement arose in Turkey. It abolished the caliphate in 1924, set up a republic, and secularized the country. Persian and Indian rulers were deposed or made into mere figureheads. The aftermath of colonial rule established in many cases artificial borders drawn more according to the desires of outside powers for control than in the interests or national groupings of people in these diverse regions. The continuing domination in the region by Western (Europe and the United States) and Eastern (China and the former Soviet Union) powers created a great deal of social and religious bitterness and economic inequity. The United Nations' founding of the State of Israel in 1948, displacing thousands of mostly Muslim

Palestinians from lands owned by their families for generations, just added fuel to the fire.

The Western-initiated process of secularization or marginalization of religion from the active social, economic, and political realm to the private and personal realm has created a great deal of uncertainty and social upheaval on the one hand and political repression on the other hand. The Iranian Revolution of 1978–79, led by the Ayatollah Khomeini, was just one reaction to the perceived attack on Islam by the secularization movement of the "godless" West. Many Muslim intellectuals have been engaged in active efforts to retain

Ayatollah Khomeini

important principles and find visible interpretations to keep their faith vital in ways that meet the demands of modern life. In this, Muslims' efforts are in many ways similar to the striving of members of other religious traditions around the world.

➤ What do you think it would be like to be ruled by a government that was totally Catholic?

➤ What do you think it would be like to be ruled by a government that espoused a religion different from your own?

The Nation of Islam

In 1930, an African-American man calling himself W. D. Fard Muhammad founded a temple (not a mosque) in Detroit and called it Temple No. 1. His followers called him God, Allah, or the Great Mahdi. He taught that the white man and his "white religion" (Christianity) were the "devil." Fard called for the establishment of a separate, African-American homeland on American soil where his group called the Nation of Islam could be a "nation within a nation."

After Fard's mysterious disappearance in 1934, Elijah Muhammad, head of the temple in Chicago, succeeded Fard as leader of the Nation of Islam. Elijah Muhammad was called the Messenger of Allah and the Holy Prophet by his followers. Elijah Muhammad expanded the Nation of Islam to other urban cities of the North, as well as state and federal penitentiaries. He continued Fard's anti-Christian teachings regarding the nature of Allah as the "Supreme Black Man," African-Americans as the "Lost-Found Nation of Islam," black supremacy, the resurrection of the mind, and separation from the white race. The Nation of Islam appealed to many on the margins of society. Its membership was mostly poor, urban African Americans. Adherents were called to live a moral life, which included not smoking or drinking, treating members of their families and neighborhoods with respect, holding a steady job, and staying off of government assistance.

Elijah Muhammad

In the 1960s, Malcolm X, leader of the Nation of Islam Temple in New York, went on a pilgrimage to Mecca, where he met Muslims from all over the world and from every race and ethnic background. He began to challenge Elijah Muhammad's leadership in his teaching of Islam and exclusivity of the Nation before he was assassinated by Nation of Islam rivals in 1965.

After the death of Elijah Muhammad in 1975, one of his sons, Wallace D. Muhammad, agreed with Malcolm X and aligned the Nation of Islam with the more universal, orthodox Islam. Taking the name Warith Din Muhammad, he succeeded in bringing most of the Nation of Islam into union with Sunni Islam. The Five Pillars of Islam were enforced. The temples were renamed mosques and non-black people were admitted for worship. But a faction led by Louis Farrakhan disagreed with the younger Muhammad's reconciliation with orthodox Islam.

Malcom X

Louis Farrakhan purchased the main temple of the Nation of Islam located in Chicago. Because this temple was the same location from which Elijah Muhammad led the Nation of Islam for forty-one years, this gave Farrakhan a power base. There were some members of the Nation of Islam who had felt betrayed by Warith Din Muhammad and were pleased to have Farrakhan resume leadership in the organization. Warith Din Muhammad had let white people into the mosques, had become patriotic, and relaxed the dress code. Some adherents to the Nation of Islam believed the changes made by Warith Din Muhammad degenerated into a

Louis Farrakhan

relaxed moral standard and wanted to see the "old" Nation return. Others felt that Warith Din Muhammad and his followers were becoming more middle class and abandoning the poorer African Americans. Poorer African Americans found the separatist ideology and strict moral codes of the Nation of Islam more appealing than the universal brotherhood of orthodox Islam.

In contrast to Elijah Muhammad, Farrakhan's rhetoric regarding European Americans was toned down, but the separatist doctrine continued. He believed that race problems in the United States were detrimental to all American citizens. Farrakhan admired the civil rights leaders of the 1960s, but believed their integrationist ideas were misguided.

Whatever goodness it may possess, the Nation of Islam does not represent the beliefs or practice of Islam. Islam is universal, not separatist. It advocates a worldwide community of people, not racism.

■ Section 1 Summary

■ Muhammad is the final messenger of God. He lived in present-day Saudi Arabia from about 570 to 632 CE.

■ Under the first four or "Right-Guided" caliphs, the Muslim state expanded from the Arabian Peninsula to Northern Africa, the borders of China, India, and to the Pyrenees in Europe.

■ From the eighth to the twelfth centuries, Muslim culture contributed many achievements in art, architecture, philosophy, literature, science, medicine, and technology.

■ In modern times, Western imperial powers, particularly the British and the French, eroded the Islamic caliphates and, thus, Islamic influence. In the twentieth century, weakened and dismantled Muslim states contributed to the erosion of Muslim influence.

■ The Nation of Islam is an African-American separatist movement emphasizing self-help and self-improvement. It is not recognized as an Islamic movement by the world Muslim community because of its adherents' lack of acceptance of many Islamic teachings, practices, and principles.

■ Section 1 Review Questions

1. Explain how Muhammad received his first revelation.

2. As a messenger of God, what was Muhammad's chief message to humankind?

3. What was the major cause of the rise of the two major groupings of Muslims—the Sunni and the Shi'ah?

4. On a map, locate the capitals of the following: the first capital of Islam, capital established by 'Ali, Umayyads, Abbasids, Fatimids, Mughals, Safavids, remnant Umayyads, Ottomans.

5. Summarize some of the major contributions of Islamic civilization to Western culture during its Golden Age.

6. What were some of the major causes of the decline of the Muslim states in the early modern period?

7. Summarize the historical development of the Nation of Islam in the United States.

2. Sacred Stories and Sacred Scriptures

The Qur'an is the most sacred book for Muslims. It contains a collection of the revelations Muhammad received directly from God in Arabic over a twenty-two year period in both Mecca and Medina. After the Qur'an, the *Sunnah* is the second authentic source of authority for Muslims. The Qur'an and the Sunnah are indispensable sources of instruction for religious and moral life for Muslims.

Muslims also acknowledge the revealed writings of Judaism and Christianity. However, these books (the Torah, the Psalms, and the Gospels) are believed to be only human words, not the direct words of God. Because they are human words, they are corrupted by human error. Muslims believe that the words of the Qur'an are God's words and thus infallible, uncorrupted by human intervention. The sacredness of the Qur'an to Muslims is such that it should not be placed under anything and one should perform ritual washing before touching or reading it.

Qur'an

The word *Qur'an* means "recitation." Muhammad was unschooled, unable to read and write. As he received the revelations, he memorized them, and then passed them on to his followers. They memorized what was passed on to them and wrote some of the recitations down. The third Rightly-Guided caliph, 'Uthman, took up the task of having the various copies and fragments of the revelations collected and put into one authoritative text. He wanted to make sure these words of God were passed on uncorrupted to the coming generations of Muslims.

As Islam spread, a growing number of its adherents had other Arabic dialects as well as other languages. Changes to God's words were inevitable, and 'Uthman did not want the sacred words lost. 'Uthman assigned this task to Muhammad's secretary, Zayd ibn Thabit. He was charged with compiling the written text and comparing it against the recitation of those who had memorized the revelation and recited it in Muhammad's lifetime. When this was completed, Uthman had what came to be known as the Qur'an. It was published and distributed to all the provinces.

surahs

Chapters or sections in the Qur'an. Each surah is a separate revelation received by Muhammad.

Muslims commonly classify the **surahs**, or "chapters," as a revelation that occurred to Muhammad in Mecca or in Medina. The content of the earlier Meccan revelations tend to speak about God's unity, power, and glory, right living, the end times, and Judgment Day. The later Medinan revelations have some of the themes found in the Meccan revelations, but also have practical matters important to the infant community. Hence, themes from the Medina period of revelations tend to be in the areas of what makes a good society, relations with non-Muslims, as well as financial and legal matters.

The Qur'an is divided into 144 surahs. In general, it is neither in chronological order by when Muhammad received the revelations, nor is it arranged by theme or subject. However, there is some continuity that can be detected with the surahs. In some surahs, the last verse of one chapter and the first verse of the following chapter may have similar underlying themes.

Since Muslims believe the Qur'an is a word-for-word message from God to Muhammad in Arabic, they remain hesitant to translate the Qur'an into other languages. A translation into any other language would be an interpretation in which even if the correct meaning was retained, the sacred words would not be.

From an early age, Muslim children learn to recite and memorize the Qur'an, for proper recitation and memorization of the Qur'an is a religious duty. As noted above, memorizing the entire Qur'an dates back to Muhammad's earliest followers.

Those who do accomplish such a task earn an honorary title of **hafiz**. Today there are Qur'an memorizing contests held in big stadiums in many parts of the Muslim world. Ironically, many of the winners are not ones who speak Arabic.

hafiz

A Muslim who has memorized the Qur'an.

Sunnah

The Sunnah is what Muhammad approved and prohibited, as well as his words and deeds. In short, the Sunnah is Muhammad's way of life. The Qur'an and the Sunnah go hand in hand. One needs both to fully understand and live as a Muslim. For example, while the Qur'an may say that Allah commands all to pray, the Sunnah shows Muslims how to pray through the example of Muhammad.

The **Hadith** is similar, but not identical, to the Sunnah. Muhammad's followers painstakingly recorded and transmitted oral and written accounts of his teachings and actions. These reports were compiled by the second century of the Islamic calendar.

Hadith

A word meaning "story," the sayings and stories of Muhammad that are meant to form guidance for living out religion.

While the Qur'an and the Sunnah are sources of authority for all Muslims, the Shi'ah Muslims have a third source of authority. For Shi'ah Muslims, the teachings and writings of a number of early charismatic leaders called Imams, descended from the Prophet's cousin and son-in-law 'Ali, are an additional source, since they believe these descendants are infallible and consider their words and explanations nearly as authoritative as the Qur'an and Sunnah.

➤ Give examples from Sacred Scripture that you have memorized or that easily come to mind when you pray.

■ Section 2 Summary

■ The Qur'an is the literal word of God to humanity. It is the most perfect scripture for Muslims, though Muslims read and respect the Torah, Psalms, and Gospels.

■ The Sunnah is the example and lifestyle of Muhammad, much of it recorded in the Hadith.

■ The Hadith are the recorded non-prophetic words and deeds of Muhammad.

■ Section 2 Review Questions

1. What does the word Qur'an mean?

2. Why is the Qur'an the most sacred writing for Muslims? What are other sacred writings Muslims revere?

3. Why can it be said that the Qur'an and Sunnah go hand in hand?

4. Compare the Hadith to the Jewish Talmud. How are they alike?

● 3. Beliefs and Practices

Belief in one God is at the center of Muslim belief. Along with Judaism and Christianity, Islam is a monotheistic religion. Reciting the Arabic words *La ilaha ilia Allah, wa Muhammadun rasul Allah* ("There is no god but God; Muhammad is the Messenger of God"), Muslims proclaim this belief daily and in many ways. Islam holds that:

■ God is the creator and sustainer of the universe.

■ God is all-loving, all-powerful, all-knowing, all-merciful, and present everywhere.

■ Not only does God give life, but God also takes life away.

■ God is the judge of all. It is God who determines whether a person will spend eternity in heaven or hell.

Also, Muslims believe God is not merely transcendent: God is very involved as a guide in human history and human affairs. Muslims believe in divine providence. God knows what happened in the past, what is presently happening, and what will happen in the future. However, God does not predetermine what is going to happen. Rather, God knows what choices people will make before they make them. Free will is an integral part what it means to be human. People are to be obedient to God but not coerced into submission. Surrendering to God's will brings freedom, not bondage.

As covered previously, Muslims also believe that Muhammad is the "Messenger (or Prophet) of God." Islamic understanding of "Prophets" differs from the Judeo-Christian understanding. Islamic teaching is that all the Judeo-Christian prophets were Muslims because they submitted to the will of God. Among some of the prophets mentioned in the Qur'an are Adam, Noah, Abraham, Moses and his brother Aaron, Jacob, Joseph and his brothers, Job, and Jesus.

Muslim practice is based on belief in God. Behavior is guided by the Five Pillars of Islam, religious duties that each person is to perform. Muslims practice their faith living in community. These areas of Muslim living are explored in more detail in the sections that follow.

➤ How do you understand God's providence in your life?

Pilgrims trace the steps of Prophet Mohammad in Mecca.

The Five Pillars of Islam

Five Pillars

The foundational principles and practices of Islam that were set forth by Muhammad and are practiced by all Muslims.

As Islam is to be understood as a "way of life" and not merely a formal religion, the **Five Pillars** serve as the religious duties that each Muslim is to perform. In fact, Muslims understand the word *Islam* to mean the very essence of religion, that is, submission to God. Muslims believe that performing certain acts and forms of worship, such as prayer and fasting, are part also of the guidance revealed to the prophets. Five specific acts, and ways of performing them, form the basis of Muslim practice and worship. These acts are found in the Qur'an and the Sunnah. They are called the Five Pillars because performance of these acts as perfectly as possible is the key to upholding the faith. More than just formalities, these acts contribute to purify believers in certain ways. Each has a physical and a spiritual, a worldly and other-worldly, and a personal and a communal dimension. Together the Five Pillars have greatly contributed to defining the *ummah*, or Islamic community. Each of the Five Pillars is detailed below.

1. *Shahadah* (Witnessing)

Reciting the Arabic words *La ilaha ilia Allah, wa Muhammadun rasul Allah*, translated as "There is no god but God; Muhammad is the Messenger of God," is the first and most important of the Five Pillars of Islam. The other four pillars are outward expressions of the first. This first pillar is akin to the Jewish Sh'ma. Muslims declare this belief in the absolute oneness of God several times a day.

A "crier," called a *muezzin*, proclaims this creed from the tower, or *minaret*, of every mosque. A father whispers these words into the ears of the newborn child so that they are the first words heard on earth. A dying person attempts to have the *shahadah* be the last words on his or her lips. A convert to Islam recites these words as a statement of belief. This public declaration of faith defines a person as a member of the Islamic community.

2. *Salah* (Prayer)

Submitting to God is at the heart of Islam. The Qur'an commands Muslims to pray or worship at fixed times during the day. Muslims ritually pray five times per day called *salah*.

Before Muslims pray, they must cleanse themselves physically and symbolically. In the ritual washing, called the **wudu**, the mouth, nose, ears, face, hands, arms, and feet are washed. This ritual washing opens and closes with a prayer.

In addition to a clean body, the person must be wearing proper clothing. Men must be clothed from the navel to the knees. Women must be clothed from head to toe. Shoes are not worn. To ensure that the place of prayer is clean, Muslims often use a prayer mat. Whenever a Muslim prays they face the direction of the Ka'bah in Mecca. This direction, marked in the mosque by a niche in the wall, is called the *qiblah*.

wudu

The ritual washing of the face, hands, arms, top of head, and feet that a Muslim must perform before salah, the second pillar of Islam.

The five fixed times for prayer are 1) between dawn and sunrise, 2) after mid-day, 3) between late afternoon and sunset, 4) between sunset and the end of daylight, and 5) night, until dawn. Five times a day Muslims chant:

> God is most Great.
>
> I bear witness that there is no god but God.
>
> I bear witness that Muhammad is the Messenger of God.
>
> Come to prayer.
>
> Come to success.
>
> (*At the first prayer of the day the following line is added:* "Prayer is better than sleep.")
>
> God is most Great.
>
> There is no god but God.

In countries where Muslims are a minority, it is more difficult for them to stop and pray. But many Muslims in school and work settings do reserve times to fulfill this religious requirement.

Anywhere a Muslim is, they may pray, as long as the spot is clean. One may find Muslims stopping to pray in their homes, in a corner at the airport, out where they are tending the fields or their flock, or in a library. Even in regions where Muslims are a minority, where it is more difficult for them to stop and pray, conscientious Muslims will stop what they are doing and pray. With no muezzin about to call the community to prayer, modern technology may help. Today, computer programs, digital watches, and special clocks fill in for the muezzin. Whatever the difficulties, many Muslims take the obligation to pray seriously.

Friday is the special day of prayer for Muslims, though Fridays are not understood to be the equivalent of a Sabbath. On Fridays, the second prayer time is made in a mosque and called *Jum'ah*, or "Assembly." Besides the regular midday prayer, the *imam*, or prayer leader, delivers a sermon. Since Islam has no clergy, anyone whom the community considers knowledgeable about Islam can be a prayer leader and deliver a sermon. As might be imagined, Muslims in non-Muslim countries find it difficult to attend Jum'ah in the middle of a Friday work or school day. In the United States, efforts are being made to make schools and businesses aware of this difficulty and, at least in larger cities, small mosques are being built near business areas to accommodate Muslims working there.

3. *Zakah* (Almsgiving)

Muslims give alms to the needy as an act of worship. Almsgiving is not an option, but an obligation. Muslims believe that almsgiving, called *zakah*, is one way a person can be freed from those things that are obstacles to Allah. The Qur'an does not specify how much wealth one should share with others, but two and one half times one's savings is the norm. Rather, it states: "They ask you how much they are to spend. Say: 'What is beyond your needs'" (Surah 2:219).

Other acts of charity are also encouraged. An act of charity can mean anything from a smile to removing an obstacle from the road. Thus, in Islamic teachings, charity lies within the reach of both the rich and the poor.

4. *Sawm* (Fasting)

All Muslims who have reached the age of puberty and are not ill or traveling are required to keep a month-long fast, called *sawm*, each year during the ninth Islamic lunar month called **Ramadan**. It is the month in which Muhammad received his first revelation from God. The fast reminds Muslims to fulfill their obligations to care for the poor and needy. To fast in Islam means to abstain from food, drink, and

Ramadan

The fourth pillar of Islam, which is a month of prayer and fasting that commemorates the Night of Power, the first revelation to Muhammad by God.

marital relations from dawn to sundown. The person who fasts should also avoid arguments and try to focus on positive thoughts and deeds.

Just before dawn, most Muslims have a light meal. At the break of dawn, the first prayers of the day are recited. After sundown, the fast is broken with a meal. Later in the evening, special prayers and passages from the Qur'an are read and shared at the mosque. During the four weeks of Ramadan, the entire Qur'an is recited in the mosque. Ramadan ends with one of the two major celebrations of Muslims, Eid al-Fitr, the Festival of Breaking the Fast. For Muslims, fasting is not a somber experience, but a joyous event. Even if one is not a very strict Muslim, Ramadan is a very special time during the Islamic year to enter as a member of the worldwide Muslim community.

5. *Hajj* (Pilgrimage)

The *Hajj* is a pilgrimage to the city of Mecca, Saudi Arabia, where Abraham submitted to the will of Allah. It is held annually in the twelfth month of the Islamic calendar. Hajj is required only once in one's lifetime and only of those Muslims who are physically and financially capable of completing it. The rituals performed on the hajj reflect rituals and actions similarly performed by Abraham and his family.

For Muslims, the events of Abraham's life are different from the biblical account. In the Islamic tradition, Abraham left his native city of Ur in Mesopotamia when he was unable to convince the inhabitants of that city to do away with their belief in many gods and believe only in one God. They traveled through many parts of the Middle East and then found themselves in Egypt. After Abraham and his wife Sarah had grown old, unable to have children, Sarah offered Abraham her Egyptian servant, Hagar, in hopes that Abraham may have an heir. Hagar bore their son, Ishmael. Not long after Ishmael's birth, Abraham called upon Hagar and Ishmael to prepare for a long journey. He led them to a valley in the desert of Arabia and left them there, trusting God would care for them as promised. Their food and water soon dried up, and Hagar grew desperate for the welfare of her young son. She ran up one hill and then a second, back and forth between the two hills, trying to hail a traveling caravan for help. Exhausted, she prayed to God for help, and soon water miraculously gushed from near the foot of Ishmael. Today this place is called *Zam Zam*. Caravans finally arrived and asked that their camels be able to drink from the spring. Hagar graciously assented. Over time, traders settled in that desert valley, which flourished into the city of Mecca.

Meanwhile, Abraham came to visit from time to time. Upon one visit, when Ishmael reached puberty, Abraham told Ishmael he had a dream in which God told him to sacrifice his son. Ishmael agreed to submit to God's will. When Abraham was just about to sacrifice Ishmael, he heard a voice from heaven saying that he would be rewarded for his good deed. So Abraham and Ishmael got a ram, slaughtered it, and celebrated. Desiring that the people of that desert valley worship the one God rather than many, Abraham and Ishmael rebuilt the Ka'bah once built by Adam for the worship of God. Through the Angel Gabriel, God showed Abraham the rituals of hajj and Abraham spent the rest of his life calling upon the people to submit to God's will.

It is important to know how Muslims understand the story of Abraham for the rituals of hajj to make sense. Some of the rituals include circling the Ka'bah to mark its centrality to the Muslim community, running seven times between the two hills, drinking from the springs of Zam Zam, and throwing stones at a pillar representing Satan, who tried to dissuade Abraham from sacrificing Ishmael. The centerpiece of the hajj is for the pilgrims to go out to the Plain of Arafat where Muhammad gave his last sermon. Over two million pilgrims spend the day at the Plain of Arafat in prayer for forgiveness and fervent devotion. The array of pilgrims throughout the region clad in white garments and offering prayers to God is believed to be a foretaste of the Day of Judgment. The pilgrimage ends with the *Eid al-Adha*, or Festival of Sacrifice, in which a lamb is sacrificed in commemoration of Abraham's willingness to sacrifice Ishmael.

Muslims around the world celebrate Eid al-Adha.

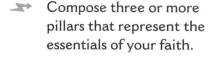 Compose three or more pillars that represent the essentials of your faith.

Islamic Living

The Five Pillars are practiced in the Islamic community, or *ummah*, a collective term meaning "nation." There is no long process in becoming a Muslim. To be considered a member, one merely has to state the *shahadah* as a sign of belief and submission to Allah. In turn, the individual becomes a member of the worldwide ummah. Being a Muslim entails duties and responsibilities to other members and to humankind as a whole, as well as the right to the support of the community. Accepting Islam is not an end, but a beginning. It is a lifetime endeavor to practice and perfect one's submission to and belief in Allah.

Islam entails a complete way of life covering spiritual, social, personal, political, economic, and physical aspects of existence. Allah is not only ruler of the earth, but of every aspect of a Muslim's life. The Qur'an has much to say about what an Islamic society should look like overall, as well as in the day-to-day concerns of family, life, and the specific roles of women and men in family and society.

According to the Qur'an, Muslims who spend time thinking about the small things in life are losing sight of God. In addition, thinking that charitable giving results in depriving the giver of basic needs is incorrect. Those who worry about money are not trusting that Allah will provide for the needs of all creation. Islam calls upon each Muslim to care for those in need, as held in the third pillar. The *zakah*, or "poor tax," is a required contribution to charity. In some Muslim countries, the *zakah* is enforced by law.

Islamic law (*Shar'iah*) is the centerpiece of Muslim life. It is the guidance provided by God on how to live the way God desires both an individual and a society to live. The primary sources of Shar'iah are the Qur'an and the Sunnah. The Qur'an does have some obligations, permissions, recommendations, and prohibitions regarding some aspects of a Muslim's life. For example, the Qur'an teaches against murder, drunkenness, and sexual relations outside of marriage. It also spells out obligations for prayer, fast during Ramadan, and giving to the poor. In other matters, Muslims look to the Sunnah for rules for Islamic practice.

ulama

A Muslim scholar trained in Islam and Islamic law.

There are many issues in a Muslim's life that are not addressed in either the Qur'an or the Sunnah. Neither are codes of law. For Sunni Muslims, Islamic scholars, **ulama**, are responsible for the interpretation of shar'iah. They use consensus and analogous reasoning to come to decisions. Consensus, though not used much today, was used frequently in the early days of Islam. It was the consensus of the scholars with regard to particular questions that became law. An example of analogous reasoning is with the issue of drinking alcoholic beverages. The Qur'an says that one should not drink wine, but mentions no other alcoholic beverage. By analogy, the ulama came to the decision that a Muslim was not to drink any intoxicating beverage. As the centuries went on, further rulings were necessary to include other intoxicating materials such as recreational drugs. While Shi'ah Muslims, too, have the Qur'an and the Sunnah as the primary sources for shar'iah, they do not use consensus or analogy. Rather, Shi'ah have the works of imams, starting with 'Ali, as well as other leaders they regard as sole authorities in interpreting what behavior God wishes from the people.

Recall that Islam sees no distinction between one's spiritual and temporal life. Hence, shar'iah covers all aspects of a Muslim's life, both personal and public. Shar'iah also contains the principles of how one is to live as well as the practice or implementation of the foundational principles. Ulama do not see themselves as creators of Islamic law. On the contrary, God is the only lawgiver. Ulama see their role as interpreters of shar'iah, that is, God's law, God's path for the believer.

As can be imagined, there are many variations of shar'iah. Not only are there differences between Sunni and Shi'ah, but there are geographic, cultural, and historical differences. While some want to reinterpret shar'iah for the age at hand, others see any change in interpretation as abrogating God's law. Whatever the differences, the goal is the same—teaching how to live one's life in accordance with God's will.

Women in Islam

The role of women in a Muslim society is a very complex issue. The role of women in Islam has become very controversial because of the worldwide challenges to traditional ideas about women.

Women are mentioned frequently in the Qur'an and the Sunnah. The rise of Islam dramatically raised the status of women by giving them the right to own, inherit, buy, and sell property, to free choice in marriage and the right to divorce, the right to maintenance and education, independent legal personhood before a court of law, and the right to any earnings from their effort of which their husbands cannot take charge without their permission. This listing does not cover every

detail of her Islamic rights and duties, nor does the shar'iah define women's roles as a specific topic. The legal scholars did not state that her exclusive place is in the home as wife and child bearer, for example. Instead, guidance about Muslims defined in connection with specific roles that may be common to men or women, such as being a parent or a child, property owner, or employer.

The topic of women's dress has been a touchstone of debate, because many Muslim women have persisted in wearing long, loose, and modern clothing and head coverings despite the influence of Western fashions. While a few decades ago it was common for sophisticated, urban women in Muslim countries to wear Western fashions and traditional Islamic dress was associated with rural women, this is no longer true today. Women who cover in an Islamic fashion and those who do not may be doctors, engineers,

teachers, or even member of parliaments or heads of state. Modest dress, though not necessarily head covering, is also enjoined upon men, who, too, are to guard their chastity, avoid unnecessary mixing of the sexes, and reserve sexual relations for marriage.

Women have been prominent in Muslim history as artists, teachers, scholars, spiritual and political leaders, and investors, among many other fields. Historical and textual research shows also that many of the traditions that have isolated and discriminated against women are not part of Islamic teachings, but entered into Muslim cultures from pre-Islamic practices. The extreme segregation and isolation of women from mainstream society, especially among the wealthy urban classes, is one such practice. Today, women's opportunities and social roles vary widely among Muslim countries, cultures, regions, and economic classes. Modern social change has made available to men and women broader choices about education, professions, marriage, and religious self-expression. Families are still the backbone of Muslim life, and women play very influential roles in this setting, in addition to their growing roles in the larger society. Other than that, Muslim women share many of the same struggles and uncertainties that face men and women everywhere.

■ Section 3 Summary

- ■ Muslims proclaim the absolute oneness of God
- ■ Muhammad is the Messenger or Prophet of God whose message is revealed for all humankind.
- ■ The major religious duties of every Muslim are the Five Pillars of Islam: profession of faith, prayer, fasting, almsgiving, and pilgrimage.
- ■ The Islamic community is known as the ummah.
- ■ The shar'iah is the sacred law of Islam, which gets is source from the Qur'an and the Sunnah and is both a legal and a moral guide for Muslims.
- ■ The role of women in Islam is a very complex topic.

■ Section 3 Review Questions

1. Explain what Muslims believe about the two main sections of the Islamic Profession of Faith.
2. Name and explain each of the Five Pillars of Islam.
3. How does one become a Muslim?
4. What are the sources of shar'iah, and what is its role in Islam?
5. Discuss the role of women in Islam.

4. Sacred Time

Muslims would say all time is sacred because all time belongs to God. If pressed, they would say that the five times reserved for prayer each day are more sacred.

The Islamic calendar begins with the year of Muhammad's Hijrah. Like the Jewish calendar, the Islamic calendar is based on lunar months. Whereas the solar calendar used by Christians and the Western world is 365 days, the lunar calendar is 354 days. The Jewish calendar is adjusted for the difference so that the various Jewish festivals will always fall in the same season each year. For example, Jews adjust their lunar calendar so that Passover will always take place in spring. The Islamic calendar does not adjust for the eleven-day difference. The Muslim lunar calendar sets the annual celebrations so that they move through the seasons of the solar year over the course of about two decades.

There are sacred times on the Islamic calendar that have special significance. Two of the most important Islamic festivals are *Eid al-Fitr* (Festival of Breaking the Fast) at the end of Ramadan, and *Eid al-Adha* (Festival of Sacrifice), celebrated at the conclusion of the hajj rituals each year at Mecca. Another special festival is *Ashura*, a type of day of atonement.

Eid al-Fitr (Festival of Breaking the Fast)

Eid al-Fitr marks the end of Ramadan, occurring on the first new moon twenty-nine or thirty days after the start of the month. Families come together, dressed in their finest clothes, for a festive meal in the homes of relatives. Cards are sent out, homes are decorated, and children receive presents. Those who are less fortunate are also remembered through charitable giving.

Eid al-Adha   (Festival of Sacrifice)

Eid al-Adha is the second of the major festivals in Islam. This feast, celebrated at the end of the hajj, commemorates the willingness of Abraham to sacrifice his son Ishmael (not Isaac, as in the Hebrew Bible), in accordance with the will of Allah. As the Angel Gabriel substituted a ram for Ishmael, Muslims also slaughter an animal to commemorate their willingness to sacrifice their lives for God. Muslims like to make clear that the slaughter of an animal is not related to washing away sin, as in Judaism or Christianity, but a symbol of their willingness to sacrifice themselves in order to live in the will of God. It is usually a sheep or goat that is slaughtered, with most of the meat shared with those in need. Muslims not on pilgrimage celebrate this four-day Feast of Sacrifice from their homes in solidarity with those on pilgrimage to Mecca with prayer and gift giving.

Ashura

The feast of Ashura marks the day God freed Moses and the Hebrew people from the grips of the Egyptian Pharaoh. Muhammad fasted on this day and requested that his followers do the same. Ashura is marked by all Muslims as a day of fasting, similar to the Jewish Yom Kippur, Day of Atonement.

Shi'ah Muslims especially commemorate Ashura as remembering the martyrdom of Husayn at Karbala in 680. Adherents mourn the massacre of Husayn and reenact his death through passion plays. Some Shi'ah Muslims parade through the streets of Karbala wearing black, chanting, and striking their chests. A small number of Muslims strike themselves with ropes or chains, emulating the suffering of Husayn.

➤ How do religious seasons and festivals contribute to the rhythm of your life?

■ Section 4 Summary

■ The two great feasts of Islam are Eid al-Fitr and Eid al-Adha.

■ Eid al-Fitr commemorates the end of Ramadan.

■ Eid al-Adha remembers Abraham's willingness to sacrifice his son Ishmael.

■ Ashura is a day of fast for all Muslims and a day of remembrance for the martyrdom of Husayn for Shi'ah Muslims.

■ Section 4 Review Questions

1. Explain the difference between the Jewish calendar, the Christian calendar, and the Islamic calendar.

2. What are the two great Islamic festivals, and what do they celebrate?

3. What are the two main significances of Ashura?

5. Sacred Places and Sacred Spaces

Of all the sacred places in Islam, the mosque is the most common. There are mosques in almost every urban area and several rural areas in the world. In addition, the holy cities of Mecca, Medina, Jerusalem, and Karbala have special significance to Muslims.

Mosque

Mosque translates to *Masjid*, "a place of prostration." It is the building of public worship for Muslims. The main purpose of a mosque is prayer. Prayer at a mosque can be either communal or private.

Traditionally, mosques are built from stone or brick in the form of a square. The distinctive exterior feature is the minaret. Generally, the minaret is a tower where the muezzin proclaims

adan, that is, the call to prayer. In some
areas where Muslims are a minority group,
the adan is confined to the area immediately near the mosque.

adan

*In Islam, the "call to
prayer."*

The mosque can be used also for other social occasions like
weddings or meetings. In non-Muslim countries, the mosque is
a place where Muslim children learn to recite the Qur'an in
Arabic. In addition, the mosque can be the place where funeral
arrangements are made and a body is prepared for burial.

➤ **In your opinion, how should a person
prepare himself or herself before entering your place of worship?**

Mecca

Mecca, Saudi Arabia, is the holiest city in Islam. It is the
birthplace of Muhammad and the area from which he received
his first revelations. From Mecca, Muhammad was forced to
emigrate for several years because of persecution, but was later
able to return in triumph. Mecca is the site of the Ka'bah and
the place of pilgrimage for all Muslims who are able. For
Muslims, the place of the Kab'ah is similar in importance to the
Holy of Holies for the ancient Jews. It is the geographic center
of Islam and the symbolic place of the Divine Presence. After
the death of Muhammad, a mosque was built around the
Kab'ah, called the Grand Mosque. For Muslims, Mecca is a
symbol of their faith in the One God as well as God's faithfulness to the covenant with the prophets, and through them, all
humankind.

Medina

Medina, Saudi Arabia, is only three hundred miles from
Mecca. It is the second most holy city in Islam. This was the city
to which Muhammad immigrated due to the strong opposition
he faced because of his preaching in Mecca. During their pilgrimage to Mecca, many Muslims today take the opportunity to

travel to Medina for a visit to pray at Muhammad's mosque, visit his place of burial, and see other historical sites of the early ummah's development.

Jerusalem

The city of Jerusalem is holy not only for Jews and Christians. Muslims believe Muhammad made his "Night Journey" to this holy city. It refers to the night Muhammad was taken miraculously on a winged horse to the Temple Mount in Jerusalem (seen at left). There Muhammad prayed at the head of the assembled but long deceased prophets such as Abraham, Moses, and John the Baptist. This event includes Muhammad's brief ascension into heaven. It is in this ascension event that Muslims believe God called upon Muhammad to institute the practice of praying five times a day.

At the end of the seventh century, Muslims restored the ruined Temple Mount area, which they call *Haram al-Sharif*, or the Noble Sanctuary. Honoring Muhammad's Night Journey experience, Muslims built a shrine called the Dome of the Rock, whose golden dome is a jewel in the skyline of old Jerusalem. Later the *Mosque al-Aqsa*, or "the Farthest Mosque," referring to the farthest of holy places from the Kab'ah in Mecca, was built. With the capacity for five thousnd people, it is the largest mosque in Jerusalem.

Karbala

Karbala, Iraq, is the site of the massacre of the grandson of Muhammad and son of 'Ali, Husayn, and his companions and family. They were on their way to Kufa, Iraq, to lay claim to what they considered as the legitimate leadership of the Muslim people when they were besieged and killed by the Umayyad faction, who also claimed legitimate leadership.

Supported by Shi'ah Muslims, the death of Husayn is understood as the martyrdom of those upholding the purity of Islam shared with them by Prophet Muhammad. As such, an element of a people persecuted for the true faith underlies some Shi'ah Muslims. A golden dome was constructed to surround the tomb of Husayn. To this day, Karbala is a major place of pilgrimage for Shi'ah Muslims.

Section 5 Summary

- The mosque is the place of public and private prayer for Muslims. Its primary use is communal prayer, but it also can be used for other social, educational, and business functions.

- Mecca is the holiest city for Muslims. It is the site of Muhammad's birth. In addition, Mecca is the location of the Ka'bah and is the place where pilgrims make their hajj, fulfilling the fifth of the Five Pillars of Islam.

- Medina is the second-holiest city. It is the place where Muhammad and his first followers emigrated after it became intolerable to stay any longer in Mecca.

- Jerusalem is a holy site for Muslims, as well as Christians and Jews. In Jerusalem, Muhammad's miraculous Night Journey and ascension occurred.

- Karbala is a place especially sacred to Shi'ah Muslims. It is Karbala where one can find the tomb of the martyred grandson of Muhammad, Husayn.

Section 5 Review Questions

1. Define mosque.
2. How did Mecca become a holy place for Muslims?
3. Why are Medina and Jerusalem also holy cities for Muslims?
4. What is the significance of Karbala, Iraq, for Shi'ah Muslims?

6. Islam through a Catholic Lens

The plan of salvation also includes those who acknowledge the Creator in the first place, amongst whom are the Muslims; these profess to hold the faith of Abraham, and together with us they adore the one, merciful God, humankind's judge on the last day (*CCC*, 841).

While visiting Morocco in August 1985, Pope John Paul II met a group of Muslim youth. There he said, "Dialogue between Christians and Muslims is today more necessary than ever." The truth of this statement has not dissipated. As two religious traditions with a common heritage, dialogue between the faiths with the two largest numbers of adherents in the world is late in coming. Yet, as children of Abraham, along with the Jews, Catholics have more in common with Muslims than we may think.

In 1965, the Second Vatican Council instructed Catholics on the similarities between Catholics and Muslims. It said:

> The church has also a high regard for the Muslims. They worship God, who is one, living and subsistent, merciful and almighty, the Creator of heaven and earth, who has also spoken to people. They strive to submit themselves without reserve to the hidden decrees of God, just as Abraham submitted himself to God's plan, to whose faith Muslims eagerly link their own. Although not acknowledging him as God, they venerate Jesus as a prophet, his virgin mother they also honor and even at times devoutly invoke. Further, they await the Day of Judgment and the reward of God following the resurrection of the dead. For this reason, they highly esteem an upright life and worship God, especially by way of prayer, alms, deeds, and fasting. (*Nostra Aetate*, 3)

There are also significant differences between Catholic and Muslim belief. One major difference is in the understanding of the nature of God. Though Muslims believe in one God,

Catholics believe in one God who is in Three Persons—Father, Son, and Holy Spirit. This is the central mystery of Christian faith, the doctrine of the Holy Trinity. This unity of persons within the One God is foreign to Muslim understanding, which cannot conceive of God manifesting self in any way.

Of course, Catholics and Muslims also have a basic and essential difference in their understanding of Jesus. Catholics believe in the divinity of Christ and that he was at once both divine and human. Through the Paschal Mystery of his suffering, death, and resurrection, he won for humankind its redemption and salvation. Muslims do believe that Jesus existed; however, they do not acknowledge his divinity. Rather, they hold that Jesus was a prophet second only to Muhammad. More particularly, Muslims believe Jesus was born of the Virgin Mary but did not suffer a human death by crucifixion. Muslims believe that what seemed to be a crucifixion was an illusion created for some of Jesus' enemies and that God raised Jesus to heaven.

As Catholics engage in dialogue with Muslims, there are two things to remember from the point of view of Muslims. First, Muslims are acutely aware that most Catholics have an understanding of Muslims gleaned from the Western media. The negative images of Muslims connected with the events of September 11, 2001, and other terrorist attacks is a skewed view of the almost one billion Muslims in the world who subscribe to peaceful solutions and lifestyles. Second, Islam continues to react in many different ways in response to the Western colonialism of the seventeenth to twentieth centuries. Many Muslims believe that the fall of the great Islamic empires was due to their own religious laxity. For this reason, Muslims have attempted to purify their religion at least somewhat by isolating themselves from dialogue with other religions.

Effective dialogue between Catholics and Muslims begins at the starting point of common beliefs. The nature of one God, the heritage of peoples formed from Abraham, and the sharing of positive and peaceful human values is the best place to start. Another important area is the common struggle both religions have with some modern "isms" such as secularism, materialism, and racism. Family life is central to both Catholics and Muslims. Preserving religious values and practices while avoiding these creeping outside pressures and strategies to do so are worthy goals of discussion. Issues like systemic prejudice, poverty, and the care of the environment also form common concerns. As the Second Vatican Council asserted, "there must be a sincere effort on both sides to achieve mutual understanding" (*Nostra Aetate, #3*).

■ Section 6 Summary

- ■ There are a number of similarities between Muslims and Catholics.

- ■ Two major differences between Muslims and Catholics must be clarified—the doctrine of the Trinity and the two natures of Jesus Christ.

- ■ When Muslims dialogue with Catholics, Muslims have two major areas of concern: that many Western Catholics have a view of Muslims presented by the media and that dialogue with those of other religions might negatively influence their faith.

- ■ Major areas of dialogue are family, social justice, the biblical prophets, Jesus, and Mary.

■ Section 6 Review Questions

1. List some similarities between Catholics and Muslims.

2. Explain two major differences between Catholics and Muslims.

3. What are two areas of concern when Muslims engage in interreligious dialogue with Catholics?

3. List some suggested areas of dialogue with Muslims.

Faith and Football at Notre Dame

Certainly the heading of this feature has been dissected before. Faith and football at Notre Dame have gone hand in hand since the famous Fighting Irish started playing college football in 1887.

As part of its Catholic tradition, Notre Dame players go to Mass before games. Just prior to processing from the chapel to the stadium, the players are given a religious medal, usually of a saint. Theology courses are also part of any student's curriculum, including the curriculum of football players.

But during the 2002–2006 seasons, the faith and football connection took a new twist. Ryan Harris, an offensive tackle from St. Paul, Minnesota, was not only an All-American player, but he was also a practicing Muslim. His parents, who had explored a few different religions themselves, allowed Ryan to make his own decision about which religion he would practice.

It was in an eighth grade social science course that Ryan's interest in exploring Islam more closely was sparked. "At the time, I was searching for my beliefs and what I believe about God. I looked into it and decided that I believe in God, Jesus, Moses, and Abraham. And I believe that Muhammad brought the last message," Harris said.

While at Notre Dame, Ryan took several classes in Arabic. "I speak Arabic just a little bit. I know the alphabet and I can give you some words I know from the mosque, but I could not carry on a conversation."

Ryan was also very involved with his teammates in the local community, including volunteering to teach and coach football at a local Catholic parish and at the Boys and Girls club. Along with his teammates, he kept the Notre Dame tradition of attending Mass before games and receiving a religious medal.

"I go to Mass with the team. I feel very fortunate to be able to spend time with my teammates, especially time to relax and place God in my thoughts before a game. It makes me feel thankful for all the blessings I have received," he says.

Ryan said that later in his life, he would like to make a hajj to the holy sites of Islam.

• Conclusion

Though Muslims believe Islam was present from the beginning of time, it did not come to the forefront until the seventh century CE at the time of Muhammad, making it in this sense one of the world's youngest religions. It is also now the second largest religion in the world. Islam is marked by zeal for the will of God. Some of the attraction to Islam is its seeming clarity in what is expected. There are the duties of the Five Pillars of Islam as well as the Qur'an and Sunnah as guides for fulfilling life's duties. However, placing Islam in specific cultural contexts makes performing the duties of Islam difficult. If one does not live in a predominantly Muslim country, the structures that support Islamic life are not present and Muslims have to look elsewhere for support.

Muslims can find support in each other, in the ummah, a term that describes the worldwide Muslim community. The egalitarianism of the ummah attracts a number of people to Islam. A person is a leader in the Islamic community through his or her knowledge of Islam, not because of an ordained leadership.

Through the centuries, Muslims have made tremendous contributions to Western civilization. In fact, some scholars claim that the European Renaissance would not have happened if it had not been for the contributions of Muslims, especially those of medieval Spain. Islam stands for the equality of all members. In fact, during the hajj at Mecca, the first thing a male pilgrim is to do is change the clothes he came with for a simple white robe. All Muslims are equal before God. And all honor is due to God and God alone.

■ Chapter 4 Summary

- ■ The history of Islam begins with a rapid expansion in all directions from its beginnings in Mecca under the inspiration of Muhammad.

- ■ Muhammad is the final messenger of God, the Seal of the Prophets.

- ■ Belief in the oneness of God is central in Islam. Every other idea or action must center on this belief.

- ■ Muslims view the Qur'an as the infallible, direct Word of God. The hadith forms the main body of information called the Sunnah, or example of Muhammad. The Sunnah is the second major source of Islamic teachings.

- ■ Muslims express their beliefs through the duties of the Five Pillars of Islam.

- ■ Attention to God and caring for others are the most important duties of a Muslim.

- ■ The ummah is the name of the universal Islamic community.

- ■ The two major Islamic festivals are Eid al-Fitr and Eid al-Adha.

- ■ Mecca is the most important place for Muslims. Medina and Jerusalem are two other holy places.

■ Chapter 4 Review Questions

1. Briefly outline the life of Muhammad.

2. Why is Muhammad called the "Seal of the Prophet"? How was he chosen as a prophet?

3. Name five biblical prophets recognized by Muslims as prophets.

4. What is the difference between Muhammad's Night Journey and Night of Power?

5. Who are the Rightly-Guided caliphs?

6. What was the catalyst for Islam to split into two major factions so early in its history?

7. What is the major difference between Sunni and Shi'ah Muslims?

8. What is the difference between an imam and a caliph?

9. Name the starting date and center for each of the following Islamic empires: Umayyad, Abbasid, Fatimid, Safavid, Mughal, and Ottoman.

10. What was the Golden Age of Islam?

11. What are some of the struggles some Muslims have with contemporary Western society?

12. How does the Nation of Islam as a movement differ from Islam as a world religion?

13. What is the importance of the Qur'an to Muslims?

14. Explain how the Qur'an is organized.

15. What types of writings can be found in the Qur'an?

16. What is the significance of the Sunnah?

17. What, to Muslims, is God's most important attribute?

18. Name the Five Pillars of Islam and the duties associated with each.

19. What are the characteristics of the universal ummah? What are the rights and responsibilities of the individual Muslim?

20. What are the two major sources for shar'iah?

21. When did the Islamic calendar begin? Why do Islamic festivals fall on different dates each year?

22. Compare and contrast the Judeo-Christian and the Islamic story of Abraham and his sons Isaac and Ishmael.

23. What are the prominent features of a mosque?

24. Explain why Mecca is the most sacred city for Muslims.

25. Why is the city of Jerusalem significant to Muslims?

26. In engaging in inter-religious dialogue with Muslims, what must be considered?

27. Name three major categories of topics in which Catholics and Muslims find common ground for dialogue.

28. What commonalities did Ryan Harris find between Islam and Catholicism while at Notre Dame?

■ Research & Activities

■ Research what happens on a hajj.

■ Research and write an essay on one of the following topics:

> The difficulties in being a practicing Muslim in the West
>
> The similarities between Islam, Judaism, and Christianity
>
> The various groupings of Shi'ah Muslims
>
> Islam in Spain before 1492
>
> The Palestinian-Israeli conflict over the city of Jerusalem
>
> What Muslims believe about Mary
>
> What Sufism is

■ Prepare an oral presentation on at least one of the following:

> Islamic architecture
>
> Islamic geometric art
>
> Islamic calligraphy

■ Prepare an interview of a Muslim teenager, asking him or her to share the attractiveness of Islamic life as well as the difficulties of being a Muslim teen in Western society.

■ Do research on the Islamic "Ninety-Nine Names for God" and create an artistic rendering of these names.

■ Give a class presentation on each of the following symbols found in Islam:

> Crescent moon and the star
>
> Prayer mat

Prayer beads
Minaret
The color green

Prayer

The Fattiha is often called the "Lord's Prayer of Islam." It is taken from the opening Surah of the Qur'an.

In the Name of Allah
The Compassionate
The Merciful
Praise be to Allah, Lord of the Creation,
King of Judgment Day!
You alone we worship, and to you alone
we pray for help.
Guide us to the straight path
The path of those whom you have favored,
Not of those who have incurred your wrath,
Nor of those who have gone astray.
     (Surah 1:1–7)

Hinduism

5

● Modern Religion with Ancient Origins

Hinduism may be the world's oldest living religion. Its origins are from approximately 1500 BCE on the subcontinent of India. Unlike Judaism, Christianity, and Islam, Hinduism did not begin with a founder or a particular event that marked its beginnings. Rather, Hinduism is a synthesis of many factors including the Vedic religion of the Indo-Aryans, the brahminical sacrificial rituals called *bhakti* (from a Sanskrit word meaning "devotion"), and the asceticism and meditation of, among others, the Jains and Buddhists.

The word *Hindu* comes from the Sanskrit word "sindhu" meaning "river" (specifically the Indus River in northwest India). Hindu originally referred to people living in the Indus Valley region. Later, the British designated Hinduism to refer to all the religious beliefs and practices of the people of India who were not Buddhists, Jains, Sikhs, Parses, Muslims, Jews, or Christians. Though Hinduism moved beyond the Indian subcontinent in the nineteenth century, over 95 percent of the world's Hindus still live in India. Most Indians would not call themselves Hindus, however. Rather, their self-identification would be to what caste they belong, their family heritage, their town or village of origin, to what philosophical school they adhere, or what rituals they practice.

Hindus accept the premises or parts of several religions. Yet Hindus hold that no one religion can possibly claim knowledge of the absolute truth. To Hindus, the ultimate reality that other religions may name as God is unknowable. In fact, Hinduism encourages its believers to imagine a god that is best for them, even if that god comes from another religion. Though Hinduism is mostly confined to India, its many practices and loosely held beliefs merit study because of Hinduism's long history, the focus of Section 1.

➤ **What images do you associate with Hinduism?**

BCE

ca. 3000	Indus Valley civilization
ca. 1500	Aryan migrations into northern India
ca. 1200	Beginning of compilation of *Vedas*
ca. 900	Beginning of compilation of *Upanishads*
ca. 500	Indo-Aryan migration into Sri Lanka
ca. 500s	Buddhism and Jainism founded
ca. 483	Traditional date for death of Siddhartha Gautama
ca. 400	Beginning of compilation of *Mahabharata*
ca. 300	Classical Period of Hinduism begins
327	Alexander the Great invades India
ca. 200	Beginning of compilation of *Ramayana*

CE

ca. 300	Beginning of compilation of *Puranas*
ca. 320	Beginning of Gupta dynasty
ca. 500	Beginning of *Tantras*
711	Muslims invade India
1175	Muslims set up government in Delhi
ca. 1400	Birth of Kabir

1469	Birth of Guru Nanak, founder of Sikhism
1498	Vasco de Gama lands on Indian soil
1526	Beginning of Mughal Empire
1542	Birth of Emperor Akbar
1608	Establishment of British East India Company
1666	Birth of Gobind Singh
1858	British conquer Mughal Empire
1863	Birth of Vivekananda
1869	Birth of Mohandas K. Gandhi
1893	First Parliament of Religion in Chicago formed
1897	Foundation of Ramakrishna Movement
1947	India gains independence from Britain; partition of India and the founding of Pakistan
1960s	Maharishi Mahesh Yogi, founder of Transcendental Meditation Movement, brings his program to the West

1. A Brief History of Hinduism

Besides sharing no doctrinal statements, Hinduism has no founder and no set date for its beginnings. Rather than speak about how Hinduism *began*, it is more correct to speak about how Hinduism *emerged* as a religion. What is now called "Hinduism" has continually grown and expanded over hundreds of centuries. The banyan tree is often used as an analogy to explain Hinduism to non-Hindus. A banyan tree does not only have branches that grow up. Some of its branches grow down into the ground, become roots, and sprout new trunks alongside the old. In an old banyan tree, it becomes difficult to distinguish which is the original trunk. So too, religions in India have expanded and changed so much that what we now call Hinduism does not have a linear path to a beginning.

How might the banyan tree be symbolic of some aspect in your life?

The Indus Valley Period (3000–1500 BCE)

Before the Aryans invaded northwest India in about 1500 BCE, there was a thriving civilization in the Indus Valley area of India, now including present-day Pakistan. It is likely that later Hinduism contains elements of this ancient civilization. Archeological finds of the nineteenth century point to a collection of cities, many of which contained a large public bath in the middle of the city as well as baths in many homes. These baths suggest the value of ritual purity. Female figurines were found depicting characteristics that suggest fertility and regeneration. A number of seals that would be pressed into clay were found. Many are male animals, suggesting regeneration. Other seals appear to be a man sitting in a meditative position. Still other seals depict a figure that could be a precursor of the Hindu god Shiva. Few weapons were found, suggesting a relatively peaceful civilization. The Indus Valley civilization seemed to be in decline in the 1500s BCE while the nomadic Aryan society began to enter the Indus Valley region from Central Asia around that time and brought with it its own culture. The two prominent contributions of the Aryans to Hinduism were their language and their scriptures.

Vedas

Ancient scriptures that are the foundation of Hinduism. They were composed in Sanskrit. The most important part of the Vedas is the Rig Veda, which consists of 1,028 hymns praising the gods of the Aryan tribes who invaded India from the northwest around 2,000 BCE.

We know very little about the Aryan settlers to the Indus Valley except through a collection of their writings called **Vedas**, meaning "divine knowledge." Later known as Indo-Aryans, they brought with them an oral tradition that was transmitted only by their priests. They believed that the timeless wisdom of the Vedas was revealed to seers called *rishis* in the primordial past. The Vedas were not written down for thousands of years, for the priests believed the spoken word had the power for both good and evil and only the priests were to be the custodians of the power. They believed the spoken word had to be pronounced perfectly in order to be efficacious and that incorrect speaking could be a danger to the people. In addition, transforming the oral words into written words would be a defilement of the sacred. It was not until after the arrival of the Muslims that the Vedas were compiled and written down. Even though the Vedas were in written form, it was still in the hands of the priests for centuries before they became the sacred scriptures for Hindus. The Vedas were not translated into European languages until the arrival of the British in India in the eighteenth century.

The Brahminical Period (1500–300 BCE)

Indo-Aryans intermarried with the indigenous population and migrated south to the Ganges River area where they created an even more elaborate civilization by 900 BCE. During this period, the ritual sacrifices of the **Brahmins**, the Vedic priests, were so elaborate and expensive that only the rich could afford them.

Various "schools" of Brahmins began to specialize in certain types of sacrifices. Home ritual sacrifices also emerged. As the rituals became more complex, Brahmins found it important to compose commentaries on the school rituals, which became known as the *Brahmanas*. Eventually many of these commentaries, other reflections of the Brahmins, and the *Vedas* were included in the **shruti**, the oldest of the Hindu scriptures.

From about 550 BCE to 300 CE the mediating role of the Brahmin decreased as **gurus** emerged, training disciples in **bhakti**, personal devotion to the gods. Two Hindu gods, Shiva and Vishnu, gained great prominence during this time. In addition, there was a rise in ascetical practices.

Brahmins

Hindu priests. The term is also used to describe the highest social class in the Hindu caste system.

shruti

A canon of Hindu scripture, it is from a word that means "what is heard."

gurus

From the Sanskrit for "teacher," Hindu teachers and guides in philosophical and spiritual matters.

bhakti

In Hinduism, the devotional way of achieving liberation from the cycle of death and rebirth, emphasizing the loving faith of a devotee for the gods.

Classical Period (300–1200 CE)

Sanskrit

An ancient language of India that is the language of Hinduism and the Vedas. It is derived from a word that means "perfected."

The Classical Period is called such because it is the period in which Hinduism became recognized as a religion. Ritual forms changed dramatically during this period. There was the establishment of Hindu temples and the continual growth of home-based rituals. **Sanskrit**, the liturgical and scriptural language of Hinduism that only a few understood, gave way to the vernacular. Though the *shruti* scripture, which contained the Vedas, became the authoritative scripture believed to be written by the divine, another body of literature that the populace found more appealing emerged. Known as *smriti*, it includes two great epics, the *Mahabharata* (which includes the *Bhagavad Gita*) and the *Ramayana*, which deals with the struggle between good and evil.

karma

Based on the belief in reincarnation, the Hindu and Buddhist belief that the form the soul will take in the next life is determined by its behavior in this life.

Most dramatic during the Classical Period was the shift from emphasis on the transcendent to emphasis on the immanent. Rituals dealing with the cosmos became less important and personal transformation became more important. The Hindu concepts of **karma** and reincarnation emerged during this time. *Samsara*, meaning "to flow together," was the belief in an ongoing migration between life and death and new life. In Hinduism, samsara is seen as ignorance of the Brahman (True Self), and thus the soul is led to believe in the reality of the temporal, phenomenal world. Hindus established three non-exclusive ways to deal with samsara: the Ways of Action, Wisdom, and Devotion.

caste system

The social class system that is prevalent in Hindu India.

It was during the Classical Period that the Aryan division of labor was transformed into the complex **caste system** of Hinduism. In addition, the proper behavior of men and women at particular stages of life within and between castes was more clearly regulated within Hindu society.

> The idea of personal transformation was emerging in Greece, Mesopotamia, and Israel around the same time as it was in India. Why do you think the West never adopted the concept of reincarnation?

The Hindu-Muslim Period (1200–1600 CE)

Muslim traders reached the borders of India at the end of the seventh century. By 1021, Muslims had conquered the northwest section of India. The newly arrived Muslim leaders did not try to convert Hindus to Islam. However, they did implement a tax similar to the way they taxed the Jews and Christians they ruled in other places. Throughout the twelfth and thirteenth centuries, Muslim sultans had moved into the northern and central sections of India, administrating the region from Delhi.

In the sixteenth century, the Mughals, also Muslims, over-ran the Muslim rulers of Delhi and expanded Islam even farther into India. Some Muslim rulers were tolerant of Hinduism while others took to destroying Hindu temples and statues. The ruler Akbar (1556–1605) attempted to syncretize the religions of India, even holding high-level discussions on the topic, but was unsuccessful. After Akbar, Muslim toleration for Hinduism deteriorated. In fact, compromise on either side was negligible. For the most part, Hindus during this period established practices that clearly distinguished them from Muslims.

The tension between Hindus and Muslims also produced great creativity. The Hindu poet Kabir (1440–1518) was influenced by Islamic mysticism, while his disciple Nanak (1459–1539) began the new religious tradition, Sikhism, a synthesis of Hinduism and Islam.

The Modern Period (1600–Present)

In the eighteenth century, the British defeated the Muslim rulers of India and set up India as a colony of Britain. With the coming of the British came Western culture, Western values, and Western religious traditions. This influx of the West onto the subcontinent of India was perhaps more disruptive to the social fabric of India and its inhabitants than the invasion of the Muslims, especially in the cities. The caste system, the social boundaries, and religious practices and beliefs of Hinduism all came into question under British rule.

The next significant events affecting Hinduism's history occurred in the twentieth century. Hinduism's tensions with Islam did not cease in the so-called Modern Period. In 1947, Muslims broke away from India and established Pakistan as a separate Muslim country. Not all Muslims chose to become part of Pakistan. There are still a sizable number of Muslims in India, especially in the northern area. Also, Kashmir, a region between the two countries, remains disputed between Pakistan and India with both Muslims and Hindus. At the same time, Britain's colonization of India ended.

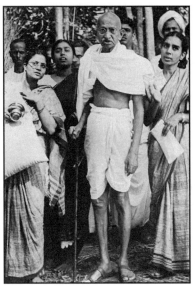

Mahatma Gandhi with his grand-daughter Ava (on his right) and his personal physician Dr. Sushila Nayar (on his left).

Though Christians were on Indian soil from the late first century CE on, it was not until the sixteenth century that a steady flow of Christian missionaries came to India. The influence of Christianity on Hinduism can be seen in the rise of Hindu reformers of the nineteenth century. Sri Ramakrishna (1836–1886) began the Ramakrishna movement with the belief that all religions are paths to God. Mohandas Gandhi (1869–1948), more popularly known as Mahatma ("Great Soul"), Gandhi advocated the equality of all religions, *ahimsa* (non-violence), and *satyagraha* (passive resistance) to British rule. Gandhi was a key figure in helping India become independent of Britain. Yet Gandhi was against the partition of India into India and Pakistan. Gandhi worked hard to alleviate tensions between religious traditions. Like most Hindus, Gandhi was open to spiritual truths, no matter the source. Sadly, in 1948, Mohandas K. Gandhi was assassinated by a fellow Hindu who believed Gandhi had acquiesced to Muslims.

In the Modern Period, Hinduism has been clearly influenced by rulers that came from outside India. Only recently did many from outside India know about Hinduism. The First Parliament of Religions was held in Chicago in 1893. A Hindu named Swami Vivekananda was present there and then toured many parts of the United States as a missionary of Hinduism. Since then, a number of Hindu leaders have traveled throughout the world, especially to the West, preaching their understanding of Hinduism to whoever would listen.

In the 1960s, the British rock group The Beatles brought Maharishi Mahesh Yogi and his advocacy of **Transcendental Meditation** to the world's attention. In Transcendental Meditation, a person is given a **mantra** on which to meditate daily. Also during the 1960s, A.C. Bhaktivedanta Prabhupada (1896–1977) founded the International Society of Krishna Consciousness (ISKON). More popularly known as the *Hare Krishnas* because of their continual "Hare Krishna" chant, devotees could be commonly seen wearing saffron-colored robes in airports, on street corners, and on college campuses in the 1960s and 1970s.

Transcendental Meditation

A technique derived from Hinduism that promotes deep relaxation through recitation of a mantra.

mantra

A sacred verbal formula that is repeated in prayer or meditation.

➤ Is there a cause in which you would be willing to non-violently demonstrate the truth of your situation, the justice of the cause?

Jainism

Mahavira

Mahavira founded Jainism in the sixth century BCE. Born a Hindu, Mahavira ("the Great Hero") reacted against some of the practices of Hinduism, including the elaborate sacrificial rituals. Jainism contains some elements from both Hinduism and Buddhism.

Jains are most noted for the establishment of *ahimsa*, or non-violence, an attitude that influenced many other Hindus, including Mahatma Gandhi in the twentieth century. Jains practice non-violence or non-injury to the point that they will eat only those things that will not kill plants or animals. Thus, they are vegetarians whose diet consists mostly of milk, fruit, and nuts.

Most Jains reside in India, with others scattered in the United States and Canada, Europe, Africa, and East Asia.

■ Section 1 Summary

- ■ Hinduism is a major world religion that has no clear beginning or founder. Rather, it has expanded from various religions on the subcontinent of India.

- ■ The Vedic religion of the Aryans who entered northwest India around 1500 BCE left a lasting legacy of language, scriptures, and gods, the forerunners of Hinduism.

- ■ Home sacrificial rituals increased as the rituals of the brahmins grew in elaboration and expense.

- The Classical Period (300–1200 CE) was the first time Hinduism could be recognized as a religious tradition.

- Muslim rule influenced Hinduism, but not to the point of compromise.

- In 1947, a Muslim nation, Pakistan, was formed from India.

- During the Modern Period, Hinduism has expanded due to various unique movements, including those connected with Transcendental Meditation and Hare Krishnas.

Section 1 Review Questions

1. What was the Aryan influence on the origins of Hinduism?
2. Who were Brahmins and what was their main function?
3. What makes up the shruti?
4. Describe Jainism.
5. Why are the years 300 to 1200 CE known as the Classical Period of Hinduism?
6. What happened when the Muslims came to India?
7. What are some of the beliefs major Hindu figures of the nineteenth and twentieth centuries advocated?
8. Describe one movement of Hinduism that contributed to its expansion outside of India.

2. Sacred Stories and Sacred Scriptures

Of the two categories of sacred scriptures introduced earlier, shruti are considered the more sacred. Hindus believe that they have been revealed to ancient seers by the gods and not one syllable is to be changed. Smriti, the second category of scriptures, is a word that means "that which is to be remembered." Though less authoritative, the smriti texts contain Hindu traditions originally passed down orally through the ages and are more popularly read. Examples from each category follow.

Shruti Scriptures

The earliest scriptures in this category—the Vedas—are from the Aryan era. The main form of worship for Aryans was a fire sacrifice to the gods in which the priests chanted hymns known as Vedas. Only the priests knew and chanted these hymns from memory. The Vedas were considered "sacred knowledge" that was not to be passed on to anyone but other priests. There are four Vedas.

The *Rig Veda* is the oldest and most sacred. The Rig Veda is a collection of more than one thousand hymns to various gods composed in Sanskrit about 1300 BCE. There are various accounts of creation, hymns of praise to various gods, and mantras used in the fire sacrifice. The *Soma Veda*, compiled around the ninth century BC, is a collection of hymns that are chanted at the **soma** sacrifices. The *Yajur Veda* is more of a prose form instructing the priests in the proper manner of fire and soma sacrifices. The *Atharva Veda*, compiled around the seventh century BCE, is a collection of hymns intended for domestic use. In addition, this Veda contains a number of charms, spells, and incantations to bring about healing or remove curses. Some of the healing is to correct the mistakes done during a sacrificial ritual.

soma

A hallucinogenic beverage that was used as an offering to Hindu gods and used in Vedic ritual sacrifices.

The *Upanishads* are another type of shruti scriptures. They are writings concerned with the cycle of rebirth as it is contingent on a person's actions, liberation from the cycle of rebirth, and the mystical relationship between *Brahman* (Ultimate Reality) and *atman* (soul). *Upanishad* translates "to sit down beside"; these stories were often shared in a dialogue between guru and student. The following story about a boy named Svetaketu is from the *Chandogya Upanishad*. Svetaketu's father is instructing his son on matters that cannot be seen, heard, or thought. It continues in this way with his father saying:

> "Place this salt in water, and in the morning come to me." He did exactly so, and he said to him, "The salt that you put in the water last night, bring it hither."

But while he grasped for it he could not find it, since it had completely dissolved.

"Take a sip from the edge of it. What is there?"

"Salt."

"Take a sip from the middle. What is there?"

"Salt."

"Take a sip from the far edge. What is there?"

"Salt."

"Set it aside and come to me." And [the boy] did exactly that, [saying,] "It is always the same."

He said to him, "Being is indeed truly here, dear boy; but you do not perceive it here.

"That which is the finest essence, the whole universe has that as its soul. That is Reality that is the Self, that thou art, Svetaketu."

—Chandogya Upanishad 6.13:1–3

Smriti Scriptures

The *Mahabharata* is a Hindu epic poem in the smirit category with more than 200,000 verses. The Mahabharata tells the story of the war between two families over inheritance. Krishna, an **avatar** of the god Vishnu, supports the righteous family. Within the Mahabharata is the *Bhagavad Gita*, the most popular of Hindu scriptures and the best known Hindu scripture outside Hinduism. The *Bhagavad Gita* is the story of Arjuna, one of the brothers in the righteous family, who is caught between his duty to fight as a member of the warrior caste and his dedication to nonviolence. He debates this

avatar

The incarnation of a Hindu god, especially Vishnu, in human or animal form. According to Hindu belief, Vishnu has been incarnated nine times. The tenth time will usher in the end of the world.

dilemma with his charioteer, who turns out to be Krishna, the incarnation of the Hindu god Vishnu. The message of this epic is that one must cultivate being disinterested, detached from desires or personal agendas, in performing one's duties.

> But if a man will worship me, and meditate upon me with an undistracted mind, devoting every moment to me, I shall supply all his needs, and protect his possessions from loss. Even those who worship other deities, and sacrifice to them with faith in their hearts, are really worshipping me, though with a mistaken approach. For I am the only enjoyer and the only God of all sacrifices. Nevertheless, such men must return to life on earth, because they do not recognize me in my true nature. (*Bhagavad Gita* 30–32)

Hindu five-headed sculpture

The second of the great Hindu epics is the *Ramayana*. This epic is about Prince Rama, who is forced into exile with his wife and brother. The evil Ravana kidnaps his wife, and Rama goes on a long journey to find her and bring her home. After he rescues her, the three return to their kingdom, where Prince Rama becomes king.

The *Puranas* are a collection of stories about the three great gods of Hinduism—Brahma, Vishnu, and Shiva. Further, the Puranas contain stories and myths about creation and the history of the world. The Puranas are especially popular among people in the lower castes, in part because they contain miracle stories and an emphasis on personal devotions.

■ Section 2 Summary

- ■ There are two main categories of Hindu scripture—shruti and smriti.

- ■ There are four Vedas containing various types of hymns, prayers, mantras, spells, and the like.

- The *Bhagavad Gita* is the most beloved of all Hindu scriptures and the best known by non-Hindus.

- The *Upanishads* are mystical, philosophical writings.

■ Section 2 Review Questions

1. What are shruti scriptures?
2. What are smriti scriptures?
3. What is the dilemma of Arjuna in the *Bhagavad Gita*?
4. What are the *Puranas*?

Knowledge of the Heart

Svetaketu had just returned from twelve years of studying with the learned men of his religious tradition. Though he had "head knowledge," Svetaketu lacked knowledge of the heart. His father recognized this and used the lessons of a nyagrodha tree to show him that in the larger scheme of life, his personal importance is only equal to other things created.

The following is one of the most quoted passages of Hindu scripture:

> When Svetaketu was twelve years old he was sent to a teacher, with whom he studied until he was twenty-four. After learning all the Vedas,[2] he returned home full of conceit in the belief that he was consummately well educated, and very censorious.

> His father said to him, "Svetaketu, my child, you who are so full of your learning and so censorious, have you asked for that knowledge by which we hear the unhearable, by which we perceive what cannot be perceived and know what cannot be known?"

> "What is that knowledge, sir?" asked Svetaketu.

His father replied, "As by knowing one lump of clay all that is made of clay is known, the difference being only in name, but the truth being that all is clay—so, my child, is that knowledge, knowing which we know all."

"But surely these venerable teachers of mine are ignorant of this knowledge; for if they possessed it they would have imparted it to me. Do you, sir, therefore, give me that knowledge, knowing which we know all."

"So be it," said the father. "Bring me a fruit of the nyagrodha tree."

"Here is one, sir."

"Break it."

"It is broken, sir."

"What do you see there?"

"Some seeds, sir, exceedingly small."

"Break one of these."

"It is broken, sir."

"What do you see there?"

"Nothing at all."

The father said, "My son, that subtle essence which you do not perceive there—in that very essence stands the being of the huge nyagrodha tree. In that which is the subtle essence all that exists has its self. That is the True, that is the Self, and thou, Svetaketu, art That."

—Chandogya Upanishad

Svetaketu's father taught him that there is no distinction between himself and all other creation. All share in the same essence. Though Svetaketu could not perceive the tree from nothing, it is possible to intuit such knowledge. Svetaketu's father hoped his son could understand his oneness in the nothing from which all things flow.

➤ Give an example of when you thought
you knew everything until intuition and
experience taught you otherwise. How
did you respond to your new insight?

3. Beliefs and Practices

While there are no absolute statements that all Hindus would
believe, there are a set of beliefs and practices that most Hindus
hold in common and accept as true. Included in these are beliefs
about gods and goddesses, the cycle of rebirth, and the sacredness of life. Hindu practices include participation in a communal life that includes the caste system and an understanding of
the stages of life. These sets of beliefs and practices are detailed
in the following sections.

Deities

Ask a Hindu how many gods there are in Hinduism, and the
answer is likely to be 330 million. This answer is meant to say
that there are so many gods and goddesses in Hinduism that
they cannot be counted. Yet most Hindus also hold that all the
gods and goddesses are the myriad images of the one Ultimate
Reality or Absolute Reality, also called
Brahman. While the gods and goddesses
have attributes (for the most part human
attributes), Brahman has no attributes.
Brahman is **transcendent**, beyond reach.
The five senses combined cannot grasp
Brahman. The mind, even that of a genius,
falls short of fathoming Brahman.
Brahman is the life-force of the universe,
permeating it with an all-pervading presence. All things in the material and imma-
terial world are of one essence, and that
essence is Brahman.

Brahman

*In Hinduism, Ultimate
Reality or Absolute
Reality.*

transcendent

*A term that means
"lying beyond the
ordinary range of
perception."*

Brahman is manifested in creation as the many Hindu gods and goddesses. Three primary forms of Brahman symbolize the cycle of life: Brahma is the Creator god, Vishnu is the Preserving god, and Shiva is the Destroying god. These and other gods and goddesses are worshipped as forms of Ultimate Reality or Absolute Reality, Brahman. So, too, avatars are forms of Ultimate Reality. An avatar is the incarnation of a god or goddess who has descended from the heavenly world to earth to rid the world of evil.

The two most popular avatars are those of the god Vishnu named Krishna and Rama. Interestingly, Krishna himself is considered a god. Also, Gautama the Buddha, the founder of Buddhism, is also considered an avatar of Vishnu.

➤ **What images come to mind when you hear the term "lifeforce of the universe"?**

Female Goddesses

Ultimate Reality also assumes female forms.

Parvati, the Divine Mother, often represents the goddess Devi, the Great Goddess, when she is presented in one of her milder forms. She is often connected with Shiva. However, she can be represented with a wilder side as Durga, riding on the back of a tiger, or as Kali, the black figure who is deliverer of justice.

Saraswati is the goddess of learning, literature, and music and is often linked with Brahma.

Lakshmi is goddess of prosperity, good fortune, and beauty and is often associated with Vishnu.

Parvati

Saraswati

Atman

Hindus also believe that Ultimate Reality or Absolute Reality is identical to the innermost soul, the individuals' essential nature, the real self, of each person. The name for this "real self" is **atman**. The body, mind, and emotions of a person are not considered a person's real self. These are only illusions, or **maya**. Hindus strive for release from maya in order to achieve union with Brahman, that is, atman. As Brahman is elusive and hidden, so too, is our true self elusive and hidden. It is only through rigorous physical and mental discipline an individual can achieve true self-realization, which is identical with Brahman realization. True self-realization is *moksha*, that is, "liberation" from the endless cycle of rebirth.

atman

In Hinduism, the individual soul or essence.

maya

Sanskrit for "illusions." A teaching of the Upanishads that says that only Brahman is permanent; everything else is only an illusion.

➤ What effects does conceiving the divine have on a society as a whole? On the women within a society?

Cycle of Rebirth

For Hindus, life is cyclical, not linear. Bodies in the heavens are round. Nature shows its cycle every year of birth, death, and rebirth. Every person is on a cycle determined by karma, the moral law of cause and effect. Under **karma**, who one is and how one now acts is determined by deeds in the person's previous lives. In addition, how one acts now determines one's fate for the future. Death and rebirth are part of the cycle known as **samsara**, or the transmigration of souls, more commonly known as reincarnation.

karma

Based on belief in reincarnation, it is the notion that the form the soul will take in the next life is determined by its behavior in this life.

samsara

The experience of birth, life, and death over and over again until one has achieved oneness with Brahman.

In this cycle a soul passes from one body to another, for example, from a human body to an animal or insect. Though the physical body dies, the eternal atman lives on in another body. Good actions merit migration to a better situation in the next life, while bad actions merit migration to a worse situation. There is no cosmic judge, no god who determines one's circumstances in the next life. Like a seed, the karma that is sown in this lifetime determines one's circumstances in the next.

yoga

A Hindu discipline aimed at training the consciousness for a state of perfect spiritual insight and tranquility.

Hindus believe there is liberation, moksha, from this samsara. Moksha is achieved by removing the karmic residue that has accumulated throughout countless deaths and rebirths. The three practices or "disciplines" that a person can choose to erode the negative karmic effects and move toward liberation are knowledge, good deeds, and devotion. These disciplines are called **yoga**.

➤ What questions do you have about the transmigration of souls?

➤ In what areas of your personal or societal life do you see a need for liberation?

The Sacredness of Life

Hindus believe Brahman is in all things—humans, plants, animals, and insects. With Ultimate Reality present in all things, all things are sacred. *Ahimsa* is the name that describes the desire not to harm any form of life. Ahimsa is the basis for the Hindu's belief in nonviolent means as a solution to problems. It

satyagraha

The policy of non-violent resistance initiated by Gandhi as a means for pressing for political reform.

is because of ahimsa that most Hindus are vegetarians and that the cow is considered sacred. Mohandas Gandhi had his own form of ahimsa he called **satyagraha**, where he and his followers practiced passive resistance toward British attacks when trying to free India from British rule.

Three Paths to Liberation

Yoga is a type of training designed to discipline the entire human person—body, mind, and spirit. The goal of yoga for Hindus is to make the identity between the atman and Brahman a reality, for there, moksha or liberation is complete. The three paths to moksha are the Path of Action, the Path of Knowledge, and the Path of Devotion.

The Path of Action is *karma yoga*, in which selfless service to others brings liberation from the endless cycle of rebirth. In this path, the devotee resolves that his or her right actions and deeds will be performed not for personal gain, but for the sake of Brahman. Even the person's desire for liberation must be purged, for Brahman is more powerful than the noblest desire.

The Path of Knowledge is known as the *jnana yoga*. There are three steps involved in this path: learning, thinking, and viewing oneself in the third person. Learning is the information the person receives from outside oneself. Thinking is the internal reflection on what one learned. Viewing oneself in the third person is like seeing from God's point of view. Meditation is the most common instrument in jnana yoga. Through meditation a person can see the truth in how he or she is attached to this world.

The Path of Devotion, known as *bhakti yoga*, is the Path followed by most Hindus. A pure, long devotion to Brahman can bring liberation. Devotees of bhakti yoga perceive that Brahman is more immanent than transcendent.

➤ Of the paths to liberation mentioned above, which is most appealing to you? In what areas of your life or societal life do you see a need for liberation?

Caste System

Though Hindus have very diverse views of what they believe, the typical actions of Hindus are more uniform. There are four stages of life laid out for typical Hindu males. Hindus also believe there are four major pursuits of life, with the fourth being moksha. Of course, all discussions on Hindu living, pursuits of life, and stages of life must be understood in light of the caste system.

While Hindus are very tolerant of individual beliefs, they are less tolerant of straying from one's social group in Hindu society. These groups are commonly known as castes. The Aryans first introduced a three-fold caste system into India, and later a fourth caste was added. The castes are related to karma and samsara in that caste is dependent upon actions in a previous life. The castes are ranked from highest to lowest:

Brahmins are priests who make up the highest caste. They are from families who are considered the purest, wisest, and most learned.

Kshatriyas are warriors. They help protect and rule society.

Vaishya, the third level, are made up of those families who are farmers and merchants.

Shudra are servants, the lowest in the caste system. Shudra serve those in other levels of castes. Unlike the other three castes, Shudra are not permitted to study scripture.

Besides these four levels of caste, there is a fifth group that is deemed so low, it is not even part of the caste system. These are the *asprishya* or "untouchables." They are the families that are considered defiled because they have the degrading jobs in society, such as cleaning up human waste. In addition, to be an untouchable means that actions in one's previous lives were in some way vile. As part of his nationalistic movement in the twentieth century, Mohandas Gandhi worked to uplift the untouchables from their degrading status in society.

Even though discrimination against the lowest castes is illegal in India today, the caste system still has a strong hold on Hindu society. A person is bound to the caste he or she was born into until death. The person must dutifully submit to all requirements (clothing, habits, religious practices) defined for that caste.

Though how one lives differs widely depending on the caste, the reasons for living are the same. Hindus subscribed to three major pursuits of life until the time of the Buddha, when moksha was added as a fourth pursuit. The pursuits are:

1. *Dharma*—a person's duties in life, especially those related to social obligations within one's caste;

2. *Artha*—the pursuit of both material and political wealth;

3. *Kama*—the pursuit of artistic, recreational, and sensual pleasure;

4. *Moksha*—the pursuit of liberation from the cycle of rebirth through actions, thoughts, and devotions.

> ➨ **What group stratifications similar to the Hindu caste system can you find in your society or other institutions?**

> ➨ **How do the "castes" affect how a person practices his or her religion?**

The Stages of Life

The four stages of life (called *ashramas*) are general patterns for Hindu males of the first three castes to follow, though most progress through only the first two stages. Men are to fulfill their obligations to family and society before pursuing these ascetic disciplines. Traditionally, women are to be daughters, wives, and mothers and live under the protection of a man. The stages for males are:

> *Brahmancarin*—the student learns about the Hindu tradition, usually at the feet of a guru.

> *Grihastha*—the stage of the householder, when he marries, raises a family, and contributes to society.

> *Vanaprastha*—literally, the "forest dweller." This is the stage when a man begins to move away from ordinary life to life as a hermit in order to pursue more otherworldly desires.

> *Sannyasin*—a spiritual pilgrim who renounces absolutely everything in this world for the purpose of pursuing moksha. In this stage, the man abandons family and even family name and lives as if he has no memory of his previous life.

> ➤ What would it be like to progress through these four stages in your own religious tradition?

■ Section 3 Summary

■ Hindus believe in literally millions of gods and goddesses. These gods are merely images of the one Ultimate Reality, known as Brahman.

■ The Ultimate Reality is interchangeable with atman, a person's innermost self.

■ Every human person is on a cyclical life pattern determined by karma.

- Liberation from the life cycle is known as moksha. The three paths to liberation are action, knowledge, and devotion.

- Hindus are born into one of four castes, each of which has hundreds of sub-castes. Some are born below the caste system and are called "untouchables."

- Ideally, male Hindus in the first three castes progress through four stages of life, but in reality, most progress through only two. In the third and fourth stages, Hindu males move from the ordinary life to the ascetic life. Traditionally Hindu women are called to be daughters, wives, and mothers.

- Hindus are called upon to pursue four goals in life, with the fourth being moksha.

■ Section 3 Review Questions

1. What is meant by Brahman? How is Brahman linked to atman?

2. What are the three primary forms of Brahman?

3. Describe the Hindu cycle of rebirth related to the three paths of liberation.

4. Name and describe each of the four Hindu castes. Also define the "untouchables."

5. Name and describe the four stages of life for Hindu males.

6. What are the four life goals for a Hindu male in the first three castes?

● 4. Sacred Time

Hindus use a lunar calendar, but it is one that is more complicated than the Islamic or Jewish lunar calendar. To compensate for the eleven-day difference between the lunar and solar calendars, Hindus make an adjustment of one month, but do not give the additional month its own name. Rather, the added month bears the name of either the previous month or next month. Cumulatively, about seven months are added approximately every nineteen years. Also, rather than four seasons, the Hindu calendar has six. A simplified look at the Hindu calendar follows.

Hindu Calendar

Spring:	Claitra (March–April), Vaishakh (April–May)
Summer:	Jyeshta (May–June), Aashaadh (June–July)
Monsoon:	Sharaavan (July–August), Bhadrapad (August–September)
Autumn:	Ashwin (September–October), Kaarti(October–November)
Winter:	Margasheersh (November–December), Paush (December–January)
Dewey:	Maagh (January–February), Phalgun (February–March)

Within the calendar year, Hindus celebrate several festivals. Hindus also mark various life cycle events and rites of passage with various celebrations and ceremonies.

Festivals

As Hinduism is a religion of many gods, there are also several Hindu festivals. However, there are few festivals that all Hindus celebrate in common. Descriptions of two of the largest annual festivals follow.

Diwali (Divali, Dewali, Deepavali)

Diwali is a "Festival of Lights" similar to Hanukkah for Jews and Christmas for Christians. There is no universal Hindu calendar, so there is no uniform day this festival begins. No matter what part of India, however, it is celebrated in the fall. The northern part of India tends to celebrate Diwali in five days, while parts of southern India celebrate it in one day. Besides a Festival of Lights, some consider Diwali the start of the new year.

Diwali celebrates the return of Rama, the seventh avatar of Vishnu, to his kingdom after a fourteen-year exile. People lit oil lamps to guide him and his companions on their journey home. In addition to lighting the path, symbolically the lights break through the darkness of evil. People celebrate by donning their homes with colorful lights and candles. Diwali begins at the time of darkness, so the lights truly do break through the darkness. In some

Rama and Vishnu

regions, firecrackers are set off to frighten away evil, while other regions make images of evil deities and throw them in a bonfire. No festival is complete without special foods and colorful clothes. Diwali is celebrated also by Sikhs and Jains.

Holi

Holi is a spring festival of a rather riotous nature that commemorates the love between Krishna and Radha. Often the division between castes is suspended during this time of celebration. Fun-loving pranks are part of this day as a reminder of the fun Krishna had as a boy. Hindus squirt each other with red colored liquid or throw red powder on each other during the Holi festival. Another story associated with Holi is that of the demon Holika attempting to kill the infant Krishna. Appearing as a lovely woman, Holika tried to feed Krishna poisoned milk from her breast, but Krishna sucked the blood out of her, exposing the dead Holika as the hideous demon that she was, hence the reason for the red colored powder or liquid.

➤ What are some ways in which festivals and holidays function in a society?

Life Cycles

Besides the various festivals, Hindus celebrate numerous occasions and rites of passage in the life cycle. These celebrations are called samskaras. There are sixteen samskaras. Hindus believe if they are properly observed, the person can ward off bad karma and a better rebirth will be gained. The sixteen stages in life are listed below.

Birth

1. *Womb-placing*—This is the rite of conception where the physical union between the husband and wife is consecrated with the intention of bringing into the world a child with an advanced soul.

2. *Male rite*—This is a rite during the third month of pregnancy in which there are prayers for a male child and for good health to mother and child.

3. *Hair parting*—Between the fourth and seventh months of pregnancy, the husband combs the wife's hair as a sign of love and support.

4. *Rite of birth*—At birth, the father welcomes and blesses the infant and gives the newborn a taste of ghee (a clarified butter used in temple lamps) and honey.

Childhood

5. *Name-giving*—This rite welcomes the infant into the Hindu community of the family. It takes place anywhere between three and six weeks after birth. The given name is usually the name of a god or goddess. A person who converts to Hinduism also goes through the name-giving ceremony.

6. *Feeding*—The first time the child eats solid food (usually rice) is marked.

7. *Ear-piercing*—Boys and girls have both ears pierced and gold earrings inserted.

8. *First hair cutting*—This is a rite of passage for boys.

9. *Formal education*—The child marks his or her entry into formal education by writing the first letter of the alphabet in uncooked rice.

Adulthood

10. *Fit or proper season*—For girls, this is a purification after the first menstrual period. There is a home blessing marking their coming-of-age into adulthood.

11. *Beard-shaving*—This home blessing ceremony marks the boy's first beard shaving and maturation into adulthood.

12. *Settlement of aim or word-giving*—This is a betrothal ceremony where the man and woman pledge themselves to each other for marriage. A ring is given and presents are exchanged.

13. *Marriage*—Marriage is an elaborate ceremony that lasts for days. A ceremonial fire is present throughout, the gods are called upon, and vows are exchanged.

Funeral Rite

14. *Preparation of body*—The eldest son usually washes, dresses, and adorns the body with flowers.

15. *Cremation*—The body is laid on a funeral pyre, usually located near a holy river. The fire is set and ghee is poured on the fire. Prayers are recited and people usually stay until the fire is out.

16. *Scattering the ashes*—The ashes are usually scattered over a sacred river near the funeral pyre. The Ganges is the most popular river for this ceremony.

➤ **What is a visible sign of your religious tradition that you would proudly wear in public?**

Sikhism

Sikhism is a blending of Hinduism and Islam. There are elements in each of these two religions that can be found in Sikhism. Sikhs would disagree, believing their religion to be unique, of itself.

Sikhs (a term meaning "learners") believe that God was revealed in a very special way to Guru Nanak in 1459 CE in the Punjab area that is now Pakistan. Nine other gurus believed to be the reincarnation of Nanak and succeeded him. The last one, Guru Gobind Singh, died in 1708. The Sikh community and sacred scripture, the *Siri Guru Granth Sahib*, together are considered to be the eleventh and final Guru. When Indian Muslims formed their own homeland of Pakistan in 1947, many Sikhs moved out of the newly formed nation as Muslims moved in. Many Sikhs also have the desire to found and establish their own homeland.

Akal Takht, Sikh's highest temporal seat, inside the Golden Temple complex in Amritsar, India.

Sikhism is like Islam in that it is a monotheistic religion. As in Hindu belief, God is transcendent but can be realized through nature and through the experience of each person. God is Ultimate Reality, immanent and eternally real. God is formless, eternal, having no beginning and no end. The *Mool Mantra* is the statement of the Sikhs' belief in God:

> There is One God.
> He is the Supreme Truth
> Is without fear

> Is not vindictive
> Is Timeless, Eternal
> Is not born, so
> He does not die to be reborn.
> Self-illumined,
> By Guru's grace
> He is revealed to the human soul.
> Truth was in the beginning,
>   and throughout the ages.
> Truth is now and ever will be.

Sikhs also believe in karma, samsara, and moksha, similar to Hindus. However, Sikhs reject the belief in the caste system and hold that God created all people equal, both men and women. They also reject ahimsa and any kind of idol worship.

According to Sikh scriptures, Sikhs are to perform several ascetic practices and to wear or carry with them the "five K's" as signs of devotion:

Kesh—unshorn hair, a symbol of dedication to God (men wear a turban)

Kanga —comb, a symbol of cleanliness and purity

Kacha—short pants usually worn under the outer garments, a symbol of chastity and moral living

Kara—a steel bracelet worn on the right hand as a symbol of allegiance to the guru

Kirpan—a short sword, the symbol of an unconquerable spirit.

Formal worship takes place in a temple. The service is generally led by a *granthu*, though if one is not available, anyone knowledgeable in religious affairs may conduct the service. The service, called *gurdwara*, consists of singing and reading sacred scripture passages.

■ Section 4 Summary

- Most Hindus use a lunar calendar that marks six seasons of the year rather than four.

- The diversity of Hinduism is so great that few festivals are celebrated by all Hindus. Most Hindus do celebrate the festivals of Diwali and Holi.

- The vast majority of Hindus celebrate life cycle rituals called samskaras, believing that a person can ward off bad karma and assure a better next life.

- Sikhism is a monotheistic religion that contains elements of both Hinduism and Islam.

■ Section 4 Review Questions

1. How do Hindus compensate for the different number of days between the solar and lunar calendars?

2. What do the festivals of Diwali and Holi celebrate? How are they celebrated?

3. Name and explain at least two of the sixteen stages of the Hindu life cycle.

5. Sacred Places and Sacred Spaces

Temples, public shrines, and shrines set up in individual homes are among the sacred places for Hindus. Also, as Brahman is present in all of creation, natural sites like mountains and rivers are also counted as sacred. The Ganges River is considered the most sacred place of all.

Temples

Some villages may be too small to have a temple where a brahmin can perform worship services, but most towns and all major cities of India do have temples. Temples have images of many gods and goddesses, but are dedicated to one god in particular. That special deity is often the god for a caste in that regional area.

Hindus seldom have congregational services at a temple. Though a group may be in attendance, there is still a sense of individuality on the part of the attendees. A brahmin often performs *puja*, the practice of honoring a god or goddess in a worship service with minimum participation by the people. The deity is awakened by bells and then bathed, dressed, and offered incense, food, and flowers. There are sometimes special days for the deity when the statue, picture, or other image of the god (called a *murti*) are decorated and processed along the nearby streets.

Hindu temples

Whatever size or however complex, the underlying structure of Hindu temples is simple. There is the outer hall, the temple proper, and the "womb chamber" where the main deity of that particular temple—usually Vishnu, Shiva, or the goddess—resides. In fact, a Hindu temple is the temporary residence of a deity on earth. Each of these three areas has ambulatories so that devotees can circle in a clockwise direction as a sign of veneration.

Home Shrines

Most Hindu families have a shrine or special place in their home in which they perform puja. This place may be as large as a room unto itself or as small as a little table. Whatever the case,

the household contains a *murti* of a god that has special meaning for that family. Flowers or fruit may also be part of the shrine surrounding the murti. The actual puja can be performed individually or collectively. Usually women conduct the home puja.

The home puja involves the welcoming of the god or goddess into the house by calling upon it to dwell within the murti. It must be emphasized that Hindus do not believe that the murti itself is the god. Rather, the murti *represents* the god. However, some Hindus believe the god dwells within the murti during the puja. The murti is also washed and dressed in fine clothes so that it is ready to receive guests. Fruits, flowers, and incense are offered to the murti. There may be prayers recited, hymns sung, and sacred texts read. In return for the offering, it is held that the individual or family receives a blessing from the deity. At the end of puja, those present eat the food that was offered to the deity.

➳ Catholics often place flowers or other tokens around the shrines or statues of Jesus, Mary, and the saints. What do you think is the significance of these offerings?

Honoring Is Called Puja

By Sre Sri Ravi Shankar

Honoring is a sign of divine love. That honoring is called puja. The ceremony of puja imitates what nature is already doing for you. The Divine worships you in so many forms. In puja, you offer everything back to the Divine.

Devotees during the festival of the Sun God at Juhu Beach, Mumbai, India.

Flowers are offered in puja. The flower is a symbol of love. The Divine has come to you in love through so many forms: mother, father, wife, husband, children, friends. The same love comes to you in the form of the Master to elevate you to the level of divine love, which is also your own nature. Recognizing this flower of love from all sides of life, we offer flowers.

Fruits are offered, because the Divine offers you fruits in due season. You offer grain, because nature provides you food. A candle-light and a cool camphor light are offered; in the same way nature continually revolves the sun and moon around you. Incense is offered for fragrance. All the five senses are used in puja, and it is performed with deep feeling. Through puja, we say to God, "Oh whatever you give to me, I give back to you." Puja is honor and gratefulness.

Have you seen children? They have small little pots and dishes. They sometimes pretend that they make toast or tea. They come to the mom and say, "Now, please have some tea." They serve you. There will be nothing in the cup; it is all in their imagination. They play with you. Whatever you do to them, they also do. They put the doll to sleep. They feed it and bathe it. In the same way, puja is an expression of what the Divine is doing for you. Puja is a mixture of imitation, honor, playfulness, and love. It is all these things together, made into a soup.

(Sre Sri Shankar is founder of the Worldwide Art of Living Foundation, Healing Breath Workshops, and Sahaj Samadhi meditation programs.)

Ganges River

Though Hindus are able to frequent shrines and temples more often, the Ganges River is considered the most sacred of all places for Hindus. It is the symbol for life without end. Every twelve years, a festival called Kubach attracts millions to the Ganges.

The Ganges is considered the premiere place for spiritual healing. Hindus perform ritual bathing in the river, believing the Ganges has the power to wash away the karma that destines them for another life on earth. Many Hindus will request that upon their death, their ashes be sprinkled into the Ganges River, especially near the holy city of Varanasi, also known as Benares. Hundreds of temples line the banks of the Ganges at Varanasi.

■ Section 5 Summary

- ■ Mountains, forests, and rivers are sacred spaces for Hindus.
- ■ Most homes have a special place or shrine for honoring the deity through a worship service called puja.

- Brahmins perform pujas at temples with minimal participation from other worshippers.

- The Ganges River is considered the most sacred place for Hindus.

■ Section 5 Review Questions

1. Why is everything sacred to Hindus?
2. Describe a home puja and its purposes.
3. How does a temple puja differ from a home puja?
4. Why is the Ganges River the most sacred place for Hindus?

6. Hinduism through a Catholic Lens

> Thus, in Hinduism, men contemplate the divine mystery and express it through an inexhaustible abundance of myths and through searching philosophical inquiry. They seek freedom from the anguish of our human condition either through ascetic practices or profound meditation or a flight to God with love and trust. (*Nostra Aetate*, 2)

Of all the major world religions, Hinduism has a reputation for tolerating religious diversity over the centuries. Adherents of most of the traditions within Hinduism believe there is one objective Truth, but the finitude of the human condition is an obstacle to comprehending or attaining that pure, objective, many-sided Truth. Hindus believe the prophets, sages, and contemplatives of various religious traditions over human time pointed their respective adherents to eternal Truth, but that each tradition has only a piece of the truth. While Hindus do not believe that if all the truth statements and experiences were collected the sum would equal the Truth, they do believe that the world would be closer to the Truth.

Tolerance for religious diversity finds Hindus comfortable in exhorting not only Hindus to be good Hindus, but Jews to be good Jews, Buddhists to be good Buddhists, Christians to be good Christians, and the like. Tolerance does not imply minimizing one's own religious tradition. On the contrary, in dialogue with various religious traditions, including Catholicism, clarity in the similarities and differences between the two traditions is very important to Hindus. They are very anxious to clear up the many misconceptions people, especially in the West, have about Hinduism. In dialogue, all sides are reminded to keep an open mind because a fragment of the Truth may be found in the religious tradition of the other. At the same time, dialogue enables each participant to delve ever deeper into the mystery of one's own religious tradition, drawing the person to a deeper commitment to it.

Interreligious dialogue between Catholics and Hindus has spent a fair amount of time pursuing social issues essential to human dignity. Poverty and the lack of basic human necessities do plague India. Some of these issues are due to the caste system, but the majority of the problem stems from a fragile national economy that finds it hard to compete in modern worldwide economic markets. Mohandas Gandhi spoke out against the inequities of the Indian caste system. Mother Teresa of Calcutta, a Catholic nun and founder of the Missionaries of Charity, ministered with her community to the "poorest of the poor" and the dying people of Calcutta and other areas. Many Catholic religious communities continue to minister in India today.

Among more theological issues, two topics in particular still carry much mutual misunderstanding between Hindus and Catholics. One is the topic of Jesus, while the other topic is religious images.

Jesus, The Incarnate God

Hindus gained continual exposure to Christianity with the coming of the British in the eighteenth century. However, Christianity has been on Indian soil, especially southern India, since Christianity's infancy. Legend has it that the Apostle Thomas went to India as a missionary and established a Christian community there. St. Francis Xavier, a Jesuit, ministered in India in the sixteenth century. He would walk through the streets ringing a bell to call children out of their homes to hear the Gospel.

Hindus have a wide range of views about Jesus. Some believe Jesus spent his so-called "hidden years," that is, the years between age twelve and the start of his public ministry, learning from Hindu sages in India and then incorporating what he learned into his ministry. Many Hindus see Jesus as a source of inspiration for moral or social reform, or as one who lived an exemplary life. Some Hindus have even gone so far as to commit themselves to Jesus, not as a convert to Christianity, but as one among many avatars like Rama or Krishna. Some question Jesus' historical existence, believing the stories of Jesus to be myths, like the stories of Hindu deities. Still other Hindus believe Jesus was a *yogi*. As a yogi, Jesus is seen as one who lived a disciplined, ascetic life. Whether a Hindu believes Jesus lived or not, or whether one believes he was among the great avatars or a yogi, it is the teachings of Jesus, especially his teaching and practice of the Beatitudes, that most attract Hindus to him. To Hindus, Jesus is one who is "pure of heart."

Catholics, indeed, all Christians, would agree with some views Hindus hold about Jesus. Love, compassion, kindness, sympathy, reconciliation, and justice are all virtues that each of us as individuals as well as social groupings and institutions need to perfect. Jesus' eating with sinners, healing people not of his own faith, and loving his worst enemies even to the point of dying for them are all seemingly impossible behaviors that we, as followers of Jesus, are called to practice.

However, the Catholic-Christian view of Jesus is much different from the common Hindu view. Jesus is a historical person, not a myth. He was born in Bethlehem of Judea during the time of Herod the Great and died at the hands of the Roman procurator Pontius Pilate. This biblical testimony is corroborated by independent sources such as the Jewish writer Josephus and the Roman historian Tacitus. There is no mention anywhere within or outside the Bible that Jesus ever left Judea. There is no hint of Hindu beliefs such as karma, reincarnation, or the caste system in the teachings of Jesus. Rather, Jesus taught, often through parables, about the coming reign of God and the need to prepare for that coming. Jesus performed miracles that showed his authority over both the natural and spiritual realm. Jesus was a great teacher and wonder-worker, but much, much more. Jesus was not one avatar among many avatars; Jesus is the one and only incarnation of God. Jesus is God. As St. Paul tells us in his Letter to the Philippians:

> Have among yourselves the same attitude that is also yours in Christ Jesus,

> Who, though he was in the form of God, did not regard equality with God something to be grasped. Rather, he emptied himself, taking the form of a slave, coming in human likeness; and found human in appearance, he humbled himself, becoming obedient to death, even death on a cross. Because of this, God greatly exalted him and bestowed on him the name that is above every name, that at the name of Jesus every knee should bend, of those in heaven and on earth and under the earth, and every tongue confess that Jesus Christ is Lord, to the glory of God the Father. (Phillippians 2:5–11)

Religious Images

Both Catholics and Hindus have a long history of depicting and appreciating religious images. They also share the misunderstandings by some who believe the presence of religious imagery assumes the worship of idols. Both Hindus and Catholics deny that the presence of religious imagery means the worship of idols. They find such a charge represents a misunderstanding of the purpose and function of religious imagery.

Long before the Great Schism of 1054, both the Eastern and Western Church had images of Jesus, Mary, saints, angels, biblical stories, and events within Christian history. Religious imagery could be found in the catacombs, in basilicas, churches, chapels, castles, homes, monasteries, marketplaces, and fields. It could be paintings or statuary on wood, metal, or stone. Beautiful icons in the Eastern Church were destroyed as part of the **iconoclasm** controversy. The Protestant Reformation brought about another form of iconoclasm. Some Protestants destroyed religious statuary because they equated the presence of statues of Mary and the saints with the worship, rather than the veneration, of Mary and the saints.

iconoclasm

The "breaking of icons," the belief that there should be no human depiction of the sacred for it places the icon as a source of worship rather than what the image represents.

Much of Hindu religious imagery is the depiction of its many gods and goddesses. It seems the larger the Hindu temple, the more religious imagery is found in that temple. A Hindu shrine may have only one deity, often the local village god or goddess. Besides temples and shrines, Hindu religious imagery can be found in the home, on the streets, in the stores and sidewalk shops, in government buildings, and along the roads. Like

Christians, Hindu religious imagery was not always completely safe. During the invasion of Muslims, Hindus found their temples and shrines destroyed, which meant the religious objects inside were destroyed.

Religious imagery has many functions. Seldom is religious imagery merely ornamental or artistic purposes. This may be one purpose, but seldom is it the primary purpose. Religious imagery may be used to tell a story within a religious tradition. The story may be inspirational or instructive or both. Religious imagery may be used to instruct adherents of a faith tradition, especially those who are unable to read. Still, the function of a particular religious image may be as an object of veneration.

Though Catholics and Hindus may be similar in that they use religious imagery and are misunderstood, either intentionally or unintentionally, by people outside their respective religious traditions, the content of what is depicted is very different. For clarification, we will focus only on the use of statues.

Religious images in Hinduism are not worshipped, but venerated. They are accorded the honor of a very special guest. A guest is gifted with special food, candles, perhaps flowers or incense. The veneration of a deity assists one in meditating on Ultimate Reality.

In Hinduism, the Ultimate Reality is unknown and unknowable. Yet the unknown and unknowable can be approached from the known. That is, the many Hindu **devas**, which are known, reveal some aspect of Ultimate Reality. The more images depicting an aspect of the unknown, the more Ultimate Reality is revealed. The outrageousness of the images and their various components points to that in which language is lacking. A god or goddess represented anthropomorphically helps humans enter into the mystery of Ultimate Reality. There is a danger, however, in making the deities too human, too much like ourselves. Hindu artists avoid this danger by creating images that cannot be mistaken as representing finite human beings. For example, the more arms an image has, the more powerful the deity is. The more heads an image has, the more knowledgeable or wise the deity. What an image wears, what an image is holding in its many hands, whether an animal is integrated into the image, all point to some aspect of the deity, which in turn points to some aspect of Ultimate Reality.

devas

From the Sanskrit for "sitting one," they are celestial beings in the Hindu tradition.

While the Eastern Church has a long tradition of depicting religious images as icons, that is, pictorials on flat panels that could be made of various materials, the Western Church has a tradition of depicting religious images in the form of statues. In either case, the religious images are overwhelmingly historical figures. Jesus as the Good Shepherd, Jesus as King, the crucified Jesus in the arms of his mother, Mary, are all sources of inspiration. Catholicism is a very incarnational religious tradition. With Jesus becoming man, he raised the dignity of humanity. Catholics venerate those whom the Church deems closest to God and who are exemplars of how to seek intimacy with God. Not only can religious imagery instruct and inspire us, it also can form us as a faith community. Placing flowers or lighting a candle in front of a statue is not a gesture of worship, but a gesture of veneration or honor. We pray to Mary and the saints to intercede on our behalf. We pray to, worship, and adore the Triune God alone. As art images are translated into sacred images, so, too, are we as individual believers and as a community of believers transformed into a holy people worthy of the promises of Christ.

➤ What do you respect about the Hindu tradition?

➤ Why do you think some people are so opposed to the use of religious images as a form of devotion?

■ Section 6 Summary

- Hindus believe partial Truth can be found in many religious traditions, but that no religious tradition, including Hinduism, possesses the whole Truth.

- Hindus are happy to participate in interreligious dialogue, for they believe it is one vehicle for correcting misunderstandings about Hinduism.

- There are a variety of views about Jesus among Hindus.

- According to Catholics, Jesus is not one avatar among many, but the only incarnation of God.

- Both Catholics and Hindus have a long tradition in the use of religious images, but the content of the images is radically different. Catholic depictions are mostly historical while Hindu depictions are mostly mythical.

■ Section 6 Review Questions

1. In dialoguing about human dignity, what topic in particular do Hindus have in mind?

2. Name at least three views of Jesus that can be found among Hindus.

3. Name similar views Catholics and Hindus have about Jesus.

4. List three functions of religious imagery.

● Conclusion

Hinduism is a difficult religion to define because it has no founder, no universal creed, and no widely accepted scriptures. Yet, Hinduism has a rich array of rituals, scriptures, systems of belief, and colorful deities. Important concepts of Hinduism are Brahman (the Ultimate Reality), atman (equal with Brahman as the unification with one's real self), and karma (the actions a person does that will have a direct effect on the present life and also on what type of life he or she will have after rebirth).

Hinduism has proved itself to be a religion that has gone through many ups and downs and still lands upright. Though the caste system still has a great influence on Hindu life, the individual *person* remains more important than individual *beliefs*. For this reason, life cycle rituals play a very important role in Hinduism. Most Hindus are not interested in converting other people to Hinduism. Because Brahman has many faces, Hindus believe that other paths people take to attain unity with Brahman are valid.

■ Chapter 5 Summary

■ The history of Hinduism shows its continual expansion and absorption from other religious traditions on the subcontinent of India.

■ Hindus believe in millions of gods, yet each god helps to image Ultimate Reality known as Brahman.

■ Karma, samsara, and moksha are mostly universal beliefs within Hinduism.

■ Hindus are born in one of four caste systems, each with hundreds of sub-castes. Some Hindus, called "untouchables," have the misfortune of not being born into any caste.

■ Male Hindus of the first three castes progress through four stages and are called to pursue four goals.

■ There are two categories of Hindu scripture: shruti and smriti.

■ Besides nature, Hindu sacred spaces include temples, home shrines, and the Ganges River.

■ Hindu life cycle rituals are more universal than festival celebrations.

■ Most Hindus celebrate the festivals of Diwali and Holi along with life cycle rituals called samskaras.

■ Jainism, Buddhism, and Sikhism all derived from Hinduism in some way.

■ Hinduism is very tolerant of religious diversity.

■ Many views of Jesus can be found among Hindus, but Catholics would agree with very few of them.

■ Both Hindus and Catholics suffer from the misunderstanding of their use of religious imagery.

■ Chapter 5 Review Questions

1. Briefly summarize the main characteristics of each of the five main Hindu historical periods.

2. What is the difference between shruti and smriti scriptures?

3. What was the major dilemma for Arjuna in the *Bhagavad Gita*?

4. What do Hindus mean by Ultimate Reality?

5. How are Brahman and atman related?

6. There is a perfume that is sold called Samsara. Why would Hindus find that strange?

7. What is moksha?

8. What are the three main paths to liberation for Hindus? Which of the three paths is the most prevalent among Hindus?

9. How are the caste system and the cycle of rebirth related?

10. Name and explain the four stages of life for Hindu males in the first three castes.

11. Why is the Ganges River so sacred to Hindus?

12. What is the significance of the city of Varanasi to Hindus?

13. What are the four pursuits in life for Hindus? Which of the four is the most important?

14. What elements of Hinduism can be found in Sikhism?

15. Describe the various views about Jesus that can be found among Hindus.

16. What are the "five K's" of Sikhism?

17. Why can Mohandas Gandhi be called a Hindu social reformer?

18. Why are both Catholics and Hindus accused of worshipping idols?

19. List and give examples of three reasons for the use of religious imagery.

20. What was the lesson Svetaketu's father was trying to teach him?

21. How are karma, moksha, and samsara related?

22. What are the two festivals most celebrated by Hindus? Why are they celebrated?

Research & Activities

Research and give an oral presentation on one of the following topics:

The practice of sati

The caste system in India today

The "untouchables" in India today

The former Indian prime minister Indira Gandhi

Mohandas Gandhi

The Self-Realization Fellowship

Transcendental Meditation

The International Society of Krishna Consciousness

Sacred cows in India

Sikhism or Jainism in India today

Prayer

Gayatri Mantra (the mother of the Vedas), the foremost mantra in hinduism and hindu beliefs, inspires wisdom. Its meaning is "May the Almighty God illuminate our intellect to lead us along the righteous path."

> Oh God! Thou art the Giver of Life,
> Remover of pain and sorrow,
> The Bestower of happiness,
> Oh! Creator of the Universe,
> May we receive thy supreme sin-destroying light,
> May Thou guide our intellect in the right
> direction.

Buddhism

6

A Human-Centered Religion

Buddhism—from the Sanskrit word *budhi*, meaning "to wake up"—is a human-centered religion, not a god-centered one. The responsibility for spiritual development in Buddhism rests totally upon the individual. A purpose of Buddhism is to be awakened or enlightened about that which is real.

Unlike Hinduism, Buddhism can be traced to a founder. He is Siddhartha Gautama, a Hindu who was born into the warrior caste in what was then India and is now present-day Nepal. Called simply the "Buddha," meaning "Awakened One," Siddhartha Gautama taught that if people followed his teachings, they, too, could be enlightened and attain **Nirvana**. Siddhartha Gautama was neither a god nor a messenger of a god. He was a human being who pointed to his teachings and not himself. Though some Buddhists believe Siddhartha Gautama had some divine element to him, what appears to be their

Nirvana

Meaning "to extinguish" or "to blow out," it refers to the extinction of suffering, impermanence, delusion, and all that keeps the life cycle (samsara) going. Nirvana is the spiritual goal for all Buddhists.

233

worship of him is rather a symbol of deep respect for who Buddhists believe to be the most compassionate person in history. For some, bowing to the image of the Buddha is bowing to the buddha nature that is within each individual.

Buddhism is more than 2,500 years old. Over the centuries, Buddhism has grown into two main branches of Theravada and Mahayana Buddhism with a vast array of subdivisions in Mahayana Buddhism. The history of Buddhism is complex, and its library of sacred texts is vast. Ritual and meditative practices cover the spectrum from the simple to the elaborate. Though most Buddhists live in Asia, a steadily growing number of Buddhists can be found on the continents of Europe, Australia, and North America.

BCE

ca. 560	Siddhartha Gautama is born
480	The first of Four Councils
383	Emergence of Theravada Buddhism in India
100	Emergence of Mahayana Buddhism

CE

50	Buddhism in China
400s	Translation and editing of Tripitaka into Pali
552	Buddhism in Japan via Korea
1203	Destruction of final Buddhist institutions in India by Muslim ruler Muhammad Ghuri
1578	Sonam Gyatso, first Dalai Lama in Tibet
1852	First Chinese Buddhist temple established in America in San Francisco
1949	Communist takeover of China
1959	Tibetan Buddhists flee to India and Nepal
1989	Tenzin Gyatso, fourteenth Dalai Lama, wins Nobel Prize for Peace
1998	Terrorists commit a deadly suicide attack on Sri Lanka's most sacred Buddhist site, the Temple of Tooth, where Buddha's tooth relic is enshrined.

➤ **Where do you see Buddhism in popular culture?**

1. A Brief History of Buddhism

The origin of Buddhism begins with the birth of Siddhartha Gautama in approximately 560 BCE. The history continues with the preservation of the Buddha's teachings through four succeeding "councils" of his followers. It then fans out in a number of directions across the Asian continent. Though Buddhism began in India, it extended to Central, Eastern, and Southeastern Asia. Today there are Buddhists worldwide, including the Western world where many are attracted to Buddhism's focus on meditation, spirituality, and wisdom.

Siddhartha Gautama

There are a number of stories about the life of Siddhartha Gautama, sometimes called Shakyamuni, meaning "sage of the Shakya clan." Born a Hindu of the warrior caste, his father was king of a small village located in present-day Nepal. His mother, Queen Maya, dreamed that an elephant touched her right side and she conceived. Brahmins, the priestly Hindu caste, interpreted the dream for her: she would bear a son that would either be a great king or a great holy man.

Siddhartha Gautama

According to Buddhist tradition, Queen Maya traveled to her father's house around the middle of the sixth century BCE to prepare for the birth. In her travels, she stopped in Lumbini Gardens. There she stepped off her chariot and held the branch of a tree for support and to rest. Immediately her child emerged from her right side without any help and took seven steps. He stopped and said, "No more births for me." He was named

Siddhartha. Seven days later, Queen Maya died. Siddhartha's father went to great lengths to shield him from the world's pain and suffering. He lived the life of a pampered prince, having as many women and servants at his disposal as he wished.

At age sixteen, Siddhartha married Yasodhara, and they had a son named Rahula. When he was nineteen, Siddhartha had his charioteer take him beyond where his father permitted. On these travels, Siddhartha saw things that his father had tried to shield from him. These were later known as the **Four Sights**, and they would change the course of the prince's life. Siddhartha saw an old man, a very sick man, a corpse, and a wandering holy man without possessions. Each of these sights made a dramatic impression on Siddhartha. One night, at age twenty-nine, Siddhartha quietly kissed his sleeping wife and son and had his charioteer take him to the edge of the forest. There Siddhartha donned the simple robes of a holy man and had his charioteer take all his princely clothes and jeweled possessions back to his father.

For the next six years, Siddhartha took up the life of a wandering **ascetic**, meditating for hours each day and eating only enough to stay alive. In fact, he had become so emaciated that he said he could put his finger in his belly button and feel his backbone. At one point, Siddhartha sat under a **bodhi tree** and sought answers to questions about life, especially suffering. In his meditations, Siddhartha was tempted by Mara, the stealer of Wisdom who left one with ignorance and delusion. Mara

Four Sights

The inspiration to become a monk for Siddhartha the Buddha, the four sights were an old crippled man (old age), a diseased man (illness), a decaying corpse (death), and finally an ascetic that Siddartha encountered on an unannounced journey outside of the palace.

ascetic

A person who renounces material comforts to live a self-disciplined life, especially in the area of religious devotion.

bodhi tree

The large, sacred fig tree at the Mahabodhi Temple at Bodh Gaya where Siddhartha the Buddha arrived at enlightenment.

tempted Siddhartha with thirst, lust, discontent, and sensuality, but to no avail. Going even deeper into meditation about suffering and the cycle of rebirth, Siddhartha finally reached the enlightenment he sought. He struggled with the thought of whether to share his new insights with others or not.

Returning to the Deer Park near where he lived, Siddhartha delivered his first sermon to five ascetics who had first traveled with him, but later abandoned him. He told them that neither indulgence nor asceticism could release people from *samsara* (the cycle of birth, death, and rebirth). Rather, it was the **Middle Way**, life in the middle of the spectrum between indulgence and asceticism, that led to *moksha*, that is, freedom from the cycle. The Middle Way consists of following the Four Noble Truths, the fourth of which is the Noble Eightfold Path, eight practices dealing with wisdom, morality, and meditation.

Middle Way

The Buddhist teaching that liberation from samsura comes neither through severe ascetical practices nor through wild indulgences, but in the middle of the spectrum between those two opposites.

Those first five wandering ascetics Siddhartha preached to in the Deer Park decided to be disciples of the Buddha. They formed a community of monks called the **sangha**.

sangha

At first just the Buddhist monastic community, later it came to describe the entire community of monks, nuns, and lay persons.

Siddhartha continued his travels and preaching and gained a number of followers. He returned to his homeland, where he converted many fellow countrymen to his Middle Way, including his wife, son, and cousin.

At age eighty, Siddartha died of food poisoning. As he lay on his right side dying, he asked the gathering crowd whether anyone had any questions. There was no response. He told the people that nothing in the world was permanent and that they had to work out their own salvation with diligence. Then Siddartha died and entered Nirvana. The year was about

relics

Items of religious devotion, especially a piece of the body or personal items of an important religious figure.

483 BCE. He was cremated and his **relics** were divided and distributed to places where he had travelled. Stupas, dome-shaped monuments, were erected over his relics, and their presence became places of Buddhist pilgrimages.

➤ Which is more appealing to you: life lived to the extreme or life based on the Middle Way? Why or why not?

The Four Councils

Dharma

From the Sanskrit, meaning "uphold," in Hinduism it is that which is in accordance with the laws of the cosmos and of nature such as righteous acts. In Buddhism it is the teachings of the Buddha.

Siddhartha left neither a successor nor writings of any kind to his followers. His legacy was the **Dharma**, which he shared with all who would listen. After his death, the Buddha's followers carried on his practice of teaching, but there was a concern that the purity of the Buddha's teachings and practices be preserved. According to Buddhist tradition, a council of Siddartha's, longtime followers—five hundred monks—gathered about a year after the Buddha's death with the intent to preserve his teachings through the recitation of memories. They recited to each other, revised the recitations, and tried to come to some agreement on Siddhartha's teachings. After this First Council, periodic recitation gatherings were held to maintain the purity of the memories and to pass the recitations on to others.

About one hundred years later, the Second Council was called. This council was held to address questionable practices of some "liberal" monks who sought a relaxation of monastic discipline, including permission to store salt, to eat after noon, to drink palm wine, and to accept silver and gold. The Council found these practices unlawful, but the decision was likely a seed for a major split between the more conservative *Sthaviras* and the more liberal *Mahasanghikas*. These two groups continued to subdivide over the next few decades until there were eighteen sects, ten belonging to the Sthaviras and eight belonging to the Mahasanghikas. Only the Theravada sect from the Sthavira group survives to this day. However, the Mahasanghikas are a forerunner of **Mahayana Buddhism**, which is in existence today.

Mahayana Buddhism
Literally the "Great Ox Cart." This branch of Buddhism differs from Theravada Buddhism because it accommodates a greater number of people from all walks of life.

The Third Council came about upon the conversion of King Ashoka of the Mauryan dynasty of India in the third century BCE. After carrying out various military campaigns, he became disenchanted with the military and the devastation war left on people, communities, and the environment. He converted to Buddhism and ruled his country by the Buddhist ideals of moral living and pacifism. Ashoka was both a patron and a promoter of Buddhism, though he supported also the religious traditions of Hinduism and Jainism. Ashoka had the original stupas of Siddhartha created after his death opened and subdivided the relics into very small elements. In this way, Ashoka was able to create thousands of stupas as pilgrimage places to honor Siddhartha throughout the land. He built thousands of monasteries and sent missionaries as far south as Ceylon (present day Sri Lanka). Buddhist tradition holds that Ashoka's son, a Buddhist monk, was sent with companions to Sri Lanka as missionaries. There King Tissa and many of his nobility converted to Buddhism. Buddhist missionaries went deep into the Hellenized world of the West. Edicts of Ashoka inscribed on rocks and pillars indicate that missionaries went to the Seleucid King Antiochus II and the Egyptian King Ptolemy II in the third century BCE as well as a number of other Western rulers. The growth of Buddhism was so swift under Ashoka that a number of questionable teachings flourished.

Buddhist tradition relates that King Ashoka called for a Third Council to purify the sangha of its various irregularities. Ashoka's efforts extended and preserved Buddhism beyond India, for by the time Muslims invaded India in the twelfth century and Buddhism disappeared from its land of birth for centuries, it had been established in many other regions of Asia.

Stupa Buddhist shrine in Sri Lanka

By around 100 CE Mahayana Buddhism, with its emphasis on lay participation, had emerged as a distinct branch of Buddhism. Increased lay participation also brought a variety of interpretations of Buddhist scriptures.

Buddhism in India

Buddhism made great strides in India during the first few centuries of the Common Era, especially during the **Gupta dynasty**. Rulers of this dynasty continued the practice of supporting Buddhism by creating an atmosphere where Buddhism could thrive, helping to build monasteries and funding great stupas for the relics of renowned and holy Buddhists. It was during the Gupta dynasty that the rise in Buddhist universities as part of monastic centers became prominent. The universities boasted an extensive curriculum with students taking courses not only in Buddhism, but logic, science, mathematics, medicine, and music. One of the most famous Buddhist universities was Nalanda, located not far from where Shakyamuni first attained Enlightenment. Continuing the work begun by Ashoka, universities became the training places for missionaries. The rise in the number of universities prompted also the rise in Mahayana as a dominant expression of Buddhism.

Gupta dynasty

240–550 CE, when the Gupta Empire ruled India with political peace and prosperity.

A negative factor of large monasteries and universities was that they tended to make the monks more elitist. Concurrently, the laity began to drift away from Buddhism, and move toward the resurgent bhakti movement in Hinduism. Coupled with the Huns' invasion of India in 470 that destroyed thousands of monasteries, Buddhism was nearly rendered extinct. Though the Huns were defeated in 528, Buddhism never fully recovered in India. It was during the time of the gradual decline of Buddhism in India that some Chinese Buddhist pilgrims came to India. They returned to China with a wealth of knowledge and a number of Buddhist texts.

After the invasion and removal of the Huns, Buddhism was able to revive itself to some extent in India. The **Pala dynasty** came a generation after the Gupta dynasty. Kings of the Pala dynasty were patrons of Buddhism, building a number of great monastic centers. As Tibet rose as a vibrant Buddhist region, Pala kings shifted their external focus from China to Tibet.

Pala dynasty

The empire that controlled the Indian subcontinent from the eighth to twelfth centuries. The word **pala** *means "protector."*

The end of the Pala dynasty was simultaneously the end of Buddhism in India until the twentieth century. The Muslim invasions into India at the end of the twelfth century sealed that result. Though there were remnants of Buddhism in India for a few more centuries, it had all but disappeared from the land of its birth.

Surprisingly, after centuries of absence, Buddhism is slowly returning to India. With the positive and inspirational example of the exiled Tibetan Buddhists in India who were, and still are, persecuted by Communist China, as well as a statement of protest against the caste system, conversions to Buddhism have experienced a revival in India. At the beginning of the twenty-first century, a small but steady number of people in India are converting to Buddhism.

Buddhist Expansion Beyond India

Not long after the death of the Buddha, Buddhism was introduced to Central Asia and eventually into countries with the present day names of Afghanistan, Uzbekistan, and Tajikistan as well as Pakistan and parts of Iran. While Buddhism played an important role in Central Asia for centuries, it shared its religious landscape with a number of other religious traditions including Christianity. However, eventually Islam became the dominant religious tradition in Central Asia.

Buddhism was introduced to Southeast Asia via Sri Lanka. In Malaysia and Indonesia it joined Hinduism to provide two strong religious traditions in the region until around the tenth century (when Islam eclipsed both religious traditions except among the Chinese minority). Thailand and Myanmar were predominantly Theravada Buddhist strongholds. Kampuchea and Vietnam, influenced by China, were predominantly Mahayana. A revival of Theravada Buddhism in around the eleventh century moved Kampuchea in that direction around that time. In the last few centuries, European colonialism over-whelmed Buddhism and Communism devastated it. However, Buddhism was never completely lost and there are small signs of revival today.

Buddhism found its way to China around the beginning of the Common Era. It took a while to find a home there, but when it did, it became very much part of the religious landscape along with Confucianism and Taoism. To the many schools of Buddhism, China contributed Ch'an and Pure Land Buddhism (discussed in the next chapter). From China, Buddhism moved to Korea where the *Tripitaka*, early Buddhist scriptures, were very revered. Buddhism then moved from Korea to Japan. To Japan from China came Pure Land Ch'an Buddhism, called Zen Buddhism, as well as two sects of Buddhism that became distinctly Japanese. Japanese rulers readily patronized Buddhism, but the practitioners of Shinto, the indigenous religious tradition of Japan, was less welcoming, at first. Eventually, it became difficult to distinguish between Shinto and Buddhism.

In Tibet, **Vajrayana Buddhism**, also known as Tantric Buddhism, a branch of Mahayana Buddhism, emerged. Vajrayana Buddhism puts a great emphasis on the person doing mantras, rituals, and meditations as a way to strive for Enlightenment. In the fourteenth century Tibetan Buddhists came to believe that the leaders of their monasteries were reincarnations of great **bodhisattvas** who chose to postpone their own opportunity to enter Nirvana and

Vajrayana Buddhism

Literally "Diamond Vehicle," it is the prominent branch of Buddhism in Tibet.

bodhisattva

A being that compassionately refrains from entering nirvana in order to save others and is worshipped as a deity in Mahayana Buddhism.

helped others enter Nirvana before they would go. Leaders of monasteries in Tibet became known as **lamas**. The head of Tibetan Buddhist monastic leaders was known as the **Dalai Lama** who was also the political leader of Tibet until the Chinese communist government forced them out of Tibet in 1959. They set up their exiled community in Dharamsala, India.

lamas

In Tibetan Buddhism, teachers and often heads of monasteries.

Dalai Lama

The head lama of Tibetan Buddhism who was the spiritual and political leader of Tibet until its takeover by Chinese communist leaders and a forced exile to India.

What are ways you consciously "share the religious landscape" with people of other religious tradtions.

The Dalai Lama

The Dalai Lama, who is the exiled spiritual and political leader of Tibet, received the 1989 Nobel Peace Prize in recognition of his nonviolent campaign to end the Chinese government's forty-year policy of genocide and persecution in his homeland. The Nobel committee praised him "for advocating peaceful solutions based upon tolerance and mutual respect in order to preserve the historical and cultural heritage of his people." Receiving the prize, he modestly said,  "The basic human spirit is getting the upper hand. I am a simple Buddhist monk, no more, no less."

It has been said that the name for the quality that describes the Tibetan people individually and collectively is the "good heart." The gifts of Tibet are especially evident in the areas of spirituality, peace, nonviolence, relationship to the natural world, and human relations.

Expressing his beliefs, the Dalai Lama says:

> Through mental peace there is a greater possibility to achieve lasting world peace . . . Through hatred or extreme competitive attitudes a genuine peace is difficult. Through mental peace, through a general sense of brotherhood, sisterhood, there is greater possibility to achieve real world peace. . . . True religion must be a sort of destroyer. Understand? Compassion and tolerance, we call destroyers of anger, destroyers of hatred? If you apply different religions in the right way then all have the same aim; that is, a better human being. [3]

Buddhism in Modern Times

Buddhism has attracted interest in Western nations, inspiring writers and thinkers of other religious traditions, including Christianity, with Buddhist approaches to meditation, wisdom, and spirituality. Buddhism did not take hold in the West until modern times.

There were sporadic encounters between the West and Buddhism, mostly with Christian missionaries. St. John of Damascus translated a life of Buddha around the beginning of the eighth century, which traveled through Europe during the Middle Ages. Titled *Barlaam and Josephat*, Barlaam was the Buddha-like character who was seen as a Christian saint. Missionaries such as Francis Xavier in Japan and Mateo Ricci in China encountered Buddhism.

It was not until the British were building their empire and sending people to set up trade routes that there was a sustained interaction between Buddhism and the West. The translation of Buddhist texts into European languages brought Buddhism even deeper into the West, especially to Western intellectuals.

In the United States, the poet Henry David Thoreau translated a French translation of a sutra into English. The expansion of the railroads during the nineteenth century brought thousands of Chinese immigrants, a number of whom were Buddhists, to the western part of the United States to help in that endeavor. At the end of the nineteenth century, one could find Japanese Buddhists among Japanese immigrants in Hawaii and California as field laborers.

The World Parliament of Religions held in Chicago in 1893 was another opportunity for Buddhists to be on Western soil. The Japanese Zen master D. T. Suzuki translated his books on Zen Buddhism during the middle of the twentieth century. American authors Allen Ginsberg and the Trappist monk Thomas Merton kept in contact with Suzuki and were influenced by him.

During the twentieth century, the rise of communism triggered the demise of Buddhism in a number of countries. The attempt to eradicate Buddhism was felt first in the former Soviet Union. After World War II, the communist takeover in Asia affected Buddhism in China, Tibet, and parts of Southeast Asia. However, as history has shown, the decline of Buddhism in one region sees a rise of Buddhism in another.

Buddhism's worldwide popularity grew even more at the start of the twenty-first century. With its tendencies toward individualism, self-help, and self-realization, many westerners find at least some aspects of Buddhism interesting, if not helpful. Others appropriate some aspect of Buddhism into their own religious tradition while others convert outright to Buddhism. Buddhism is one of the fastest-growing religions in select areas of the world, including England and the state of California.

■ Section 1 Summary

- ■ Siddhartha Gautama, called Shakyamuni by his followers, was the founder of Buddhism.

- ■ As Gautama was a Hindu, Buddhism has its roots in Hinduism.

- The first councils of early Buddhism were assembled to codify monastic discipline and unify Buddhist scriptures.
- Buddhism received imperial patronage from King Ashoka.
- Two major branches of Buddhism are Theravada and Mahayana.
- The invasion of the Muslims into India eventually drove Buddhism from India, though Buddhism is reemerging there today.
- In its first few centuries of existence, Buddhism spanned much of the continent of Asia.
- Though there were sporadic encounters with Buddhism over the centuries, Buddhism did not take hold in the West until modern times.

■ Section 1 Review Questions

1. Briefly summarize the birth, Enlightenment, and death of Siddhartha Gautama.
2. What were the main issues addressed by each of the Buddhist councils?
3. What attracted King Ashoka to Buddhism?
4. Why were the Japanese attracted to Zen Buddhism?
5. List countries in Asia where Buddhism took hold, at least for some time.
6. Who is the Dalai Lama?

● 2. Sacred Stories and Sacred Scriptures

Siddhartha wrote no texts, nor did his immediate followers. Rather, for a number of generations after the death of the Buddha, stories about him and his teachings were kept alive through passing on the memories at recitation gatherings.

Like sacred scriptures of other religious traditions, the sacred texts of Buddhism developed over a number of centuries.

There is an enormous corpus of texts employing a wide variety of literary genres. Texts were originally written in a number of languages and translated into other languages with little regard for accuracy. The liberal translation of texts and the addition of other texts tended to bring tension, and sometimes division, within Buddhism. There is no agreement among, or even within, the various branches of Buddhism as to which texts are considered sacred and which texts are not. The following is a very brief survey of the major texts used within Buddhism.

Scriptures of Theravada Buddhism

The early Buddhist scriptures known as **Tripitaka**, or "Three Baskets," were passed down orally in Sanskrit before they were written down around the first century BCE in the Pali language. Thus, besides being called the Tripitaka, it is called also the **Pali Canon**. The "Three Baskets" to which the Tripitaka refers are the *Vinaya Pitaka*, *Sutra Pitaka*, and *Abidharrna Pitaka*. The Tripitaka is the authoritative scripture for Theravada Buddhists. They believe the Tripitaka contains the words of the historical Buddha.

The Vinaya Pitaka is the code of monastic discipline for monks and nuns. There are 227 rules for monks and 311 rules for nuns. The rules highlight offenses in descending order of seriousness. Each rule is accompanied by a story that explains the reason for the rule. This basket also records the life and ministry of the Buddha.

The Sutra Pitaka is primarily made up of discourses attributed to Siddhartha Gautama. Many of the topics of the discourses, such as morality, later became part of Buddhist doctrine. The story of the Buddha's birth and attainment of Nirvana can be found in this Pitaka.

Tripitaka

From the Sanskrit meaning "Three Baskets," and also known as the Pali Canon in Theravada Buddhism, the compilation of three collections of early Buddhist texts.

Pali Canon

The authoritative Buddhism scripture of Theravada Buddhists written in the Pali language, and important, but not definitive, for Mahayana Buddhists. Another name for the Tripitaka.

The Abidharma Pitaka examines the Buddha's psychological teachings. It spends a great deal of time analyzing Buddhist doctrine in detail. The Abidharma Pitaka is of more interest for monks or serious students than the average lay Buddhist. The Mahayana and Vajrayana versions of this Pitaka contain additional treatises.

The Way to Happiness

Examine these statements on happiness from the "Dhammapada", or "Sayings of the Buddha," found in the Tripitaka:

- Let us live happily, then, not hating those who hate us! Among men who hate us let us dwell free from hatred!

- Let us live happily, then, free from [moral] ailments among the ailing! Among men who are ailing let us dwell free from ailments!

- Let us live happily, then, free from greed among the greedy! Among men who are greedy let us dwell free from greed!

- Let us live happily, then, though we call nothing our own! We shall be like the bright gods, feeding on happiness!

- Victory breeds hatred, for the conquered is unhappy. He who has given up both victory and defeat, he, the contented, is happy.

- There is no fire like passion; there is no losing throw like hatred; there is no pain like this body; there is no happiness higher than rest.

- Hunger is the worst of diseases, the body the greatest of pains; if one knows this truly, that is Nirvana, the highest happiness.

- Health is the greatest of gifts, contentedness the best riches; trust is the best of relationships, Nirvana the highest happiness.

- He who has tasted the sweetness of solitude and tranquility is free from fear and free from sin, while he tastes the sweetness of drinking in the law.

- The sight of the elect (Arya) is good, to live with them is always happiness; if a man does not see fools, he will be truly happy.

- He who walks in the company of fools suffers a long way; company with fools, as with an enemy, is always painful; company with the wise is pleasure, like meeting with kinsfolk.

- Therefore, one ought to follow the wise, the intelligent, the learned, the much enduring, the dutiful, the elect; one ought to follow a good and wise man, as the moon follows the path of the stars.

(Chapter 15, 197–208)

↪ **What is one lesson you learned about happiness from this reading?**

Scriptures of Mahayana Buddhism

Besides their own version of the Tripitaka, Mahayana Buddhists have a great number of texts they consider sacred. Most popular is *The Lotus of the True Law*, more popularly known as the **Lotus Sutra**. Mahayana Buddhists attribute the Lotus Sutra to the Buddha, but it was more likely composed over several generations. Mahayana Buddhists believe the Lotus Sutra contains the final teachings of the Buddha, placing the Tripitaka in a secondary yet still-important status.

Lotus Sutra

A Mahayana Buddhist text where Enlightenment is made available not only to monastics, but to all because of the great compassion of bodhisattvas.

The popularity of the Lotus Sutra is due to the universality of its message. With the belief that all living things possess Buddha-nature, the Lotus Sutra teaches that all people, not just religious professionals or monastics, can attain Enlightenment. In addition, the Lotus Sutra advocates the bodhisattva ideal in which while working on one's own Nirvana, a person helps others attain Nirvana through the sharing of wisdom and compassion.

The other very popular Mahayana sutra is the *Perfection of Wisdom*, which is a treatise on how to achieve the perfection of wisdom of a bodhisattva. It teaches that to attain perfect wisdom, one must go beyond knowledge of the ordinary and rational. One must transcend the world of existence and resolve seeming contradictions by treating them as paradoxes. For example, we would say light and darkness are opposites. In the *Perfection of Wisdom*, light and darkness would be seen as essentially the same for both are ultimately naught.

Scriptures of Vajrayana Buddhism

tantric

A word to describe Hindu literature written in Sanskrit and concerned with rituals acts of body, speech, and mind.

Vajrayana Buddhists use Mahayana scriptures but add to them their own **tantric** texts from India and China. As with Theravada and Mahayana Buddhism, Vajrayana Buddhism has scriptures of its own. The *Kanjur*, or "Teachings," contains the Theravada and Mahayana scriptures, plus scriptures unique to Vajrayana Buddhism. The second is the *Tanjur*, or "Translation of the Treatises," which are commentaries on the Kanjur. The Kanjur has a number of sutras or discourses on the Buddha's teachings. Unlike Theravada and Mahayana Buddhism, Vajrayana Buddhism places a great value on the tantric tradition of India. In Hinduism, tantrism is that in which some forms of worship and ritual are employed to appropriate and harness the powerful energies of that which is Ultimate Reality in order to some day be one with Ultimate Reality. In Vajrayana Buddhism, tantric texts are more how to do the rituals or meditations to gain Enlightenment.

Two examples of Vajrayana tantric techniques are the use of the *mandala* and the use of the *mantra* to help focus one's meditation. As we saw in Hinduism, a mantra is a sacred word or phrase that assists one in focusing during meditation. The mandala is a sacred geometric symbolic of the universe.

The more popular scripture within Vajrayana Buddhism, however, is the *Tibetan Book of the Dead*. It contains various writings on death, dying, and rebirth. It describes what life—specifically consciousness—is like between death and rebirth. The popularity of the *Tibetan Book of the Dead* partially stems from the fact that it is read while someone is dying, if possible, or when a person has recently died.

> ➤ Christians have a closed canon, meaning they are not able to add books to the Bible. Buddhists do not have a closed canon. What do you think are the advantages of each practice?

■ Section 2 Summary

■ Each of the major branches of Buddhism has their own sacred scriptures.

■ The one scripture used by all major branches of Buddhism is the *Tripitaka*, though the attribution of authority varies.

■ One of the most popular scriptures in Mahayana Buddhism is the *Lotus Sutra*.

■ Vajrayana Buddhism has a number of tantric texts.

■ Section 2 Review Questions

1. In English, what does the term *Tripitaka* mean?
2. What is the most popular Mahayana sacred text?
3. What is the most popular Vajrayana sacred text? Why?

● 3. Beliefs and Practices

The center of all Buddhist beliefs is the *Four Noble Truths*, from Siddhartha Gautama's earliest sermons. If one is ignorant of the Four Noble Truths, she or he will remain on the endless cycle of samsara. Oppositely, understanding of the Four Noble Truths leads to the *Noble Eightfold Path*, the Middle Way, which reminds a person to avoid extremes, to take everything in moderation. These beliefs and subsequent practices are at the heart of Buddhism. Members of the sangha traditionally fell into the categories of monks or nuns. However, recent understandings have incorporated lay people as being equally important as monastics. These areas are explored in the sections that follow.

Four Noble Truths

The Four Noble Truths are named and described as follows:

1. *Life is filled with suffering.* Suffering refers not only to physical suffering, but also mental suffering that comes with facing the various traumas of life. We begin this life with the birth trauma. Then there is physical, mental, and emotional pain, illness, injury, old age, and fear of death. Samsara is the endless cycle of suffering through death and rebirth, and karma is the cause of samsara. Suffering even goes beyond life's physical and mental pains. The reason for suffering includes concepts of impermanence, incompleteness, imperfections, and discontent.

anatma

The Buddhist doctrine of "no soul" or "not self" that means a permanent, unchanging, independent self does not exist, though people act as if it does. Ignorance of anatma causes suffering.

All life is impermanent. Physical beings, both earthly and heavenly, are constantly changing. Human beings age, wood begins to rot, and stars are constantly being formed. Our thoughts, feelings, and attitudes are also impermanent. This is the Buddhist doctrine of **anatma**. While Hindus taught that self or soul was God (atman), Gautama taught that if the soul was purely God then it is not a soul at all. Therefore, it is "no-soul" or "not self."

2. *The cause of suffering is desire.* Because people believe the individual self is real, they have cravings. People constantly want things. When they do not get them,

they are frustrated or disappointed. Even if a person gets what he or she wants, the resulting happiness is impermanent. Ignorance of the nature of the not-self and, thus, believing the self to be real (that is, permanent and unchanging) is the fundamental cause of suffering.

3. *To cease suffering, one must cease desiring.* To end suffering is to end samsara and achieve Nirvana. That is what is real in Buddhism. Everything is suffering, impermanent, and incomplete. The only thing permanent and thus real is the end of suffering. Suffering ceases when we free ourselves of the bondage of desires and cravings and stop believing that our individual self is real. This freedom brings people happiness and contentment. Nirvana is the "extinction" of that suffering through the endless cycles of rebirth.

4. *The path to the end of suffering is the Noble Eightfold Path.* This is the Middle Way between indulgence and self-denial. The Noble Eightfold Path is the moral standard of Buddhism.

While both Buddhists and Hindus believe in samsara, their concept of the cessation of samsara differs significantly. The cessation of samsara for Hindus is moksha, while for Buddhists it is Nirvana. Moksha is liberation from samsara and the realization that the individual self, atman, is one with Ultimate Reality, Brahman. While there is immortality in Hinduism, there is no immortality in Buddhism because there is no-self, no soul. For Buddhists, the liberation from samsara is Nirvana, meaning to "extinguish," referring to putting out the flames of desires, cravings, or passions. This extinction is neither a positive nor a negative experience. Rather, Nirvana is. One is awakened to the reality of the human condition, no longer ignorant or delusional.

➤ Do you think that the ceasing of all desires is possible? Is even the desire to cease all desires itself a desire?

The Noble Eightfold Path

As the fourth of the Four Noble Truths, the Noble Eightfold Path are the central practices of Buddhism. When a person has perfected these eight practices, he or she is awakened or enlightened and attains Nirvana.

1. *Right Understanding.*

   The first step of the Noble Eightfold Path requires that one see things as they really are. Right understanding is the understanding of the causes of suffering, the end of suffering, and the way one endures suffering. In short, this step is summation of the Four Noble Truths.

2. *Right Thought.*

   The mind must be purified of all that moves it away from enlightenment. Right thought is not just getting rid of wrong thoughts. It is replacing wrong thoughts, like hatred and desire, with right thoughts, like loving kindness and renunciation. Right thought can be equated with the Christian beatitude of single-heartedness.

3. *Right Speech.*

   All forms of lying, slandering, gossiping, and using harsh words must be eliminated. Instead, a person must speak truthfully and kindly about others.

4. *Right Conduct.*

   Right conduct calls on people not to cheat, steal, murder, or engage in any kind of sexual misconduct.

5. *Right Livelihood.*

   This path calls upon people not to earn a living through actions that would harm other living things. For example, one's livelihood is not to be earned by slaughtering animals, doing anything involving weapons, or manufacturing or selling any kind of intoxicants such as drugs and alcohol.

6. *Right Effort.*

   This path has to do with a person's thoughts. He or she is to be diligent in getting rid of bad or delusional thoughts, while cultivating good, wholesome thoughts.

7. *Right Mindfulness.*

   A person is to be aware of everything he or she is thinking and doing. Right mindfulness is being aware of thoughts, feelings, and actions at all times. Right mindfulness means knowing oneself.

8. *Right Concentration.*

   This final path is a form of meditation in which a person concentrates on one object, like a flickering candle, in order to give full attention to the object and dispel other distractions. This is the type of concentration that enables a person to see things as they really are and thus gain enlightenment.

The Noble Eightfold Path is categorized by three main practices—morality, meditation, and wisdom. Moral actions bring about meditation, meditation brings about wisdom, and, completing the circle, wisdom gives rise to good actions.

> On a scale of 1 to 10, how well do you know yourself?

Community

Traditionally, sangha referred to a Buddhist community of monks or nuns. Only in the monastic life could one properly practice the teachings of the Buddha. Lay people took care of the material needs of the monastics, gaining merit for a better rebirth. Recent developments have expanded sangha to mean the community of all Buddhist practitioners: monks, nuns, and lay people. Sangha is one of the Three Jewels of Buddhism. The two other jewels are the Buddha and Dharma. The Three Jewels are considered the core of Buddhism. In becoming a Buddhist, one proclaims refuge in these Three Jewels:

I take refuge in the Buddha.
I take refuge in the Dharma.
I take refuge in the Sangha.

Though the monastic and lay lifestyles are very different, each is dependent upon the other. Theravada monks are celibate and provide spiritual nourishment to the laity. The laity provide physical nourishment to monks, who seek their daily food through begging at the households of Buddhist devotees.

arhat

From the Sanskrit for "worthy one," it is a concept of Theravada Buddhism which refers to one who has attained Nirvana in their present lifetime, thus, liberated from the cycle of rebirth.

To be enlightened and reach Nirvana is an important goal of a Buddhist. For Theravada Buddhists, **arhat** ("worthy one") is the name that describes such a person. However, only those who have heard the teachings of Buddha can become arhats. Mahayana Buddhists likewise accept the status of arhat as an ultimate goal. However, the exemplar person in Mahayana Buddhism is a bodhisattva who has chosen to defer full enlightenment until all other humans have first reached nirvana. Because of their great compassion for all persons, bodhisattvas, who are not necessarily monks or nuns, will transfer merit they have gained to others so others can reach nirvana. The bodhisattva will enter nirvana last.

Mahayana monks abide by the same rules as Theravada monks. However, they add to the rules by witnessing about Siddhartha Gautama, his way of life, and emulating his attitudes of peace and compassion to others. The Japanese Mahayana Buddhist sect of Zen does not beg for alms. Rather, they earn their own livelihood. Another Japanese Mahayana sect known as Shin permits their monks to marry and raise a family.

■ Section 3 Summary

- ■ The foundations for Buddhist teachings are the Four Noble Truths and the Noble Eightfold Path.
- ■ Sangha is the Buddhist community of monks and lay people.
- ■ The Three Jewels are considered the core of Buddhism.
- ■ Monastic and lay lifestyles are different but dependent on one another.

■ Section 3 Review Questions

1. Name and explain the Four Noble Truths.
2. List the three major categories of the Noble Eightfold Path.
3. What are the Three Jewels of Buddhism?

● 4. Sacred Time

Buddhists do not have a special day of the week for congregational worship. Theravadan Buddhists can make offerings to images of the Buddha at any time.  Mahayanan Buddhists can do the same and also make offerings to images of other buddhas and bodhisattvas. In areas where there are no temples, Buddhists make offerings at home. For both home and temple, the items offered might be flowers, candles, or incense. A recitation of the Three Jewels is usually part of the offering. The scent of incense reminds Buddhists of the influence of good virtue. Flowers, which soon wither, remind people of the impermanence of everything. Because Buddha is not a god, bowing to an image of the Buddha is a sign of profound respect rather than submission to a deity.

Meditation

Meditation is central to every branch of Buddhism. The last three paths of the Noble Eightfold Path are categorized as meditation. By following the paths of right effort, right mindfulness, and right concentration, Buddhists believe they are well on their way to enlightenment. For Buddhists, meditation is also a means of heightened awareness. Meditation helps people cultivate the awareness of their dreams, goals, and self-identities and the means to engage in good karma. Siddhartha Gautama taught his disciples a number of types of meditation. Two of the most common are *Mindfulness of Breath* and *Meditation of Loving-Kindness*.

Mindfulness of Breath is one of the first forms of meditation Buddhists learn. As might be imagined, Mindfulness of Breath focuses on breathing as the person learns to pay close attention to the ebb and flow of breath. As one focuses on breathing, other thoughts and distractions try to intrude. The person who persists in practicing this form of meditation over a long period of time finds that the power of concentration becomes stronger, and that inner calm enters not only the mind, but the whole person.

Most Buddhist meditations, including the Meditation of Loving-Kindness, begin with Mindfulness of Breathing. When the mind has been calmed, a person then focuses on the self and says loving things about himself or herself. For example,

"May I be a loving person."
"May I have a heart filled with love."
"May I be a peace-filled person."
"May I be a fulfilled person."

After focusing on self, attention is then turned to others: first to one the person loves, then to one whom the person is neutral about, and finally to one whom the person dislikes. In the Meditation of Loving Kindness, each of these three people is wished well over a long period of time.

A Place for Meditation

According to Buddhist thought, one of the main goals of each person is to gain wisdom and new insight through meditation. In meditation, the mind is cleared of all worldly concerns so that the person can concentrate on God, or in Buddhism, that which might allow one to move to a higher stage of spiritual awareness. The following news account describes an unusual setting for Buddhist meditation:

> It's a shocking image—even to the accustomed eye.
>
> Fourteen children, the oldest of whom is eleven, are lined up, marching with hands clasped behind their backs at Central Juvenile Hall in East Los Angeles. The youngest child, eight years old, is outfitted in bright orange prison garb, signifying he is a high-risk violent offender, a category that includes murder, assault and armed robbery. . . .
>
> It's the spiritual realm these young offenders are being helped with today, as a team of Buddhist monks and teachers spends an hour teaching the children how to meditate and how meditation might help those who will need to survive extended time in the California prison system. . . .
>
> Benzamin-Masuda rings a bell and asks the children to focus now on the center of the room.
>
> The children settle down and begin to practice meditating.
>
> "Part of the trouble is that these kids' defense systems are very high to begin with," says Kusala, who is with the International Buddhist Meditation Center in Los Angeles, which has been instrumental in bringing Buddhist spiritual practices into the juvenile halls. "Remember, people often had deceptive motives when they paid any attention to them. Some classes are more chaotic than others, and some are smooth as silk."

He says it's generally the older boys—15 and up—"who realize a little better what their reality is and know they need help and seem to catch on very quickly."

A visit to the meditation class of the "KL" group (boys 16 to 18 who are standing trial for murder) finds students who are attentive, intelligent and polite.

"When I stress about my case, and my situation, and the things that have happened, I can focus on my breathing and get a respite," says a 17-year-old boy who has been in the KL unit for a year. "Sometimes not having any word [to meditate on] is better."

Javier Stauring, Central's Catholic chaplain, thinks the silence and meditative practices have a more profound result for troubled youngsters "rather than just having supportive people who show up to listen to their problems. The discoveries these kids are making about themselves is amazing. Our hope is that these discoveries will remain, and I think the silence has helped a lot. They don't get a lot of silence in this institution."

Quoted from "Soul Searching," by Janet Kinosian
(*Los Angeles Times*, June 2, 1998)

➤ What are obstacles in your life that keep you from gaining the benefits of meditation?

Puja

Like Hindus, puja is part of the daily life of a practicing Buddhist. Recall that for Hindus puja is a worship service to honor the deity held in homes and temples. For Buddhist monks, puja takes place in monasteries, while for Buddhist laity, puja also generally takes place at a home shrine.

Contents of a home shrine generally consist of an image of the Buddha and, in some countries, representations of ancestors.

In a typical puja ritual, participants offer flowers, fruit, a bowl of water, incense, and lighted candles to revere, respect, and honor the Buddha. The significance of each offering is explained below.

Puja Offerings and Their Significance

Flowers	Though initially offering beauty, they wither and, thus, point to the impermanence of all life.
Fruit	A reminder of what good conduct brings.
Water	A sign of purity, which is the example of the Buddha and the goal of all.
Incense	The sweet odor of incense is a reminder of what good conduct brings.
Candlelight	Dispels the darkness of delusion and ignorance.

In addition, Buddhists offer gratitude to the Buddha for the Dharma, which points to the way of Enlightenment and Nirvana. Reverence and gratitude to the Buddha is shown through the gestures of removing one's shoes before beginning, folding one's hands and bowing, and in some traditions, prostration. Prayers are said, a mantra may be chanted, and a time for meditation on some aspect of the Dharma may be included. In addition, the Three Jewels and the **Five Precepts** are generally recited.

Honoring the Buddha and his Dharma are not confined to the home. Buddhist shrines and temples are also places for puja. In addition, especially in predominantly Buddhist nations, one can see

Five Precepts

A basic moral standard by which all Buddhists are to live. They are:

1. *Do not take the life of any living creature.*

2. *Do not take anything not freely given.*

3. *Abstain from sexual misconduct and sexual overindulgence. (For monastics, abstain from any sexual activity.)*

4. *Refrain from untrue or deceitful speech.*

5. *Avoid intoxicants.*

images of the Buddha everywhere. The images of the Buddha may be statues cast in bronze, stone, wood, metal, or other materials. It may be two inches tall or two stories tall. Images may be in the form of paintings of many styles and many mediums. Buddha's image can be found in small shrines on street corners, in shops, on roadsides, in public parks, and the like. In countries where adherents are predominantly Mahayana Buddhists, not only images of the Buddha, but images of bodhisattvas are ubiquitous. These images are not only reminders of exemplary lives, but sources of power and good karma.

> ➤ **What are similarities to home shrines in the Hindu, Buddhist, and Catholic traditions?**

Festivals

There are two categories of Buddhist festivals. One is centered around the life of the Buddha, while the other major category is centered around the sangha. Minor festivals mark the seasons, particularly spring and autumn. However, these are not specifically religious categories, and they are connected more with countries and regions than that which is specifically Buddhist. An examination of one festival from each of the two major categories follows.

Celebrating the Buddha

Visakha, or "Buddha Day," is the most holy day of the year for Theravada Buddhists. It is celebrated on the full moon day of May. For Theravadans, Siddhartha Gautama was born, became enlightened, and died all on the same date. The emphasis for this festival is literally on en*light*enment. Theravada Buddhists light colorful lanterns and candles around the monasteries where the celebrations occur. An image of the Buddha is decorated and a monk gives a sermon on some aspect of the life of the Buddha.

Many Mahayana Buddhists celebrate these significant events in the life of the Buddha on three separate days throughout the year. For Mahayanans, the celebration of the life of the Buddha may entail a bathing of the sacred image followed by a procession. The bathing not only signifies great reverence for the Buddha, it is also a reminder that there are faults in everyone's life that need to be washed away.

Celebrating Sangha

The sangha began as a mendicant ("begging") order of monks. They wandered, preaching the Dharma during all but the three months of the monsoon season. The three-month period became known as the "Rains Retreat." Though a monastic retreat, lay Buddhists also consider the Rains Retreat to be a time of great holiness. The end of the retreat is celebrated with the great festival put on by the lay people. At a special ceremony monks are presented with new robes. Lay people believe that the monks gain great spiritual power during the Rains Retreat and hope that some of that holiness will radiate onto them and shorten samsara.

➤ **Who is someone in your life whose holiness you wish would rub off on you?**

Celebrating the Buddhist Life Cycle

Buddhism plays little role in most rites of passage, except for those at the time of death. The *Tibetan Book of the Dead* characterizes dying as a sacred act. Death rituals are important in Buddhism because of the Buddhists' great interest in life after death and the rebirth of the person. The most important interest is helping a person move from samsara to Nirvana.

There are no specific Buddhist initiation ceremonies for infants. Initiation of a newborn into a community is based on local customs. However, Buddhists do connect birth with suffering and samsara. Buddhists believe that a newborn had previous existences and that the karma of previous lives could influence the character of the person in this life.

Like birth, marriage ceremonies are performed according to local customs. A marriage ceremony for a Buddhist couple may

have no element of Buddhism. Very often a Buddhist couple is married in a civil ceremony, and a monk or the local sangha is asked to bless the marriage afterwards. The marriage blessing may take place at a temple, a shrine, or a home. The blessing may include chanting from sacred scripture and perhaps even a sermon on married life.

■ Section 4 Summary

- Meditation is a common observance in every branch of Buddhism; the two most common forms are Mindfulness of Breath and Meditation of Loving-Kindness.

- There are a number of Buddhist festivals, but few are celebrated by all Buddhists. All Buddhists do celebrate the birth of Siddhartha Gautama in one form or another.

- Lay people hope to receive spiritual benefits from monks who participate in the Rains Retreat.

- Buddhists have no specific life cycle ceremonies for birth and marriage, but they do have special funeral rituals.

■ Section 4 Review Questions

1. Why is meditation important for Buddhists?
2. Briefly describe Mindfulness of Breathing meditation.
3. How do Theravada and Mahayana Buddhists celebrate the birth of the Buddha?
4. What is the origin of the Rains Retreat?

● 5. Sacred Places and Sacred Spaces

Buddhist monasteries are often connected with temples. In Theravada Buddhism, men especially must spend part of their lives in a monastery. They may leave the monastery when it is time to marry, but often return again when their children have been raised. Also, lay people share in the merit of the monks by providing food to feed them and by maintaining the monasteries. The monastery is one sacred place for Buddhists, but there are some others.

Temple

The temple is especially sacred for Therevada Buddhists. Monks live at the temple and perform certain religious rites there. Lay people come to the temple for religious devotions, meditation, and instruction on Buddhist teachings. At a temple, there are usually images of the Buddha and stories about the life of the Buddha depicted in paintings or statues. A stupa is usually present with relics from the Buddha or his followers. Mahayana temples are likely to have a number of enshrined images of many people from the past who have become enlightened and thus are also called buddhas, but with a lower-case "b." Mahayana and Vajrayana temples tend to have a number of

Tapsa Temple, Mt. Maisan, Koroa

shrines venerating bodhisattvas, as well. A temple usually has a place for a monk to deliver a sermon on a special occasion.

Stupas

Originally, stupas were small mounds made of stone or brick that housed the relics of the historical Buddha and were usually located near a temple. As Buddhism expanded, relics of the Buddha gave way to relics of other important Buddhist figures as well as other religious objects. Stupas are still places of pilgrimage for Buddhists. In Vajrayana Buddhism, people walk around a stupa several times out of reverence. Larger stupas are called **pagodas**. Rather than a simple, small mound, pagodas are large, elaborately decorated domes.

pagodas

Towers in eastern Asia, usually with roofs curving upward at the division of each of several stories and erected as temples or memorials.

What are symbolic "relics" in your life that you revere?

Places of Pilgrimage

Swayambunath Temple, Kathmandu, Nepal

Other sacred spaces for Buddhists are places that are, in some way, connected with the life and ministry of the historical Buddha. They are located in present-day India or Nepal and described below.

Lumbini Gardens

Lumbini Gardens is the traditional site of the birth of Siddhartha Gautama. It is located in Nepal. It became a place of pilgrimage shortly after the death of Siddhartha

Gautama. In the third century CE King Ashoka had a twenty-two-foot pillar erected there as a memorial to the Buddha.

Bodh Gaya

The bodhi tree under which the Buddha meditated and gained his enlightenment was located at Bodh Gaya. The tree now located there is said to be a descendant of the original bodhi

The Bayon Temple, Angkor Thom, Cambodia

tree. Near the tree is a sandstone slab marking the place where Gautama became enlightened. A stone under the present tree has a footprint which tradition says is the footprint of the Buddha. Buddhist pilgrims often bring things to decorate the area. People make offerings of flowers. Saplings from the original bodhi tree are planted throughout India. These also are places of pilgrimage.

Sarnath

It was the Deer Park near Varanasi where Siddhartha Gautama preached his first sermon about the Four Noble Truths. This was also the place where he gained his first disciples. A stupa there was constructed by King Ashoka. Deer still roam the park today.

Kushinara

Kushinara is the traditional place of the death of Gautama. The Kushinara Nirvana Temple was built in 1956 to commemorate the 2,500th year of the Buddha's entrance into Nirvana. There is also a 1,500-year-old red stone statue of a reclining Buddha located at Kushinara.

> ➤ Name a holy place or shrine you have visited. What is one impression you had of this place?

■ Section 5 Summary

■ Monasteries are often connected to Buddhist temples. Mahayana temples include images of other buddhas and bodhisattvas besides images of Shakyamuni.

■ A stupa contains a relic or other sacred objects of Buddhism.

■ The most popular places for Buddhist pilgrims are those connected with events in the life of the Buddha. These sacred places are located in India or Nepal.

■ Section 5 Review Questions

1. Name a difference between a Theravadan temple and a Mahayanan temple.

2. How does a pagoda differ from an ordinary stupa?

3. Name the four major sites of pilgrimage related to the life of Siddhartha Gautama. Why are these significant?

6. Buddhism through a Catholic Lens

The most common sources of agreement between Catholics and Buddhists are in the areas of peace and compassion. While Christianity preaches peace and compassion and speaks out against the injustice of war, Buddhists point to the fact that seldom in their history have their adherents ever even engaged in war. One way that compassion is practiced in both traditions is through non-violent means. Both Catholics and Buddhists look to "walk gently upon the earth rather than trample the earth with heavy boots." We agree that we are to speak and act in kindness, rather than tear each other down with our words and actions.

Another similarity between the two traditions is monasticism. Living in a climate that faced a monsoon season, Buddhist monks were led to establish monasteries to shelter themselves from the weather for months at a time. In Christianity, the monastic lifestyle developed in the fourth century when hermits began to populate the caves of the Middle East before forming the great monasteries of the Eastern and Western Roman empires.

A corollary to monasticism is the practice of meditation. While the content of meditation is very different between Catholicism and Buddhism, some experiences are similar. Interreligious dialogue between Catholic and Buddhist monks has occurred for the past half-century. In 1968, Trappist monk and internationally known spirituality author Thomas Merton attended an international meeting of Buddhist and Catholic monks in Bangkok, Thailand.

As with any two religious traditions, there are several differences that co-exist among similarities in belief and practice. The next sections focus on comparing Jesus Christ and Siddhartha the Buddha and the views on suffering of the two religions.

Thomas Merton

Jesus Christ and Siddhartha the Buddha

There are some striking similarities between the stories of the life of Jesus and the life of Siddhartha. Both had miracles associated with their respective births. Both were tempted before they began their public life. Both had a group of followers, walked on water, fed a multitude of people, and shared a message and a way for spiritual freedom. Both have attributed to them the foundation of a world religion. Both religious traditions spread far and wide. While Buddhism went east, Christianity went west. During modern times, one can find Buddhism flourishing anew in the West while Christianity is making new inroads in the East. Ironically, for both, their places of origin have very few adherents of their respective religious traditions. While very few Christians can be found in their land of birth, modern-day Israel, very few Buddhists can be found in India.

As striking as the similarities are between Jesus and Siddhartha, so too are the differences. Siddhartha never claimed to be divine while Jesus was both human and divine. Jesus was born of humble means while Siddhartha was born into royalty. Siddhartha was married, and Jesus was not. While Jesus' message was about the Kingdom of God, Siddhartha's message was about the cessation of suffering.

Suffering

While suffering is a common theme between Catholics and Buddhists, they approach the topic from very different points of view. For Buddhists, all who have not reached Enlightenment and Nirvana in this world are prone to suffer. People's past lives of negative, destructive activity such as greed, hatred, and stealing subject them to return to another life of suffering. To get off the endless cycle of samsara—of birth, death, and rebirth—one must stop the desires and cravings of the heart and practice the Noble Eightfold Path.

Buddhists name three categories of suffering. The first category of suffering is physical or emotional suffering. If someone has done violence to another, that clearly is suffering. Getting in a motorcycle accident is suffering.

A second category of suffering is related to change or transition in one's life. The amount of suffering one experiences in change or transition is in direct relationship to one's attachment to the person or object. For example, there is more suffering involved when a best friend moves across country than if a simple acquaintance completes the same move. Or, there is more suffering when one's hard-earned home is destroyed in a fire than if one's clothing is permanently ruined by ink or soil.

Symbolic Prayer Flags

A third category of suffering is the kind of pain brought about even in the midst of pleasure. For instance, one may think that being a star athlete would bring pleasure, but Buddhists would say that such a feeling is an illusion. Buddhists believe that within seeming pleasure is suffering. The suffering comes from the fact that, since all things are impermanent, the pleasure of being the team captain is impermanent and illusory. The suffering is in the disconnect between that which is reality and that which is illusory.

In essence, Buddhists would say that suffering comes when one possesses the illusion that something or someone will bring pleasure, and that, in reality, it is illusory. Though seemingly negative or pessimistic, Buddhists would say that their perception of suffering is ultimately life-giving, for looking squarely and accepting wholeheartedly that which is real and turning away from that which is illusory brings great peace and true happiness to people.

Catholics understand suffering as part of the finite human condition. Some suffering is through no fault of one's own, such as natural disasters and disease. Other sufferings we bring upon others and ourselves, for one of the consequences of Original Sin is an inclination to evil (CCC, 406). Ultimately, we only have to look at the greatest moral evil ever committed— the passion and death of God's only son—and the subsequent good (Christ's resurrection and our redemption) that came from it. However, even for all that, evil and suffering themselves never become a good.

It is a mistake to think God created suffering or that God wants people to suffer. On the contrary, God desires the cessation of suffering, and sometimes we are the instruments to help alleviate the sufferings of others. Suffering is a mystery. To ask, "Why must people suffer?" is a question which all must live with and even hold in awe. The most important thing to remember about suffering is to trust God. God is in control. God knows what is happening. God is with all creation always and provides for what people need to get through life's many sufferings. It is Jesus on the cross who gives strength to those who know the promise of the resurrection. As with Jesus, all suffering ceases at one's own resurrection when one experiences eternal life with God and the saints. One should not be surprised if at the Final Judgment one may be asked: "Did you help alleviate the sufferings of your brothers and sisters?"

■ Section 6 Summary

■ There are both striking similarities and vast differences between Jesus and Siddhartha.

■ Compassion and loving kindness are important behaviors in both Buddhism and Christianity.

■ Suffering is an important topic in both Catholicism and Buddhism, but each religious tradition sees the meaning of suffering in very different ways.

■ Both Christianity and Buddhism have strong, vibrant monastic traditions.

■ Section 6 Review Questions

1. Name two similarities and two differences between Jesus and Siddhartha.

2. How is compassion manifested?

3. Why would Buddhists say there is no such thing as pure pleasure?

4. What is an opportunity for dialogue between Catholic and Buddhist monastics?

● Conclusion

Buddhism is unique among the world's religions. Though it does not deny the existence of gods, divine beings are not central to Buddhists. And whereas the human person is at the center of Buddhism, Buddhists deny the existence of a human soul. Siddhartha Gautama, the founder of Buddhism, came to the realization that suffering was part of life and that it can be extinguished through the practice of the Noble Eightfold Path.

Meditation is the method through which an individual gains the two most important virtues in Buddhism, wisdom and compassion. Through meditation one realizes that there is no permanence in life. Paradoxically, realizing that all is impermanent, unsatisfactory, and not-self brings one to that which is permanent bliss, Nirvana.

■ Chapter 6 Summary

- Siddhartha Gautama, called Shakyamuni, founded Buddhism in the sixth century BCE. Gautama was a Hindu raised in the warrior caste.

- Councils, after the death of Shakyamuni, aided in the development and expansion of Buddhism as well as its separation into Theravada and Mahayana Buddhism.

- Though already in decline, Buddhism disappeared off the landscape of India not long after Muslim invasion into that country, when Muslims gained control there.

- The Tripitaka is the sacred scripture for Theravada Buddhists. Mahayana and Vajrayana Buddhists have other sacred scriptures in addition to the Tripitaka.

- The Four Noble Truths and the Noble Eightfold Path are the foundations of the Buddha's teachings.

- The sangha comprises the Buddhist community of lay people, monks, and nuns.

- Meditation is one of the most important practices for all Buddhists.

- Most Buddhist festivals are local or regional celebrations. The Buddha's birthday is the most common festival among all Buddhists.

- Buddhists do not have specific life-cycle rites for birth and marriage, but they do for death.

- Temples are places for Buddhists to make offerings for the purpose of merit-making.

- Stupas contain relics of the Buddha, other renowned Buddhists, or other religious objects.

- Four sites in Nepal and India are connected with Gautama's life and are important sacred places of Buddhist pilgrimages.

- There are a number of similarities and differences between Jesus and Siddhartha.

- Compassion and loving kindness are highly desired attributes in both Catholicism and Buddhism.

- Suffering is part of the human condition, but Buddhism and Catholicism approach the topic quite differently.

- Both Buddhism and Christianity have long traditions of monasticism.

■ Chapter 6 Review Questions

1. Briefly summarize the life of Siddhartha Gautama.
2. What is the Middle Way?
3. Highlight the accomplishments of the first Council.
4. Outline the expansion of Buddhism beyond India into the continent of Asia.
5. How did the rise of communism in Asia affect Buddhism?
6. What is the Tripitaka? What is the role it plays in Theravada and Mahayana Buddhism?
7. What is the *Tibetan Book of the Dead* and why is it popular?
8. Compare the traditional role of monks to lay people in Buddhism.
9. Briefly compare and contrast Theravada, Mahayana, and Vajrayana Buddhism.
10. What is the difference between Hindu and Buddhist understanding of samsara?
11. What are the Three Jewels of Buddhism? When are they recited?

12. What is the meaning of anatman to Buddhists?

13. What is Nirvana? How is it attained?

14. What are the three main categories of the Noble Eightfold Path?

15. What is the festival celebrated most by Buddhists? How do Theravada and Mahayana Buddhists celebrate that festival, generally?

16. Why do Buddhists not have standard life cycle rites for birth and marriage but they do for death?

17. What is a stupa? How is it used?

18. Name the Buddhist pilgrimage sights related to the birth, life and death of Siddhartha Gautama.

19. List three similarities and three differences between Jesus Christ and Siddhartha the Buddha.

20. How do Catholics and Buddhists each explain the cessation of suffering?

■ Research & Activities

■ Research and report to the class on one of the following topics:

Buddhism and Communism in China (or Tibet, or Vietnam, or Kampuchea)

Asian Buddhism and American Buddhism in the United States

The attraction of Buddhism to people in the West

The physical and mental benefits of Buddhist meditation

Christian Zen Buddhism or Jewish Zen Buddhism

Buddhist nuns

The XIV Dalai Lama

- View one of the following motion pictures and write an essay on how Buddhism is portrayed: *Little Buddha, Seven Years in Tibet,* or *Kundun.*

- Read Herman Hesse's *Siddhartha* and write a book report summarizing its main plot and themes.

- Write an essay comparing and contrasting Theravada, Mahayana, and Vajrayana Buddhism.

- Research the similarities and differences between the role of relics in Buddhism and Christianity.

- Create a collage of images of the Buddha found in various forms of print media.

- Research Buddhist sacred places and spaces in one of the following countries: China, Japan, Kampuchea, or Thailand.

- Prepare a class presentation on the following Buddhist symbols:

    The eight-spoked wheel

    Buddha images

    Mandala

    Stupa

    Lotus

    Footprints

    Bodhi tree

■ Prayer

Buddhists do not believe in God, so their prayers are not addressed to God. Rather, traditional Buddhist prayer is a way of practicing the Noble Eightfold Path, such as Right Understanding or Right Mindfulness.

With Every Breath

> With every breath I take today,
> I vow to be awake;
> And every step I take,
> I vow to take with a grateful heart—
> So I may see with eyes of love
> into the hearts of all I meet,
> To ease their burden when I can
> And touch them with a smile of peace.

Chinese
Religions

7

● Many Forms and Practices

As you can decipher from the plural in the chapter title, "Chinese religions" does not equate with just one tradition. Rather, Chinese religions are a combination of Chinese folk religion, Taoism, Confucianism, and Buddhism. Prior to the Communist takeover of China in 1949, every one of these religious traditions was an integral part of Chinese culture. Now, as freedom and Western culture make their way back into China, the elements in these religions and the religious traditions themselves can hope for a rebirth.

Also, Chinese religions, unlike other religions, do not require strict membership rules, and Chinese may blend practices of one religion with another. For example, a person may live according to Taoist principles yet regularly visit Buddhist temples.

Another complication for studying Chinese religions is that it is sometimes difficult to determine whether each is a religion, a philosophy, or simply an intellectual exercise. Taoism clearly has an organized religious structure with priests, monks, and temples, but Confucianism does not. Many religious practices in China include a deep reverence for ancestors. Several include practices in astrology and beliefs in yin and yang.

This chapter provides a sketch of religion in China through the centuries and explains how these various religious expressions have co-mingled and yet stood apart through so many centuries.

BCE

ca. 1500	Shang dynasty
1040	Chou dynasty
500s	Birth of Lao-tzu
ca. 551	Birth of K'ung Fu-tzu (Confucius)
ca. 372	Birth of Meng-tzu
ca. 369	Birth of Chuang-tzu
ca. 250	Completion of the *Tao-te Ching*
206	Han dynasty

CE

ca. 65	Buddhism comes to China
ca. 100	formation of Taoist communities
581	Sui dynasty
618	T'ang dynasty
638	Islam comes to China
ca. 650	emergence of Ch'an Buddhism
960	Sung dynasty
1000s	emergence of Neo-Confucianism
1215	Mongols conquer China
1254	Marco Polo in China
1368	Ming dynasty
1583	Mateo Ricci in China
1644	Manchuc Ch'ing dynasty
1645	Chinese Rites Controversy
1949	Communalism takes over China
1966	Cultural Revolution

1. A Brief History of Chinese Religions

The history of Chinese religions parallels Chinese dynasties. The first historically recoded dynasty in China, the Shang Dynasty, was present from about the sixteenth to the eleventh centuries BCE. What we know about religious practices during that time comes from archeological finds left from the Shang Dynasty and others that followed. For example, artifacts from the graves of the ruling class point to a belief that the afterlife mirrored earthly life. Archeologists found items such as horses, chariots, servants, dogs, food, pottery, medicine, and the like in graves.

Rulers of the Shang Dynasty venerated their ancestors, believing their ancestors mediated between gods and descendants on earth. Ancestors had powers of healing and fertility, so the maintenance of their happiness was important to continue the flow of good fortune. There was also veneration of nature gods to assist in weather and farming. In the Shang Dnyasty, the highest god was called *Ti*, meaning "God" or "Lord."

divination

The attempt to ascertain knowledge by the interpretation of omens or supernatural events such as the use of spiritual practices like Tarot card reading or the casting of bones.

Divination was another common practice in ancient China for reading messages from the gods. The Chinese would attempt to read signs from nature—like a cloud formation or the cracks in a tortoise's shell—to determine what would happen in the future. *Astrology* was also a common form of divination. The configuration of the stars and planets were omens for either good or evil.

More information on the development of particular traditions of Chinese religions follows.

Woman touching a Chinese astrological symbol

Ancient Folk Religion

Popular Chinese religion—called folk religion before the establishment of the organized religions of Confucianism, Taoism, and Buddhism—was rich in its breadth of religious experience. Like most ancient cultures, the Chinese culture did not distinguish between religious and secular practices. All aspects of life were totally integrated.

ancestor veneration

A religious practice based on the belief that deceased family members are still living and that they have an interest in family affairs and can influence the fates of family members. Ancestor veneration refers to various ways of showing respect and reverence for family ancestors after their deaths. Family members bring offerings to their ancestors in order to obtain protection and guidance.

Under the heading of folk religion, **ancestor veneration** played an integral part from the beginning of the Chou Dynasty, the era following the Shang Dynasty, between the sixteenth and eleventh centuries BCE. Ancestors were not so much worshipped as deities, but revered as older, wiser members of the family unit. The older a person was at the time of death, the more honored. People believed ancestors had two souls. One soul would disappear at death while a second one was immortal. This second soul was the object of reverence. It was the responsibility of the male head of the household to make sure ancestors received proper care. Failure to offer proper reverence to ancestors could anger them to the point that they might destroy crops, send illnesses, or cause mental distress, including nightmares.

Ancestors were not the only ones ancient Chinese peoples revered. There was also an elaborate pantheon of gods and goddesses. While the high god during the Shang Dynasty was Ti, the high god of the Chou Dynasty was called *T'ien*, or "Heaven." T'ien ruled over a number of lower gods and goddesses. Intrinsically connected to human nature as a source of goodness, Heaven governed the destiny of both the royal class and the common people. Royal ancestors were intermediaries between T'ien and their royal descendants on earth. Ancestors had the power to grant good fortune in health, longevity, prosperity, and fertility.

As in the Shang Dynasty, both ancestors and deities required properly executed sacrificial rituals to be effective. The proper time for the ritual was sometimes determined through some form of divination. While all honored their ancestors, the ruler would offer sacrifices to the high god Heaven, while local people would offer sacrifices to their agricultural gods or household gods.

Completely new in the Chou Dynasty was the notion of the **Mandate of Heaven**. The god Heaven desired peace and harmony throughout all creation. Heaven conferred upon kings a mandate to represent Heaven on earth. To keep the Mandate of Heaven, kings were to maintain personal integrity, rule the people with care and concern, and appoint government officials on the basis of merit rather than heredity. If the kings behaved in an immoral, cruel, or corrupt fashion, Heaven granted them a chance to "clean up their act." Warnings came in the form of natural disasters or social unrest. If the kings persisted in ruling badly, Heaven took the mandate away from them and transferred it to another dynasty. At least, that is how the theory went. Theory and practice, however, are often two different things. From the ninth and eighth centuries BCE to its demise, the Chou Dynasty was ruled by corrupt leaders. The Mandate of Heaven was intended to ensure the people of a good and just ruler, and the sacrificial rituals were to ensure the people of a good harvest. Yet general warring factions, social disarray, and moral decline led to the eventual demise of the Chou Dynasty.

Mandate of Heaven

The Chinese concept of legitimacy used to support the rule of the kings of the Chou dynasty and later the emperors of China in which Heaven would bless the authority of a just ruler, but would give the Mandate to another if the ruler proved unjust.

Confucius and Confucianism

Originally named K'ung Fu-tzu, Confucius was a Chinese philosopher whose sayings in the collection *Analects* became the source of his teachings that were followed after his death. Known more as a moral philosopher than a religious figure, Confucius, nonetheless, had religious elements to his philosophy. He was more interested in helping cultivate "gentlemen" or sages for a better world on earth than preparing souls for a world to come. Yet, it is almost impossible to talk about Chinese religions without including the teachings of Confucius and his followers..

Confucius

Confucius lived from around 551 to 479 BCE during a time of a weak imperial government when different warring factions were fighting for leadership and territory. He was born in the small feudal-like state of Lu, the product of the union between his seventy-year-old father and one of his father's teenage concubines. Tradition says Confucius' father was a great military hero whom the government granted a small piece of land upon retirement from the military. Confucius's father died when he was three years old. After that, he and his mother found themselves shunned by his father's family. Poor and without social ties, they moved to a nearby town where his mother worked and taught the eager Confucius.

As a teenager, Confucius took a minor government post of keeping books for granaries. He married at age nineteen, and his beloved mother died when he was twenty. However, nothing could get in the way of Confucius's education. For Confucius, learning was not merely an accumulation of knowledge, but an important means to build moral character. As he continued his studies, Confucius began teaching groups of young men all he knew, though teaching was not his first love. Rather, Confucius spent his entire adult life aspiring for public office. He even went on a twelve-year search with a few of his students for a region that would hire him as a public official. However, since Confucius held the political idea that governments were in need of reform, existing governments saw him as a threat to their administration. Confucius spent the last years of his life teaching and compiling some ancient Chinese texts. Included in his writings were the *Analects*. Though slow to catch on, later generations of Chinese rulers and peoples would read and adopt the teachings of Confucius.

When Confucius died he believed himself a failure. He was very wrong about that.

> ➤ Recall a time when you thought your ideas would be a remedy to a problematic situation, but people rejected them. How did you feel?

> ➤ When was a time when someone else held you in greater esteem than you yourself did?

Confucius's writings revealed that he saw chaos all around him. He believed that if society would return to the values of the ancients, chaos would disperse. Confucius was especially interested in those values that were transmitted through rituals such as ancestor veneration, worship of the high god Heaven, and death rites. He believed that it was his duty to recapture these lost elements of ancient civilization and reintroduce them into his world. Proper ritual observance and moral persuasion were Confucius's formula for success.

Though Confucius is considered the founder of Confucianism, he is not a founder in the same sense as Siddhartha Gautama is of Buddhism or Jesus of Nazareth is of Christianity. Confucius regarded himself as a transmitter of ancient Chinese social values rather than as a founder of a religion or a philosophy. He studied ancient Chinese scriptures and attempted to revive their wisdom in his society. Confucius was not inventing anything new. He was simply putting his contemporaries in touch with their ancestors.

Meng-tzo

It wasn't until two centuries after Confucius's death that two of his disciples, Meng-tzo (ca. 371–289 BCE) and Hsun-tzu (ca. 298–230 BCE), were able to make significant inroads in communicating Confucian teachings to the political elite. However, they promoted completely opposite reasons for adopting Confucius's ideas. Meng-tzo advocated the intrinsic goodness of human nature, teaching that by not cultivating one's good nature, evil would slowly take over. Meng-tzo maintained that by following the Confucian teachings of self-cultivation, a person could again manifest his or her intrinsic goodness. Hsun-tzu, on the other hand, asserted the intrinsic evil of human nature. Hsun-tzu taught that it was necessary to learn how to live morally in order to avoid evil and become good.

During the Han Dynasty (206 BCE–220 CE), the teachings of Confucius became, by imperial decree, the state ideology. (This may be a major reason the Han Dynasty lasted longer than any other Chinese regime.) Confucianism was taught in all the schools and the *Confucian Classics* were required reading for all who aspired to public office (see pages 293–294.). The Confucian ideal of education being not merely for the accumulation of knowledge but also for the building of character took hold. Confucianism began to move toward egalitarianism by its claim that a person was not made noble by birth, but by character. Character building was a lifelong process of education and self-discipline. By the beginning of the Common Era, the moral idealism of Confucianism could not be separated from the overall Chinese society. Around this time, a **cult** honoring Confucius as a semi-divine figure emerged. (By the sixth century CE temples to Confucius dotted the land.)

The influence of Confucianism decreased with the collapse of the Han Dynasty (third century CE), while the

cult

Any external religious practice, observance, or devotion surrounding a deity, holy person, or religious object of a particular religious tradition.

influence of Taoism and Buddhism increased. By the tenth century, however, Confucianism was again gaining prominence. This resurgence was called **Neo-Confucianism**, and it integrated elements of Buddhism and Taoism. Scholars of Neo-Confucianism were well versed in all three religious traditions and sought to integrate the Taoist beliefs on the universe with the Buddhist beliefs about human nature in the midst of the Confucian scholarly tradition.

Neo-Confucianism

A movement in the eleventh century CE that promulgated the resurgence of Confucianism while reinterpreting it in the light of Taoist and Buddhist influences.

This trend reversed itself again during the Qing Dynasty (CE 1644–1911 CE) when there was a move to return to the more "pure" Confucianism of the Han Dynasty. Yet, because of the introduction of many European elements into Chinese society during this time, the reform of Confucianism was unsuccessful. In addition, there was a check on the cult of Confucius in the sixteenth century. Statues of Confucius were replaced with plaques with inscriptions of some of his teachings. Though there was another attempt to form a Confucian cult in the twentieth century, the advent of communism in China put a stop to it.

The Chinese communist revolution of 1949 placed Confucianism in disfavor all around. The Chinese monarchy and traditional family structures and rituals, which helped support Confucianism, were gone. After Mao Tse Tung and the communists came to power, Confucianism, along with all other religions in China, was officially banned from the nation. All religion was considered elitist, out-dated and a threat to personal freedom.

Presently, Confucianism is again stirring interest among the Chinese elite. Attempting to counter the westernization of China, Confucianism is being regarded as an important part of Chinese heritage. In fact, to many, Confucius is known as the "father of Chinese culture."

➤ What is your experience of how traditional family structure and rituals and government can support and foster a healthy religious tradition? Where do you see attempts at character building in your home, your school, and your country?

Lao-tzu and Taoism

Lao-tzu is traditionally known as a Chinese philosopher who may have lived around the fifth century BCE. He is credited as the founder of **Taoism**, a religion with roots to 2000 BCE but not expounded officially until around 500 BCE. What little we know was written by Ssu-ma Ch'ien in his *Historical Records* around 100 BCE. According to this account, Lao-tzu's family name was Li, and his given name was Erh. Lao-tzu was in charge of sacred books at the court of the Chou dynasty.

Taoism

From the root word Tao, meaning "the way." Tao is considered to be the driving force of the universe.

Disillusioned with the political and moral decline, Lao-tzu rode west to the Chinese wilderness. It is said that the guardian at the frontier pass, Yin His, asked Lao-tzu to write down his words of wisdom. Lao-tzu wrote what became known as the *Tao-te Ching*, or "The Way and Its Power," addressing it to sage-kings.

By the third century BCE, Taoist writing emphasized more concern with the individual than with rulers. A follower of Lao-tzu, Chuang Tzu (368–286 BCE), wrote a text rejecting participation in society. In 142 CE, Chang Tao-ling claimed to have received a revelation from Lao the Most High. Chang Tao-ling was named the first "celestial master" of Taoism. His successors were the spiritual leaders for Taoist priests who ministered in Taoist "churches." The period of celestial masters emphasized both political renewal and self-perfection. In the third century CE after the fall of the Han Dynasty, Chinese rulers began to turn to Taoist leaders for advice in temporal and spiritual matters. Yet, like Confucianism, the ritual aspects of Taoism tended to focus on the elite and not attract common people, until the fourth century when Taoism began to include some elements of folk religion.

In the centuries since, Taoist priests have continued to encourage methods of self-perfection and help individuals control the forces of **yin and yang**. The symbol for yin and yang has become familiar, half of which is dark with a light spot while the other half is light with a dark spot. This symbol and the notion of yin and yang itself predates Taoism. Yin and yang originally referred to the shaded and sunny sides of hills and valleys. They later came to symbolize the complementary, harmonious play of pairs of opposites in the universe. They are interdependent in the sense that one has no meaning without the other. For example, good has no meaning without evil, light has no meaning without dark, and cold has no meaning without hot. One defines the other. There is no antagonism between the pairs, for both are needed. Each contains a little of the other, as the light and dark spots indicate. Good has an element of evil, light has an element of dark, cold has an element of hot, and vice versa. For the Chinese, nature is in a continual dance to remain balanced between the yin and the yang. As with every other form of religion in China, Taoism was discredited by the Chinese Communist rulers of the twentieth century. However, elaborate Taoist rituals are still conducted in Taiwan, and elements of Taoism continue to affect all of Chinese religion and culture.

yin and yang

Meaning "shaded and sunny," they are opposite but complementary extremes in Chinese culture.

Three sages of T'ai Chi surrounding the yin-yang symbol.

➣ Name some recent people who have gained in esteem since their death as Confucius and Lao-tzu did after theirs.

Buddhism in China

Buddhism came to China in the first century CE, though it lay rather dormant until the fall of the Confucianist Han Dynasty in 220 CE. At that time, Buddhists began to build temples, monasteries, and orphanages. Though both Theravada and Mahayana Buddhism initially were present in China, Mahayana Buddhism dominated. In its early stages, Buddhism was tied closely with Taoism, with its various ascetical practices, the use of magic and the emphasis on the attainment of immortality. By the eighth century CE, Vajrayana Buddhism was present in Mongolia and Tibet.

Buddhism was slow to take hold in China. In the first few centuries of the Common Era, a number of Chinese pilgrims went to India, brought back scores of Buddhist sacred texts, and translated them into Chinese. Borrowing Taoist vocabulary to explain difficult Buddhist concepts, translations of the sacred scriptures helped Buddhism enjoy recognition from both the elite and the peasantry alike. But Buddhism's initial appeal in China was to the poor because of its strong emphasis on family. During the Sui Dynasty (581–618 CE), the Chinese government began to patronize Buddhism. However, it was under the T'ang Dynasty (618–907 CE) that Buddhism flourished the most.

Under the T'ang Dynasty the number of Buddhist monasteries increased greatly, but the ordination of monks came under the control of the state. Buddhism could not lose the perception that it was a "foreign religion." As the monasteries accumulated wealth through land holdings, a backlash against Buddhism boiled up to the point that the Chinese imperial government destroyed Buddhist temples, monasteries, and shrines in 845. Over the next two centuries, Buddhism united even more closely to Taoism and the two religious traditions converged with Confucianism and Chinese folk religion to form the underpinnings of Chinese religion. Though the Buddhist and Taoist scholars tended to remain separate, Chinese culture as a whole experienced a multi-tradition religious landscape.

A number of Mahayana Buddhist schools dotted the religious landscape of China, but only two dominate today—Pure Land and Ch'an Buddhism.

Pure Land Buddhism

Pure Land Buddhism came to China from India. Though not very popular in India, it became extremely popular in China, especially with poor people. Unable to spend the time in meditation or working for good karma, Pure Land Buddhism was a welcome alternative.

Chion-in Temple, the main temple of Pure Land Buddhism in Japan.

A number of Mahayana Buddhist traditions hold that there is more than one Buddha. Amitabha is one such Buddha. According to tradition, Amitabha was a great bodhisattva for many lifetimes. Through his accumulation of an infinite amount of merits, he was able to make a series of vows in which he would bring all sentient beings to Nirvana. To accomplish this task Amitabha, now a Buddha, went to one of the celestial realms and created a Pure Land. This celestial region was so-called because there was no evil, pain, or suffering. In addition, the environment was perpetually ideal. There were no natural disasters, the trees had jewels on them and anything one wanted one was granted. For example, if a person wanted cold water to be warm, so be it.

To be reborn into the Pure Land according to the "short" version, one need only recite the name "Amitabha," ("Amitofo" in Chinese) with great faith and devotion throughout one's life. Even though a person was morally lacking, he or she could be reborn into the Pure Land where the infinite merits of Amitabha Buddha enabled them to reach Nirvana. Another form of Pure Land Buddhism stated that only human beings could attain Nirvana. Hence, after residence in Pure Land, one must return to earth, but this time full of good karma and from there attain Enlightenment and Nirvana.

From China, Pure Land Buddhism moved to Vietnam, Korea, and Japan.

Ch'an Buddhism

Ch'an, meaning "meditation," is a Chinese form of Buddhist meditation begun in India. It emerged in China around the seventh century CE with two opinions about the attainment of Enlightenment. One faction believed Enlightenment could happen suddenly while the other believed Enlightenment could come only gradually. In either of the two approaches, it was through a master-student relationship that one learned how to meditate properly and how to deal with questions, insights, and challenges that arose. One common technique for meditation was the use of a *gong'an*, more commonly known in the West by its Japanese name, *koan*. It is a paradoxical statement or story used to clear the mind of its many obstacles so that insight and Enlightenment could come. A common gong'an is "what is the sound of one hand clapping?"

Over the centuries, Pure Land Buddhism and Ch'an Buddhism existed together side by side, often to the point of non-distinction.

> ➥ **Chinese history contributed to a blending of religions. How have some Western nations contributed to a blending of various religious traditions?**

Words of Confucius

At fifteen, I bent my will to study.

At thirty, I stood firm.

At forty, I did not doubt what was correct.

At fifty, I knew the decrees of heaven.

At sixty, my ears became docile towards truth.

At seventy, I could follow the mind's longings without stepping beyond the strict confines of a carpenter's square.

(*Analects* 2:4)

■ Section 1 Summary

■ Chinese religions are generally a combination of folk religion, Confucianism, Taoism, and Buddhism.

- Chinese folk religion has elements of ancestor veneration, divination, and astrology.

- Confucius attempted to revitalize society through the wisdom of the ancient Chinese sages.

- Attributed to Lao-tzu, Taoism refers to the Way (Tao) or that which is foundational to the temporal and spiritual.

- Buddhism had to acculturate to Chinese society before it could find acceptance. Eventually it united with other Chinese religions to form the multi-tradition Chinese religious landscape.

- Pure Land and Ch'an are the dominant forms of Buddhism in China.

■ Section 1 Review Questions

1. Briefly describe these elements of Chinese religion: ancestor veneration, divination, astrology, and yin and yang.
2. What was the Confucian ideal of education?
3. What did the celestial masters of Taoism emphasize for temporal and spiritual matters?
4. How is Buddhism linked with Taoism?

2. Sacred Stories and Sacred Scriptures

As neither Confucius nor Lao-tzu considered themselves founders of a religion, the writings attributed to them and their followers are not considered divinely inspired. Neither Confucius nor Lao-tzu ever claimed that they received revelations from any deities. So, too, their writings are not documents of revelation such as the Bible or the Qur'an. Confucius is credited with compiling and creating several volumes of Chinese literature to add to what was already in place. After his death, a large body of Confucian scriptures became sources of inspiration for centuries and the means to train students in Confucianism.

Lao-tzu

Confucius drew from the wisdom of the ancient sages. While the Tao-te Ching is attributed to Lao-tzu, it is doubtful he wrote any of it. Rather, the Tao-te Ching is the work of followers of Lao-tzu after his death who drew from age-old writings long before the birth of Lao-tzu. For this reason, it is accurate to say Taoism predates Confucianism.

Information about scriptures and stories of these religions follows.

Confucian Classics

The sacred writings of Confucianism are commonly called the Confucian Classics, though some of them are writings that predate Confucius. The Confucian Classics are divided into two main groups, the **Five Classics** and the **Four Books**.

The Five Classics traditionally are attributed to Confucius. However, they predate Confucius. He considered them classic writings of an earlier golden era of Chinese history. These were the main documents used by Confucius to teach his students. They included historical documents, an anthology of poems, a manual for divination, records of the state of Lu where Confucius was born, and works on the principles of **li**, that is, proper conduct.

The Four Books were compiled by Confucius's followers. They are texts of wisdom inspired by Confucius and Meng-tzu, Confucius's disciple. The Four Books include the *Analects* (sayings of Confucius), *The Great Learning* (details how perfection can benefit society), *Doctrine of the Mean* (philosophical utterances systematically arranged with commentaries by the compilers of the text), and *Book of Meng-tzu* (sayings of the great follower of Confucius).

Four Books

During the Ming and Qing Dynasties, the accepted curriculum that needed to be studied and passed in order to hold civil office.

Five Classics

The collection of five ancient Chinese books used by Confucianism for study. They were written or edited by Confucius.

li

From the Chinese meaning "proper" or "rites," it is the practice of proper behavior specific to one's relationship to another as well as the rituals that must be properly performed in order for one to be called a chun-tzu or "superior man."

Eventually, a student had to master these nine texts in order to pass civil exams to secure employment within the government.

Tao-te Ching

The Tao-te Ching is one of the most widely read pieces of Chinese literature in the world. It is the centerpiece of sacred scripture within Taoism. The Tao-te Ching has been translated into a number of languages. Though its authorship is attributed sage Lao-tzuLao-tzu, it is more likely that a group of people authored it several centuries after his lifetime. The Tao-te Ching is the source of Taoist beliefs. Tao is the nature of things. All that emanates from Tao returns to Tao. There is power of action without action. All are called to live a life of simplicity in harmony with Tao. The following is an excerpt from the Tao-te Ching on the Tao itself:

The tao that can be told is not the eternal Tao.
The name that can be named is not the eternal Name.
The unnamable is the eternally real.

Naming is the origin of all particular things.
The Tao is like a well: used but never used up.
It is like the eternal void: filled with infinite possibilities.

It is hidden but always present.
I do not know who gave birth to it.
It is older than God.
The Tao is called the Great Mother: empty yet inexhaustible.
It gives birth to infinite worlds.
It is always present with you.
You can use it any way you want.

The Tao is infinite, eternal.
Why is it eternal?
It was never born; thus, it can never die.
Why is it infinite?
It has no desires for itself; thus, it is present for all beings . . .

—Tao-te Ching, 1:1–2, 4, 7

■ Section 2 Summary

- Neither Confucius nor Lao-tzu created any writings, but their followers did.

- Of all the Confucian Classics, the *Analects* is the one most closely associated with Confucius.

- The Tao-te Ching is one of the most read pieces of Chinese literature in the world.

- The Confucian Classics are a set of nine works—divided into two sections—that make up the Confucian scriptures. Some of the writings predate Confucius.

- The Tao-te Ching is the main sacred writing of the Taoists. It means "the way and its power."

■ Section 2 Review Questions

1. What are the two main categories within the Confucian Classics?

2. What is *Tao*?

3. What makes up the *Analects?*

4. Who likely authored the Tao-te Ching?

The Story of Tung Yung

Once there was a young man named Tung Yung who was born into a wealthy family. Tung Yung's early years were carefree, growing up in a castle with a huge backyard. When he reached his teens, though, hard times hit his family. There were severe droughts. Crops failed year after year, and soon the family fortune had dwindled down to small change. On top of that, a disease spread over the countryside and took the lives of all of his siblings, and his father also took ill. Tung Yung was the only one left who was physically able to bring in money for what was left of his family: his mother and his ailing father. But there was no work to be found. Out of desperation, he hung a sign over his head at the market place and sold himself off as a slave. When he was purchased, he sent the money to his folks, and Tung Yung was off to a grueling life of slavery.

He was forced to work in the fields from sunrise to sunset, and when he returned home to his one-room hut, he was often too exhausted to make dinner. Day after day after day, he went through this ordeal, and soon his own health started to fail.

The Chinese god of the sun saw all this from his perch in heaven and took great pity on Tung Yung. He sent his daughter Chih Nu, the goddess of weaving, to Tung Yung's side in his hut to nurse him back to good health. She gave him some heavenly care, supper every night, and had his bed ready for him. Soon his health returned, and eventually Tung Yung married Chih Nu. They soon had a son together.

While Tung Yung was away at work, Chih Nu stayed in the hut and used her godly talents to weave absolutely wonderful tapestries with her magic loom. She would then sell them for a handsome price at the market. She soon raised enough money to buy Tung Yung out of slavery. As her tapestry business grew, more and more money was coming into the family, and soon Tung Yung and Chih Nu had their own farm.

A few years later when they were living the good life, Chih Nu realized that her mission was done and she was to return to heaven. After a tearful farewell, she climbed back into heaven and as she did, all the stars brightened and one brand new, very bright star appeared. The star we now call Vega was the new light created by Chih Nu. Next to Vega are four stars shaped like a parallelogram, which makes up Chih Nu's magic loom.[4]

> **What sacrifices are you willing to make for your family?**

3. Beliefs and Practices

Since both Confucius and Lao-tzu may have been contemporaries, it is not surprising to find that they had some of the same ideas about human nature, society, sovereignty, Heaven, and the universe. The difference was their emphasis. While

Confucianism emphasized the cultivation of a virtuous life, which in turn would spawn political leaders who could help create an ideal society, Taoism was more concerned with "the way life is." Recall that *Tao* means "way."

Confucianism

Confucius believed in the high god Heaven and various other Chinese deities. Confucius also engaged in other folk rituals and practices of his time. In other words, one might call Confucius a "practicing Chinese." However, Confucius was also wary of the various cults that were part of Chinese society. Though he did believe in the various gods and goddesses, he also believed that they should be kept at a distance. As the high god Heaven was perfect, so humans should strive for perfection. For Confucians, that perfection came not from relationships with the gods, but through people's relationships with one another. In many ways, Confucianism was a form of character indoctrination. The one who attained perfection was a **chun-tzu**, the "superior one" or "gentleman." In Confucius' time, only aristocratic men were educated, but Confucius chose to teach any male he considered intelligent enough to engage in the process of learning and character building. The period of formation included the principles of *li* and *jen*—though not specifically religious, they are nevertheless representative of Chinese culture and thought.

chun-tzu

According to Confucius, a person who lives by the ideal of jen and is neither petty, arrogant, mean-spirited, nor vengeful.

Li

Li had to do with the proper way to live, calling for courtesy, etiquette, formality, and respect. Li also called for sincerity in these gestures, teaching that they should flow from the basic goodness of the person. Li focused on an ideal way of behaving for five common relationships in Chinese society:

Emperor to subject: An emperor was to be an example to his subjects, calling them to live the same virtuous life as he did.

Father to son: A father was to be a model to his son who was, in turn, to honor his parents in this lifetime and revere them in the next.

Husband to wife: The husband was to head the household and preserve the memory of his family's ancestors; the wife was to bear sons and to obey her husband.

Elder brother to younger brother: The younger brother was to respect his older brother, for the older brother was responsible for carrying out the family rituals in ancestor veneration.

Friend to friend (males): Friends were to respect each other, with the junior friend showing deference to the elder one.

Jen

Jen refers to "humanity" or "benevolence." While li pointed outward toward behavior, jen pointed inward to one's heart. According to Confucian thought, a person should be transformed from a life ruled by passions to one ruled by enlightened wisdom. Religious and ethical rituals helped a person achieve jen.

A person who combined li with jen was in position to be a chun-tzu. A person cannot fake being chun-tzu. Being chun-tzu means having jen be so much a part of one's self that benevolence flows into action in any situation.

➤   Confucian character formation would prohibit someone from being phony or "two faced." How so?

Taoism

Though the word *Tao* can be defined as the "way, path, or course," really any definition falls short. Taoism can be thought of as the way or the nature of things. The goal of humanity, then, is to move in harmony with Tao. A "go with the flow" attitude permeates all creation, so creation flows with Tao. Taoism is a return to simplicity and harmony with all creation, for Tao is the ultimate source of all creation—an impersonal God, so to speak.

Experiencing Taoism

In order to go into Taoism at all, we must begin by being in the frame of mind in which it can be understood. You cannot force yourself into this frame of mind, any more than you can smooth disturbed water with your hand. But let's say that our starting point is that we forget what we know, or think we know, and that we suspend judgment about practically everything, returning to what we were when we were babies, when we had not yet learned the names or the language. And in this state, although we have extremely sensitive bodies and very alive senses, we have no means of making an intellectual or verbal commentary on what is going on.

You are just plain ignorant, but still very much alive, and in this state you just feel what is without calling it anything at all. You know nothing at all about anything called an external world in relation to an internal world. You don't know who you are, you haven't even the idea of the word you or I—it is before all that. Nobody has taught you self-control, so you don't know the differ-ence between the noise of a car outside and a wandering thought that enters your mind—they are both something that happens. You don't identify the presence of a thought that may be just an image of a passing cloud in your mind's eye or the passing auto-mobile; they happen. Your breath happens. Light, all around you, happens. Your response to it by blinking happens.

So, on one hand you are simply unable to do anything, and on the other, there is nothing you are supposed to do. Nobody has told you anything to do. You are completely unable to do anything but are aware of the buzz. The visual buzz, the audible buzz, the tangi-ble buzz, the smellable buzz—all around the buzz is going on. Watch it. Don't ask who is watching it; you have no information about that yet. You don't know that it requires a watcher for something to be watched. That is somebody's idea; but you don't know that.

Lao-tzu says, "The scholar learns something every day, the man of Tao unlearns something every day, until he gets back to non-doing." Just simply, without comment, without an idea in your head, be aware. What else can you do? You don't try to be aware; you are. You will find, of course, that you cannot stop the commentary going on inside your head, but at least you can regard it as interior noise. Listen to your chattering thoughts as you would listen to the singing of a kettle.

We don't know what it is we are aware of, especially when we take it altogether, and there's this sense of something going on. I can't even really say "this," although I said "something going on." But that is an idea, a form of words. Obviously I couldn't say something is going on unless I could say something else isn't. I know motion by contrast with rest, and while I am aware of motion, I am also aware of rest. So maybe what's at rest isn't going and what's in motion is going, but I won't use that concept then because in order for it to make sense, I have to include both. If I say here it is, that excludes what isn't, like space. If I say this, it excludes that, and I am reduced to silence. But you can feel what I am talking about. That's what is called Tao, in Chinese. That's where we begin.[5]

Action without Action

Taoists believed that the force through which Tao acts is **wu-wei**, or "non-action." Wu-wei may be more precisely explained as "action without actions." For example, the emotion a painting can evoke just by hanging in a gallery is a form of wu-wei. The government leader who purified himself in order to purify society is

wu-wei

Meaning "action without action," it centers on allowing nature to evolve without human interference.

wu-wei. Or, wu-wei is the non-action of a newborn whose various needs are nevertheless taken care of. The non-action evokes action. That is the way of Tao.

Immortality

While the goal of a Confucian is to be a chun-tzu, the goal of a Taoist is immortality. Taoists believe that actual physical immortality is a reachable goal. Immortality is expressed through union with Tao. To attain immortality, a Taoist engages in several practices. Breath control, good hygiene, certain elixirs, meditation, and proper rituals all contribute to immortality. Taoists often refrain from eating certain foods, like grain and meat. To Taoists, life is a delicate balance between yin and yang. If that balance could be maintained, death could be avoided and immortality achieved.

Deities and Other Spirits

By the ninth century CE, Taoists believed in a whole pantheon of gods, including, eventually, Lao-tzu. The high god of the pantheon was known as Yu Huang, the Taoist "sky god" or "Heaven" as known by the Confucians.

hsien

Means "immortal." It refers to a Taoist who has reached his or her ultimate goal—physical immortality.

Taoists were known for their celebrations, lavish costumes and temples, and complex rituals. Those who were believed to have reached immortality were known as **hsiens**. They, too, were worshipped as gods, along with Buddha, bodhisattvas, and gods of other Chinese religions.

How does "go with the flow" aptly describe one of the tenets of Taoism?

Chinese Living

For the average Chinese, the religions discussed in this chapter are not distinguishable within his or her religious experience. For example, it is not unusual to see statues of both Lao-tzu and the Buddha in the same temple and equally revered.

Confucius assured that the best way to live was as a superior person who combined li with jen. Taoists and Buddhists would say that the most virtuous person practiced wu-wei, or action without action. Each are a part of the fabric of Chinese culture. It is likely that the average Chinese person who practices them is unaware of whether one religion is being emphasized over the other.

One would think with such diverse practices and beliefs, the idea of forming a community rooted in religious beliefs would not be possible. For example, Chinese society has long been rooted in family structures, including the practice of ancestor veneration, yet monasticism was an important part of Buddhism and Taoism. How could these three very different religious traditions combine and merge to form one Chinese community? A famous cliché may help to explain. Chinese are Confucian in public, Taoist in private, and Buddhist with regard to death. Chinese have a broad spectrum of beliefs and practices that are woven so tightly into Chinese culture that the only way to make distinctions is to take the threads out piece by piece. However, systematically removing the threads would weaken the fabric of society. That is why only in a course of study like this one are these distinctions usually pointed out.

■ Section 3 Summary

- ■ Confucianism is concerned with character formation. In Confucianism, li ("proper way of living") and jen ("benevolence") are two of the most important virtues leading to perfection.

- ■ Tao permeates all creation—it is an impersonal god, so to speak.

- ■ Wu-wei is "action without action," the force through which Tao acts.

- ■ Taoists believe that actual physical immortality is a reachable goal.

- Both the jen of Confucius and the wu-wei of Taoism, and Buddhism form the fabric of Chinese living.

- The average Chinese person does not consciously make a distinction between the various Chinese religious traditions.

■ Section 3 Review Questions

1. Explain the meanings of *li* and *jen*.
2. Define Tao.
3. Explain wu-wei by giving at least one example.
4. How do Taoists picture immortality?
5. How does the saying "Chinese are Confucian in public, Taoist in private, and Buddhist with regard to death" help to describe the Chinese integration of religion?

4. Sacred Time

Chinese religions operate on a lunar calendar unique to their traditions. Like the other lunar calendars, the Chinese lunar calendar has 354 days. The Chinese name their years by combining one of the ten celestial stems with one of the twelve terrestrial branches. The stems and branches are arranged in such a way that the name of a year will recur only once every sixty years. The twelve terrestrial branches also have animals associated with them. It is with the animal name of the year that westerners are most familiar, such as "the Year of the Dragon."

Festivals

Many traditional festivals are a part of Chinese heritage. Recently, there has been some resumption of the festivals in communist China, though each has been celebrated outside of mainland China on a regular basis. Descriptions of the main Chinese festivals follow.

Chinese New Year

The Chinese New Year is the most important of all Chinese festivals. It takes place sometime between late January and late February, depending on the lunar calendar. Major celebrations occur in Hong Kong, which until recently was under British rule. A few weeks before the New Year, the Chinese prepare by thoroughly cleaning their homes and purchasing items like tangerine plants, flower displays, Chinese paintings, and calligraphy. Hong Kong is laden with brightly colored decorations, and stores are packed with shoppers.

On New Year's Eve, Chinese say prayers and pay homage to Tso Kwan, who returns to heaven to report on the behavior of the humans for the year. *Tso Kwan* means "Stove Master." He is the kitchen god of China. On New Year's Day itself, family members exchange small gifts, often money wrapped in a red packet. Another traditional part of the festival is *Kai Nien* or "Squabble Day," so-called because it is believed that if you argue on this day, many arguments will follow during the rest of the year. On the fourth day of the festival, Tso Kwan is welcomed back, and a new picture is hung in the kitchen. On the fifteenth day of the festival, a three-day lantern celebration begins. Lanterns are hung in homes promoting good fortune, health, and happiness. The celebration of lanterns ends the New Year's festivities.

Ching Ming

Ching Ming means "Remembrance of Ancestors Day." It is celebrated in April and is a day devoted to honoring deceased relatives. Chinese flock to cemeteries to clean and care for the graves of their relatives. Also, willow branches are

Family members clean the grave site of a loved one during the Ching Ming Festival.

hung in doorways to ward off evil spirits. Legend has it that those who do not hang the willow will appear as dogs in their next life.

Tin Hau

Buddha at Tin Hau Shrine

The *Tin Hau* festival is celebrated on the twenty-third day of the Third Moon (late April, early May). The day is set aside to honor a young girl known as Tin Hau, the "Queen of Heaven." She is the mother of boat people and sailors. The legend dates from the eleventh century CE when Tin Hau had a dream that her brothers were drowning. She flew over the waters on clouds and rescued her family.

There are numerous shrines and temples dedicated to Tin Hau. Chinese boat people, sailors, and those who live on the waterfront sail to Da Miao (the Great Temple) in Joss House Bay on Tin Hau's birthday, paying respect to the goddess and asking for safety in the coming year.

Tuen Ng (Dragon Boat) Festival

Dragon Boat Racing in Hong Kong

Tuen Ng, or the "Dragon Boat Festival," is held in late spring. The day honors Wut Yuan, a famous Chinese patriot who wrote many classical poems espousing Chinese nationalism. At the end of his life, Wut Yuan became disillusioned and drowned himself in the Milo River. The local people were so upset by this that they went out on the river in boats and began to beat the water with their paddles to keep the fish from eating his body. They also threw rice in the water to draw the fish away.

The Dragon Boat Festival consists of a variety of decorated, colorful boats, all including the fierce head of a dragon. The dragons symbolically search the waters for Wut Yuan's body.

Mid Autumn Festival

The *Mid Autumn* festival is second in popularity to New Year's. It recalls a time during the T'ang Dynasty when Chinese rulers carefully studied the moon. Today, to celebrate this festival, Chinese people, and citizens of Hong Kong especially, travel to high places in the region to make sure they have a good view of the moon. The hills of Victoria in Hong Kong, as well as the area beaches, shimmer in the glow of lantern lights.

Chinese Lantern during Mid Autumn Festival in Hong Kong

Life Cycles

In Chinese culture, the birth of a boy is preferred over the birth of a girl. It is a boy who carries on the family name, takes care of the parents in old age, and sees to it that ancestors are cared for. Today there is a government policy in China limiting births in an attempt to slow population growth. In this case, the birth of a girl is seen as particularly unfortunate as the couple often has no chance for a second child. Because of this, many Chinese women determine the sex of the child before birth and abort the fetus if it is a girl.

After the birth of a child, the mother is to rest for a one-month period, allowing other family members to care for her and her child. At the end of the month, there is a celebration in which the newborn is given symbolic gifts representing good health and prosperity. People eat eggs on that day as a sign of good luck.

Food also plays a part in the celebration of the "coming of age" of a child in the beginning of his or her teenage years. The celebrants eat chicken as a main course, believing chicken to be a sign of maturity. Chinese also mark other traditional times and events, including marriage and death.

Marriage

There are six stages to a Chinese marriage:

Proposal—A determination is made as to whether or not the man and woman are a good match. There is the exchange of the "eight characters" of the man and woman to check the Chinese horoscope. The eight characters are the year, month, day, and hour of the birth of each person. Also, if any inauspicious event occurs in the family of the bride-to-be during the three days after the proposal, it is taken as a sign that the proposal has been rejected.

Engagement—After the wedding date is determined with the help of the Chinese horoscope, the woman's family announces the engagement with invitations and the gift of cookies made in the shape of the moon.

Dowry—The woman's family delivers the dowry in a procession to the house of the groom-to-be. The man sends gifts equal in value to the dowry to the woman.

Procession—The man goes to the family home of the woman to escort her to his home.

Wedding—On the wedding day, vows are exchanged, and a great banquet takes place.

Morning After—The day after the wedding, the new bride serves her parents-in-law breakfast, and they reciprocate. Gifts of dried fruit are given to the newly married couple as a symbol of a good marriage and fertility.

Death

At death, the body is washed and placed in a coffin. Food and objects significant to the deceased are placed in the coffin to help the deceased enter the next world. Family members cry out to inform the neighbors of the death and put on clothes made of coarse material. Mourners bring incense and money to help with the funeral expenses. A Taoist or Buddhist priest performs the funeral rites. Sometimes a Christian minister assists. Mourners follow the coffin to the cemetery carrying willow branches, which symbolize the soul of the person who died. The branch is then carried to the family's ancestral altar and placed there in honor of the spirit of the deceased.

■ Section 4 Summary

- ■ The Chinese year is most familiarly known by the name of the animal associated with the twelve terrestrial branches of astrology.

- ■ Though there are numerous traditional Chinese festivals, few are celebrated on mainland China.

- ■ The Chinese New Year is the most important Chinese festival. The Mid Autumn festival is second in importance to the Chinese people.

- ■ The Chinese mark important life-cycle events with traditions encompassing a variety of religions.

■ Section 4 Review Questions

1. Describe the Chinese New Year's celebration.

2. Why is the birth of a boy preferred over the birth of a girl in Chinese culture?

3. Name the six stages of a typical Chinese marriage.

● 5. Sacred Places and Sacred Spaces

Whatever the number of "sacred spaces" in China prior to 1949, the number has diminished since the communist revolution. In the past sixty years, many Chinese temples have either been destroyed or turned into government facilities. Those temples left for religious practice are heavily regulated. The government also monitors the selection of religious leaders in the various traditions.

Temples

China has a number of different kinds of temples. There are Taoist and Buddhist temples, and even some Confucian temples. Temples are further defined as local or state temples. Local temples are places for people to make offerings to the gods and to the local ancestors. Before the twentieth century, the state temples were places where the emperor would make sacrifices on behalf of his subjects, usually to Heaven, other lesser deities, and, at times, to Confucius.

Shrines of Ancestors

Within the Chinese temples are typically shrines to local gods and to ancestors of the local family or families. Also, most Chinese maintain an ancestor shrine at home where offerings of food and incense are made to one or more ancestors, sometimes even on a daily basis.

Ancestor Gravesites

feng-shui

The practice of positioning objects—especially gravesites, buildings, and furniture—to achieve positive effects based on belief in yin and yang and the flow of chi, that is, air or breath.

For the Chinese, the world of the dead is a mirror image of the world of the living. This means that the needs of the deceased are similar to the needs of the living. The Chinese take choosing a burial site very seriously. A wrong gravesite would be one inhabited by evil powers and bad spirits. **Feng-shui** is the art of divining a place or date that has a positive spiritual aura. Feng-shui has become popular recently in the United States as an aspect of interior design.

Ch'u Fou is the burial place of Confucius. As Chinese reverence their familial ancestors, they also revere their spiritual ancestor, Confucius.

➤ As China's government permits more religious freedom, what do you think will be the reaction of the general Chinese population?

■ Section 5 Summary

■ Many Chinese temples were destroyed or taken over by the government after the Chinese communist revolution.

■ Chinese honor their ancestors at local temples, home shrines, and gravesites.

■ Ch'u Fou is sacred because it is the burial place of Confucius.

■ Section 5 Review Questions

1. Why are there fewer Confucian temples in China now than there were prior to 1949?

2. Define *feng-shui*.

6. Chinese Religions through a Catholic Lens

It is in the rituals surrounding death and the remembrance of those who have died where there is most clearly the confluence of the four major elements of Chinese religions—Confucianism, Taoism, Buddhism, and folk religion—with Christianity and Catholicism. Confucian li (father to son relationship), Taoist afterlife, and Buddhist karma are all elements of the folk devotional practice of ancestor veneration. The following sections further delve into these beliefs as well as offer a comparison with Catholic thought in this area.

Ancestor Veneration in Chinese Religions

When a person dies, a feng-shui master is called upon to determine the most appropriate location for the gravesite, time of the burial, and orientation of the body—that is, the yin and yang of the environment. They are seeking balance and harmony in an attempt to gain the most benefit for both the living who remain and the deceased, who is more appropriately called the "living dead."

In selecting a gravesite, the feng-shui master is looking for the proper environment, date, and orientation of the body. For the environment, the surrounding nature is important. Are the mountains favorable or inauspicious? Does the river flow in the correct direction or pattern? For a proper date of burial, the feng-shui master consults the placement of the stars as well as the date of the birth and death of the person. There can be no conflict between the present astrological orientation and the Chinese astrology of the deceased. As for the placement of the corpse, the feng-shui master determines which direction is most favorable for the corpse to face. It is believed that if the environment is not proper or the date of the burial is wrong or the orientation of the body is incorrect, misfortune befalls the family and their descendants. If they are all correct, great fortune comes.

spirit tablet

A household shrine set up to honor ancestors.

After the funeral rituals, the ancestors are cared for by way of a **spirit tablet** bearing the deceased person's name and other information that is more particular to a region. It is also now possible to have a picture of the ancestor. The tablet is placed on the family altar where family members revere the soul of the ancestor.

It is believed that the realm in which the soul resides is similar to the earthly realm. Hence, the ancestor has the same material needs in the realm of the "living dead" as they did while on earth. The eldest son is responsible for taking care of the needs of the ancestors. Offerings are placed in front of the spirit tablet. Food, especially fruit, is most common. Paper or small-scale representations of other items are included on the family altar. Cars, kitchen appliances, and paper money are examples. There may be even tools of the trade in which they engaged on earth.

The eldest son has a weighty responsibility. He is to make sure the ancestors receive regular proper care. They are to be revered before the spirit tablet at the family altar with great piety on a regular basis. Care is shown through the offerings of food as well as objects of joy such as flowers or lighted candles. At certain times during the year, family members go to the gravesite to care for the grave. The annual Ching Ming Festival is one such occasion for caring for the gravesites of ancestors

Throughout this discussion, the term "ancestor veneration" has been used rather than "ancestor worship." The former is more appropriate because ancestors are not treated as deities. Family members do not pray to them nor ask favors of their ancestors. Chinese people do not worship their ancestors, but revere them. Ancestors are part of the social fabric of Chinese culture. Though no longer visible on earth, Chinese tradition holds that ancestors are the "living dead." They are still part of the family, but located in another realm. Wherever the deceased are now, they have an influence over the good or bad fortune of a family or community. Ancestors can assist their descendants from their present location. They, too, have needs and grow anxious or restless when their needs are not met. Forgetting about the ancestor or showing little or no reverence for them brings about misfortune to their descendants. So, too, those who died untimely or violent deaths can bring misfortune to the family or community.

Catholic Belief in the Communion of Saints

In the Apostles' Creed, which predates the Nicene Creed, Catholics profess that they believe in the **communion of saints.** As the Body of Christ, Christ is the Head of the Body and the baptized are the gifted members of his Body. The communion of saints are all those who are "in Christ," both living and dead (CCC, 954).

Catholics are at times accused of "worshipping" saints. This is as inaccurate as saying that Chinese people "worship"

communion of saints

Refers to the unity of all those living on earth (the pilgrim Church), those being purified in purgatory (the Church suffering), and those enjoying the blessings of heaven (the Church in glory).

intercession

Making an offering or saying a prayer or petition to God on behalf of another.

their ancestors. Catholics honor saints, the living and the dead. They also pray to saints for **intercession** on their behalf with the Triune God. However, only God is worthy of worship.

It is common on earth for Catholics to ask other Catholics to "pray for" each other. It is just as common for Catholics to say to other Catholics, "I will pray for you." Catholics, therefore, who ask the saints in heaven to "pray for us" are doing nothing out of the ordinary (*CCC*, 956–957).

As Chinese people show reverence to their ancestors by placing items such as flowers and candles on the family altar, so, too, Catholics show reverence to saints by placing flowers or candles before an image of the saint, sometimes on a family altar. As Chinese people show reverence by bowing with folded hands, Catholics show reverence by kneeling with folded hands. Neither the Chinese nor the Catholics are worshipping the deceased family ancestor or "ancestor in faith." They are reverencing them.

To many Protestants, these gestures of reverence by both the Chinese and Catholics seem more like the act of worshipping idols. Protestants do not deny the existence of saints in heaven. They just believe that asking saints to pray to God for

St. Thérèse of the Child Jesus

their brothers and sisters on earth is a request that should be directed to God alone. They see Catholics asking saints for their prayers as asking saints to be mediators between God in heaven and people on earth, and Jesus is the only Mediator. This is a very common Protestant misunderstanding. Catholics, too, believe that Jesus is the only Mediator. There is nothing stopping Catholics from praying directly to God. Professing belief in the "communion of saints" is professing a communal rather than and individualistic relationship between the pilgrim saints on earth and the eternally living saints in heaven (*CCC*, 955).

Ancestor Veneration in Catholic Ritual

As Catholic missionaries reached the shores of China in the seventeenth and eighteenth centuries, ancestor veneration had been practiced for millennia. While some missionaries found the practice more secular than religious, they saw no need to ban the practice among the newly converted Chinese Catholics. On the other hand, other missionaries found it contrary to Christian belief and sought to ban the practice. For over two centuries, what became known as the **Chinese Rites Controversy** went back and forth between permission and prohibition. It was finally settled in 1939 under the papacy of Pope Pius XII when it was determined that veneration of ancestors was permissible for Chinese Catholics as long as there was no element of veneration contrary to Catholic doctrine, nor was there any hint of superstition.

Further, the Second Vatican Council taught that in some circumstances there was need for adaptation of liturgical and sacramental rituals to some cultures, especially those in "mission lands." In April 1998, the Ninth General Congregation of the Special Assembly of the Synod of Bishops for Asia met at the Vatican. The bishops saw **inculturation** as an important but daunting task before them. For the bishops of Asia, one way inculturation is expressed is through introducing the veneration of ancestors into the ritual life of the Church. The bishops of Vietnam, where there is a Chinese minority, were especially encouraged to begin the process. They see inculturation not as accommodating Catholicism to a particular culture, but as a means of evangelization. According to Most Rev. Etienne Nguyen Nhu

Chinese Rites Controversy

A dispute within the Church about whether or not Chinese folk religion rites and offerings to their ancestors constituted idolatry. The Jesuits believed the rites were compatible with Catholicism; the Dominicans did not. Pope Clement XI decided in favor of the Dominicans, but his teaching was relaxed in the twentieth century to allow for some participation by Catholics in those rites.

inculturation

Defined by Pope John Paul II defined as "the incarnation of the Gospel in native cultures and also the introduction of these cultures into the life of the Church."

The, quoted at the Ninth General Congregation of the Special Assembly of the Synod of Bishops for Asia:

> In the past, we had always considered the cult of ancestors like a form of belief. But in better consideration (cfr. The instruction *"Plane compertum est"*), this cult brings forth a very deep cultural and moral characteristic in the social and family life. And because of this, the Church of Vietnam must take it into consideration to be able to dialogue, proclaim the Good News and march together with their peoples. This is probably the "key" problem of evangelization in the near future. We must, therefore, courageously begin to introduce customs and traditions of veneration of ancestors into the life of the Church, especially in liturgy and sacramental rituals. Obviously, to benefit the great Work of evangelization.

■ Section 6 Summary

■ In the Chinese tradition, at the death of a person, a feng shui master is called upon to help the family find the most beneficial where, when, and how of the burial.

■ Ancestor veneration takes place mostly in the home and occasionally at the gravesite.

■ Chinese people do not worship their ancestors, nor do Catholics worship their "ancestors in faith."

■ The communion of saints is the unity of the Church on earth, in purgatory, and in heaven.

■ Recently, bishops of Asia are looking at introducing the veneration of ancestors into the liturgical and sacramental rituals of the Church.

■ Section 6 Review Questions

1. Why are feng-shui masters used by families upon the death of a loved one?

2. Why can it be said that Chinese people do not worship their ancestors?

3. In what Catholic creed is the belief in the "communion of saints" professed?

4. Why is it important to the bishops of Asia, not to dismiss the Chinese practice of venerating their ancestors?

● Conclusion

The religions described in this chapter are done so because of the place where they began. However, the overt practice of Chinese religions in mainland China today is almost non-existent. It survives with those of Chinese origin or ancestry who live outside mainland China in places such as Taiwan, Korea, Indonesia, Europe, and North America. Though there has recently been some loosening of regulations from the Chinese government, religious practices are rare. Even where Chinese religions are practiced, there is a great integration, especially among Confucianism, Taoism, and Buddhism. The average Chinese person has little knowledge of the origins of his or her religious tradition or how the different traditions vary. Religious observance often involves ancestor veneration and a respect of older, wiser family members. Oftentimes it also involves divination, offerings, and rituals designed to temper the evil spirits and reward the good ones.

In these days of increasing Western influence on China, it remains to be seen if traditional religious traditions of China will be able to revive and thrive.

■ Chapter 7 Summary

■ Chinese religions are a multi-religious tradition of folk religion, Taoism, Confucianism, and Buddhism.

■ Through much of its history, there has been a close relationship between Chinese religions and the state.

■ There is a large collection of Chinese sacred texts, but the Tao-te Ching is the most popular.

- Taoists believe that the force with which Tao acts is wu-wei, or non-action.

- Temples, homes, shrines, and ancestor graves are sacred spaces for Chinese people.

- Chinese New Year and mid-autumn celebrations are the two most important festivals to the Chinese people.

- Confucianism is a form of character formation; the one who attains perfection is chun-tzu, the "superior man" or "gentleman."

- Taoism is the "way" or "nature of things." It involves a "go with the flow" mentality.

- Chinese living is greatly influenced by Confucian teachings of li ("courtesy, etiquette") and jen ("benevolence").

- It is incorrect to say the Chinese people worship their ancestors.

- The bishops of Asia are looking at ways to integrate ancestor veneration into their liturgical and sacramental life.

■ Chapter 7 Review Questions

1. Why are ancestors so important to the Chinese people?
2. Explain wu-wei.
3. What are two common relationships on which li is focused?
4. How has Buddhism influenced Chinese religion?
5. What would a person who kept a balance between yin and yang achieve?
6. How does the ultimate goal for a Confucian compare with the ultimate goal of Taoist?
7. What are some steps a Taoist might take to achieve immortality?
8. How do li and jen compliment one another?
9. Why is it believed that Taoism in some way predates Confucianism?

10. What is the Tao Te Ching?

11. Explain why most Chinese may not be able to explain the origins of their religion or the differences between it and another religion.

12. Briefly describe these elements of Chinese religion: ancestor veneration, divination, astrology, and yin and yang.

13. List similarities and differences between Chinese ancestor veneration and Catholic veneration of saints.

14. What was Confucius's "dream job" and why was he unable to fulfill it?

15. What is the Mandate of Heaven? How could Chinese rulers abuse this mandate?

16. What is the connection between yin and yang?

■ Research & Activities

■ Read an Amy Tan novel (e.g., *The Joy Luck Club, The Kitchen God's Wife*), and write an essay on how Chinese religion is portrayed in it.

■ Watch the Disney animated film *Mulan* and participate in a class discussion on its portrayal of Chinese religion. Note whether there is one religious tradition that seems to be more emphasized than others in the film.

■ Create a multi-page portfolio that contains Confucian sayings and Chinese art.

■ Read *The Tao of Pooh* or *The Te of Piglet*, both by Benjamin Hoff. What does Hoff teach about Taoism?

■ Write an essay on one of the following topics:

"American Society Needs to Put More Yin in Its Yang"

The Chinese custom of female foot binding

Christianity in China

Urban Chinatowns in the United States

Prayer

Reflect on these word of Lao-tzu, written in the sixth century BCE.

If there is to be peace in the world,
There must be peace in the nations.
If there is to be peace in the nations,
There must be peace in the cities.
If there is to be peace in the cities,
There must be peace between neighbors.
If there is to be peace between neighbors,
There must be peace in the home.
If there is to be peace in the home,
There must be peace in the heart.

Japanese Religions

8

Heavenly Origins

In a traditional Japanese story, the heavenly gods Izanagi and Izanami descend to bring order out of the chaos of the earth, resulting in the creation of Japan:

> Many gods were thus born in succession, and so they increased in number, but as long as the world remained in a chaotic state, there was nothing for them to do. Whereupon, all the heavenly deities summoned the two divine beings, Izanagi and Izanami, and bade them descend to the nebulous place, and by helping each other, to consolidate it into terra firma. "We bestow on you," they said, "this precious treasure, with which to rule the land, the creation of which we command you to perform." So saying they handed them a spear called Ama-no-Nuboko, embellished with costly gems. The divine couple received respectfully and ceremoniously the sacred weapon and then withdrew from the presence of the deities, ready to perform their august commission. Proceeding forthwith to the Floating Bridge of Heaven, which lay between the heaven and

the earth, they stood awhile to gaze on that which lay below. What they beheld was a world not yet condensed, but looking like a sea of filmy fog floating to and fro in the air, exhaling the while an inexpressibly fragrant odor. They were, at first, perplexed just how and where to start, but at length Izanagi suggested to his companion that they should try the effect of stirring up the brine with their spear. So saying he pushed down the jeweled shaft and found that it touched something. Then drawing it up, he examined it and observed that the great drops which fell from it almost immediately coagulated into an island, which is, to this day, the Island of Onokoro [Japan]. Delighted at the result, the two deities descended forthwith from the Floating Bridge to reach the miraculously created island. In this island they thenceforth dwelt and made it the basis of their subsequent task of creating a country.[5]

Shinto

Meaning "the way of the gods," from the Chinese shin tao. *It has its roots in* animism, *a belief that says there is a spirit, or god, in all things. Japanese are especially in tune to the presence of gods and spirits in nature.*

Japanese have long felt that their island nation has heavenly origins. In fact, Japanese believe gods inhabited the land and were very much a part of the created world. Like Chinese religion, Japanese religion is an amalgamation of religions. There are the indigenous traditions of folk religion and **Shinto** as well as Buddhism, Confucianism, and Taoism. Placed in a Japanese setting, these religious traditions have a very thin, often transparent line separating them. Since the other religions have been discussed elsewhere in this text, more emphasis will be placed on Shinto in this chapter and its relationship with other religious traditions of the Japanese people.

> What is one lesson about God you have learned from examining nature?

CE

5	Establishment of National Shrine at Ise
552	Buddhism comes to Japan
594	Buddhism commissioned as a state religion
1175	Pure Land Buddhism established
1200s	Rise of samurai
1549	Jesuit missionary Francis Xavier arrives in Japan
1600s	Beginning of Tokugawa shogunate
1854	Meiji restoration and creation of State Shinto
1945	Japan defeated in World War II

1. A Brief History of Japanese Religions

The exact origin of purely Japanese religion is difficult to determine. The written history begins when Japanese culture meets with Chinese and Korean culture around the sixth century CE. With Japan's contacts with Korea around that time, Buddhism was introduced to Japan. Along with Chinese Buddhism came the sophisticated culture of China. The Chinese introduced the systematic Chinese characters to the Japanese, who adopted it as their own. Prior to that period, Japan kept no written history. It is only through archaeological finds that historians can piece together a vague idea of Japanese life before its written history.

As in so many cultures, ancient Japanese people made no distinction between the religious, social, and economic aspects of life. The Japanese people organized themselves by clans, and worship and ritual took place through the clan structure. Burial sites reveal a concern for what happens to family members after life. Other artifacts suggest the Japanese people prayed to nature spirits for the blessing of children and the growth of crops, especially rice. They celebrated festivals, especially in spring and autumn, the time of planting and harvesting.

kami

The Japanese name for any kind of Spiritual force or power.

In Japan's creation myth, Amaterasu, goddess of the sun, hid herself from the world in a cave when she felt herself insulted by her brother. To entice her out, the other gods performed a ribald dance to the sounds of much merriment. Amaterasu heard the commotion and was overcome with curiosity—she left her cave, bringing light back to the world.

Included in the psyche of the Japanese people, even to this day, is the myth of the creation of Japan and its people. According to the myth, spirits called **kami** emerged just after the beginning of heaven and earth. These first kami, in turn, created other kami. Eventually, a kami couple called Izanagi and Izanami emerged. As creators, they dipped a jeweled spear into the ocean of the amorphous earth and solid masses formed. These solid masses became the islands of present-day Japan. The myth goes on to say the divine couple inhabited earth and gave birth to the sun goddess, Amaterasu. She, in turn, sent her grandson Ninigi-no-Mikoto to earth with a sword, a mirror, and a jewel as signs of authority to reign over the earth. As the myth continues, his descendants established the imperial house of Japan. These three items are still symbols of imperial rule in Japan. According to this myth, both the mythological emperors and the historical emperors of Japan are from an unbroken line originating in the sun goddess. Not only did the land of Japan and the rule of its emperors have a divine origin, the Japanese people themselves had a divine origin. According to the myth, kami created the Japanese people. Throughout its history, the Japanese people believed that their land, their emperor, and themselves had divine origins, setting them apart from all the world. The land of Japan and those who inhabited its islands were the center of the world, and its rulers were direct descendants of Amaterasu.

➤ What is a national myth of your country? How does it help define the nation,
its leaders, and its people? If you live in
a country that does not have a national
myth, do you think you are missing
something? Why or why not?

The Chinese Influence

In the middle of the sixth century, Buddhism, Taoism, and
Confucianism were introduced to Japan. The Japanese imperial
court became interested in these new religious traditions
because they came from China, a place they perceived as having
a culture superior to Japan's. Eager to learn all things Chinese,
the Japanese ruling class adopted the Confucian model of education. They found Confucian social conventions helpful in
forging a national identity. Though present in the Japanese
social milieu, the Japanese adopted the Confucian notion of *li*.
Of particular interest was the relationship between the emperor
and his subjects and the relationship between father and son.
While the subject and son were to be loyal and obedient, the
emperor and the father were to be benevolent. For the ruling
class, the attitudes and expressions of loyalty and obedience
were a good formula for social stability.

The introduction of the Chinese culture also brought
Taoism to Japan. The Taoist traditions of harmony with nature
and divination were not foreign ideas to the Japanese people.
They used techniques of divination for some of the same purposes as the Chinese people. Divination was one way of "divining" the various signs within nature. Among other things,
people employed divination to determine the best time for an
event to take place.

Confucianism and Taoism did not become separate religious traditions in Japan. Rather, aspects of each were adopted
and adapted into the indigenous religious expressions. On the
other hand, separation between Buddhism and Shinto was
clearer. Buddhism was not native to Japan, so at times during
the religious history of Japan, Buddhism found itself at odds

with the ruling class. Nevertheless, more often, Buddhism was graciously accepted as a form of religious expression for the Japanese people. For worship, there were times when the buddhas and the kami were venerated side by side.

When Buddhism initially was introduced into Japan, Japanese leaders were the first ones attracted to the "foreign" religious tradition. Of particular interest to them was Buddhist philosophy, elaborate doctrine, well-organized priesthood, art, and literature. Buddhist rituals for the dead and memorials for ancestors were of great interest to the royal household. The Buddhist practice of cremation, begun in India, became an accepted alternative in Japanese Buddhist burial rites. In 594 CE, Prince Shotoku made Buddhism the state religion. During the next few centuries, a number of Buddhist temples and monasteries were built. Yet the Japanese indigenous religion did not disappear, for the creation myth that was told and retold made them a divine people.

With the influx of new religious traditions, the Japanese people found it necessary to name the indigenous Japanese religion. Though Shinto was the name given by the Chinese, the word kami may actually better describe Japanese religious expressions, as the Japanese believed that the kami were everywhere. At first honored in natural settings, kami eventually became enshrined at various local clan sites.

The Expansion of Buddhism

During the Heian Period (794–1185), Japan moved from a centralized to a feudal form of government, and Buddhism became the prominent religious tradition in Japan. In the ninth century, two new Buddhist sects, Tendai and Shingon, were introduced in Japan via China. Yet Japanese Buddhism was unique. These were forms of Mahayana Buddhism that saw no problem claiming kami and bodhisattvas as the same thing. Shinto shrines and Buddhist temples stood side by side in Japan. It was not unusual for Buddhist priests to perform rituals at Shinto shrines. This mutual arrangement continued until the nineteenth century, when the Meiji government forced a separation between

Shinto and Buddhism. It was during the **shogunate**
Kamakura **shogunate** (1185–1333) that
many sects of Buddhism flourished.

shogunate
A form of military government that ruled Japan until the nineteenth century.

A form of Vajrayana Buddhism known
as Shingon came to Japan. With its elaborate rituals, secret transmission of insight,
and instructive scriptures, the nobility was particularly interested in Shingon Buddhism. The appeal of Shingon Buddhism was
its belief that one could attain Enlightenment in this lifetime if
one was willing to undergo the strict discipline of ritual and
study. Shingon Buddhism strived to blend with the indigenous
religion of Japan by venerating both kami and Buddhist deities.

During the same period, Tien-tai Buddhism came from
China and became known as Tendai Buddhism in Japan.
Focusing on the Lotus Sutra for inspiration, members of
Tendai gave great faith and devotion to Amitabha Buddha,
known in Japanese as Amida Buddha. The Lotus Sutra taught
that Enlightenment was universal. In addition, Tendai
Buddhism adapted a form of devotion to Amitabha Buddha
found in Chinese Pure Land Buddhism. A further adaptation
Tendai Buddhism made in its adoption of the Chinese Tien-tai
was the addition of the worship of nature kami.

It was inevitable that Pure Land
Buddhism would also reach the
shores of Japan. Yet it was not
until the Kamakura Period that
this occurred. As in China, the
Pure Land Buddhism of Japan
advocated great devotion to
Amida Buddha. In this way, all had
the opportunity to be reborn in
the blissful Pure Land. One need
only show great faith in Amida.
One way of showing great devotion to Amida Buddha was to
recite *Namu Amida Butsu* like a
mantra or to in some way keep
Amida Buddha ever in one's mind.

The Great Buddha of Kamakura is a
bronze statue of Amida Buddha that
is located on the grounds of the
Kotokuin Temple. It is the second
largest Buddha statue in Japan.

zazen

In Zen Buddhism, seated meditation. The instructions for zazen direct the disciple to sit in a quiet room, breathing rhythmically and easily, with legs fully or half crossed, spine and head erect.

Chan Buddhism from China became Zen Buddhism in Japan around the Kamakura period. The two most noted schools of Zen Buddhism were Rinzai and Soto Zen. While Rinzai Zen believed a person could gain immediate Enlightenment, Soto Zen believed Enlightenment was a gradual process. While Soto Zen emphasized a method of **zazen**, or "sitting meditation," Rinzai placed more emphasis on the use of the **koan**. These were meant to break through logic and intellect in order for an intuitive flash, called a *satori*, to emerge and eventually lead to Enlightenment. Two notable koans are:

When a tree falls in a forest where no one is present, does it make a sound?

What was your face like before your parents were born?

➤ In what ways do you think meditating on a koan can help you in your spiritual life?

koan

A paradox to be meditated upon that is used to train Zen Buddhist monks to abandon ultimate dependence on reason and to force them into gaining sudden intuitive enlightenment.

The heart of Zen Buddhism in both schools was meditation. Zen Buddhists sat in meditation, known as zazen, and made no judgments or comments about the insights they received through their meditation practice. Zen Buddhists compared the mind to a window. The person was to look directly out of the window rather than have someone else explain to them what is outside the window. That other person would inevitably interpret the scene rather than name the person's direct experience.

Zen was more interested in a direct vision of nature than interpretations of nature. Rather than statues and pictures of the Buddha or bodhisattvas, the art of Zen Buddhism was nature. Gardens, rocks, mountains, and birds were the most popular subjects of Zen Buddhist art. The Zen connection between religion and nature was truly seamless.

➤ How does nature deepen your spiritual well being?

Shinto, the indigenous religious tradition of Japan, emerged from the vague prehistory of Japan carrying with it its beliefs in kami, its national myth, and its harmony with nature. As Japan was visited by people from other East Asian countries, Shinto adopted from and adapted to the other religions and cultures. From Confucianism it was li, from Taoism it was their calendar, divination, some festivals, and balance with nature, and from Buddhism, various forms of ritual and philosophical systems, as well as ancestor veneration.

Most prevalent was Shinto's relationship with Buddhism. Shinto and Buddhism shared in shrine rituals. To many Shinto people, Buddhist deities were just other forms of kami. It was common to have both Shinto and Buddhist worship services in Shinto shrines. Buddhist scriptures, Buddhist deities, Shinto kami, and Shinto prayers seemed quite natural together to the ordinary Japanese worshipper. Unlike the exclusivity of the monotheistic religious traditions of Judaism, Christianity, and Islam, a number of religious traditions of the East are much more comfortable worshipping in one another's sacred spaces.

The Modern Period

In 1549, the first Christian missionaries, including St. Francis Xavier, came to Japan. The missionaries were able to win converts to the faith primarily due to the Japanese interest in things Western and some government support. However, this interest did not last long. Fearing the missionaries had a political agenda, the government issued an edict in 1587 banishing all Catholics from Japan. In 1596, twenty-seven European and Japanese Catholics were executed at Nagasaki, making them the first martyrs of the Christian faith in Japan.

The Tokugawa shogunate came into power in 1603. The new rulers, military leaders called *shoguns*, had inherited a fragmented government, so they reorganized society in a manner

Christians being torturted during the Tokugawa Shogunate

influenced by Confucian values. Particularly important were the five relationships of li, especially the relationship between ruler and subject. In addition, to ensure the banishment of Christianity from Japan, the Tokugawa reformers required citizens to register with a Buddhist temple at the times of birth, marriage, and death. This meant that the number of Buddhist temples increased greatly. This also ensured that the government had control over its citizenry. An overall theme of the reformers was to purify Japan from all outside influences. Some reformers even attempted to return Japan to a time before the influence of Chinese culture. Motoori Norinaga (1730–1801) was the most famous of these reformers seeking a pure Shinto, though other religious traditions were so imbedded in Japanese culture that "pure Shinto" was impossible.

⟶ **What would it be like if your neighborhood tried to remove the influence that one culture or another has had there?**

The Meiji Period (1852–1912) restored some of the imperial power lost under the shogunates. The Meiji opened wide the doors for trade with the West. They believed the centuries of isolation advocated during the Tokugawa period put Japan far behind the industrial West. They also forced a separation between Shinto and Buddhism, and there was a concerted move toward nationalism, restoring a time when the emperor was a kami and the Japanese people were of divine origin with a divine mission. All Japanese, whatever their religious tradition, were to perform rituals as part of State Shinto, but interestingly, the Meiji decided to declare that State Shinto was not a religion. By doing so, people could practice the religion of their choice and yet remain loyal to the imperial family and to Japan. Some were more radical in striving for nationalism. They wanted to erase all trace of anything foreign. This included any trace of Chinese culture, Confucianism, Taoism, and Buddhism. However, Shinto was so entwined with these religious traditions that eradicating them was impossible without destroying Shinto itself.

> **What are the advantages and disadvantages of living in a governmental system that separates church from state?**

Two backlashes to the Meiji reform should be noted. One backlash was in the government's attempts to suppress Buddhism. Since Buddhism was such an integral part of the Japanese heritage and culture, the people of Japan revolted against its suppression, and the government relented.

Also, by allowing people to practice the religious traditions of their choice, Catholic Christians who had continued to practice their faith secretly for over two hundred years came into the open. However, the ban of practicing Christianity had not been officially lifted, and persecutions of Christians continued. When the Western world heard of the persecution of the Christians, they became antagonistic toward Japan. The Japanese government then lifted the ban on the practice of Christianity to ensure a continued relationship with the West. With the ban lifted, Christian missionaries returned to Japan, this time including Protestant missionaries. However, with the rise in nationalism, the number of Japanese people who converted to Christianity was few.

At the beginning of the twentieth century, there was a tremendous surge in what became known as "new religions" in both Shinto and Buddhism. The new religions can be described as either religious movements or religious societies. Individuals who claimed divine revelation or their own divinity founded these new groups. They were not actually new religions, for they integrated elements of the existing religious traditions of Japan into their movement or society. In the twentieth century, **Soka Gakkai** was an example of one of these so-called "new religions."

Soka Gakkai

Founded in 1930, it emphasized the power of the **Lotus Sutra** *and advocated non-violence. Today it is not only the largest of Japan's "new religions," but it is also an international organization.*

The defeat of Japan in World War II was devastating to a nation that believed itself to be at the center of creation. At the end of the war, the Allies forced Emperor Hirohito to renounce his claim to divinity, leaving the Japanese people to practice any religion they chose. Thus, State Shinto and nationalism were weakened. This left room for the "new religions" to advance. Recently, however, the more ancient forms of Shinto and Buddhism once again have attracted some Japanese devotees. Surpassing all religious revivals, however, has been the revival of Japanese nationalism. Deprived of building another powerful army by the Allies, Japan has forged an economic power second only to the United States.

■ Section 1 Summary

- Japanese religion is an amalgamation of Chinese religions and their various aspects with indigenous Japanese religion.

- Shinto, "the way of the gods," is the name given to Japanese religion. Kami (the name for any spiritual or sacred power) also describes Japanese religion.

- At various times in its religious history, the Japanese government has supported Shinto or Buddhism as the state religion.

- Zen Buddhism with its major schools—Soto and Rinzai—became popular in Japan.

- A number of new religious movements emerged in Japan at the beginning of the twentieth century. Some flourished after World War II.

■ Section Review Questions

1. What role does the Japanese creation myth play in Japanese identity?

2. Why might kami be a better word to describe Japanese religion than Shinto?

3. What was the traditional role of the emperor in Japanese religion?

4. Describe the differences between Soto Zen Buddhism and Rinzai Zen Buddhism.

5. What did the Meiji government restore?

6. What happened to Emperor Hirohito after World War II?

7. What are "new religions" among Japanese religions?

2. Sacred Stories and Sacred Scriptures

Shinto does not have any official sacred texts, that is, those revealed by the gods. However, two texts are considered authoritative and significant for both the religious and historical heritage of the Japanese people. In the eighth century CE, the Japanese government commissioned the compilation of the oral myths and legends of the Japanese people. Written in Chinese, the *Kojiki* (*Record of Ancient Matters*) was completed in 712. It includes the creation myth of Japan and concludes with a genealogy of the emperors to Emperor Temmu, who commissioned the work. A second writing—*Nihonshoki* (*Chronicles of Japan*)—was commissioned to chronicle the history of Japan. It begins with the Japanese creation myth and covers all the history through the end of the seventh century CE.

As with so many documents written in ancient times, these writers portray the elite classes, not the ordinary people. They were written to legitimize the imperial government as the direct descendant of the sun goddess, Amaterasu, so that the imperial leader could claim a form of sacred kingship.

■ Section 2 Summary

■ There are no sacred Japanese writings revealed by the gods, though two ancient texts do contain myths and legends of ancient Japan.

■ The authoritative texts were commissioned by the emperor to legitimize imperial leadership.

■ Section 2 Review Questions

1. Name the two texts that contain the national myth of Japan.

2. For whom were the texts written?

3. Beliefs and Practices

Though Shinto is the indigenous religious tradition of Japan, as can be seen through its historical development, there is fluidity between Shinto and Buddhism. It is common to find both kami and buddhas worshipped in the same home.

Kami

In connection with Shinto, kami are not gods in the sense that they are transcendent or all-powerful. Kami has to do with whatever is sacred. Nature, such as mountains, rivers, trees, or rocks, can be kami. Human beings can be kami. The emperor, as representative of sun goddess Amaterasu, great warriors, poets, scholars, and wise ancestors can be kami. The imperial leader of Japan manifested kami, and his presence reminded Japanese that all was well in this world. The focus of kami is to aid and protect. There are creative as well as destructive kami. For example, an erupting volcano is a destructive kami.

Hence, Japanese religion sees the natural world as good. The kami inhabit this world in trees, mountains, holy people, the emperor, and anything else deemed sacred or powerful. Redemption is possible because the world is imbued with goodness. Redemption comes not through good works of helping others, but through proper rituals associated with the kami or the compassion and mercy of a bodhisattva like Amida.

People pray to kami in local or national shrines, at their home **kamidana**, or in nature. Some Japanese people worship the kami that inhabit a specific mountain or other form of nature. Praying to kami may involve praise, thanksgiving, appreciation, or acknowledgment of its power. In praying to the kami, it is customary to leave the request to the end. Requests are commonly asking for the blessing of children, a good harvest, a good job, good health, protection of family members, or prosperity.

kamidana

From the Japanese for "kami shelf," it is a place for a home shrine dedicated to kami.

Mount Fuji

The mountain that most represents Japan in the eyes of the world is, of course, Mount Fuji. No peak more beautifully embodies the spirit of a nation. The elegant simplicity of its lines, sweeping up into the graceful shape of an inverted fan painted with delicate patterns of pure white snow, symbolizes the quest for beauty and perfection that has shaped so much of Japanese culture, both secular and sacred. Suspended between heaven and earth, neither rock nor cloud, the volcano appears as a cone of crystallized sky, floating above a vast landscape of fields, villages, lakes and sea. The very perfection of its form, startling in its incredible simplicity, suggests the mystery of the infinite.

The name *Fuji* probably comes from an Ainu word meaning "fire" or "deity of fire." Obviously a god of great power, the mountain had to be placated. In 806, a local official built a shrine near the foot of the volcano to keep it from erupting. The priests assigned the task of pacifying the mountain were accused of neglecting their duties because Fuji erupted with great violence in 864, causing much damage in a nearby province. The governor of that province blamed the priests for failing to perform the proper rites and constructed another shrine in his own territory, where he could make sure everything was done correctly. A fiery god of the mountain became at a later date the more peaceful Shinto goddess of Mount Fuji—Konohana Sakuya Hime—the "Goddess of Flowering Trees." Today she is worshipped at the shrine originally built for the older deity.[7]

Buddhism in Japan

butsudan

In Japanese households, the Buddhist family altar; historically, it was maintained in addition to the kamidana. It generally contains memorial tablets for dead ancestors.

As has been noted, Shinto and Buddhism are closely related in Japan. Buddhism began in India, but as it expanded throughout the continent of Asia, it adapted itself to local situations. Buddhisms influence in Japan was no exception. Some Japanese believe buddhas and bodhisattvas are just another form of kami. Likewise, some Buddhists believe kami are manifestations of various buddhas. Statues of various buddhas can be found everywhere in Japan. It is not unusual to find buddha statues within Shinto shrines. Neither is it unusual for a home to possess both a kamidana and a **butsudan**. Similar to Chinese religions, it is at the butsudan that ancestor veneration takes place.

Japanese Living

As the indigenous Japanese religion made no distinction between religion and politics, nor between religion and nature, "harmony" is an apt word to describe Japanese living. This virtue further points to the fact that for the Japanese, people and kami dwell together. Professor Ninian Smart wrote:

> If there is a central perception which prevails, it is probably that of harmony. A number of the new religious movements are keen to stress the unity of the worlds religions; and, though the Nichiren Shoshu is aggressive, most Mahayana Buddhist groups seek harmony. Shinto, too, has an interest in maintaining its harmony with other religions, partly because it does not possess any rigid system of doctrines which might bring it into conflict with them. From this point of view democracy is a method of defusing gifts, especially between religious groups, in so far as the separation of religion and the State gives a peaceful basis for the voluntary pursuit of values. It also is in consonance with the Japanese ideal in gaining consensus before any serious line of policy is undertaken.[8]

Besides harmony, another strong virtue important to the Japanese people is loyalty. The Confucian value system is very strong in the Japanese culture. In the five relationships of li, loyalty is the glue. Though it is clear that the subordinate is to be loyal to the superior, in Japanese life, the superior is also responsible to the subordinate, and, thus, ideally exhibits a certain mutual loyalty to him or her. The virtue of loyalty is still exhibited in corporate Japan, where loyalty to the clan until death has been replaced with loyalty to the corporation until retirement. Loyalty went to the extreme when **samurai warriors** were willing to commit suicide or **harakiri** rather than bring shame upon their ruler.

The clan or extended family is the most important social structure for Japanese living. Unlike the West with its "rugged individualism," the individual takes a backseat

samuri warriors

From the Japanese word for "to serve," a hereditary feudal warrior class who cultivated virtues such as loyalty, honor, and courage, and served Japanese rulers.

harakiri

Ritual suicide by disembowelment practiced by the Japanese samurai or formally decreed by a court in lieu of the death penalty.

to the family, region, or nation in Japan. Though religious experience comes to the individual, religious expression is, more often, through the context of a group. This is exhibited in two primary ways. Because of where they live, the family is a member of a local Shinto shrine. And, because of ancestor veneration, the family is a member of a local Buddhist temple.

The Japanese people themselves have been called the national clan. At one time, the emperor was the head of the clan and made offerings at the national shrine at Ise on behalf of the Japanese people. Though initially a kami for the imperial family, the sun goddess Amaterasu became the national kami. Thus, because of their divine origin, the Japanese people understood themselves as a divine people.

> Do you consider yourself pre-ordained to accomplish something worthwhile with your life? If so, what is it?

■ Section 3 Summary

- ■ The major focus of Japanese religion is the kami.

- ■ Japanese religion finds all life, all creation, and human nature intrinsically good.

- ■ Harmony is a most valued virtue in Japanese life.

- ■ Shinto and Buddhism are closely intertwined in Japan's religious expression.

■ Section 3 Review Questions

1. Besides being a name for Shinto gods, what does kami refer to?

2. Harmony and loyalty are valued virtues in Japanese religion. Why?

3. What kind of religious expression can be found in a Japanese home?

4. Sacred Time

For calculating times of many of its festivals, the Japanese use a lunar calendar similar to the Chinese, lunar calendar. However, during the Meiji period, when Japan's interest in competing in the Western world heightened, the Gregorian calendar began to be used and is in general use today in Japan.

Japanese Festivals

Matsuri is the name for Japanese festivals. As the shrines and their kami are local or regional, so are most Japanese festivals. Though most matsuri are connected with Shinto, all the religious traditions of Japan participate in the annual cycle of matsuri.

Omisoka is the Year-End Festival. It is the day of preparation for New Year's Day. People clean their homes, especially their Buddhist altars and kamidanas. The local shrines and temples are also purified, as well as the graves of the ancestors in preparing for the New Year.

The New Year, called *Shogatsu*, is the most important celebration in Japan. It is a three-day celebration held on January 1, 2, and 3. At Buddhist temples in Japan, eight bells are rung on New Year's Eve, and one hundred bells are rung on New Year's Day to purify the people of the 108 sins in Buddhism.

Hina Matsuri means "Girl's Day," and this festival is celebrated on March 3. Though Girl's Day is not a public holiday, most Japanese families with daughters celebrate the occasion. Parents arrange dolls that have been dressed in traditional Japanese court costumes on a tier to symbolize a princess wedding. The prince and princess are placed on the top of the tier, and the dolls go down in rank to the court musicians at the bottom. Offerings of rice cakes, peach blossoms, and sweet white sake are set before this tier. The daughters themselves dress in **kimonos**, and the families celebrate, wishing the girls health and happiness.

kimono

A long robe with wide sleeves traditionally worn with a broad sash as an outer garment by the Japanese.

Kodomo no Hi or "Children's Day" is a public holiday celebrated by all children. It was once Boy's Day as a counterpart to Girl's Day. The tradition of this day goes back to ancient Japan, but it became a huge festival during the time of feudal Japan when samurai was an estimable career for Japanese boys. On this day, kites shaped like carp fly in the skies of Japan. The carp was chosen for its characteristics of courage and fortitude, as a carp can swim upstream and even up waterfalls.

Obon is a three-day festival, celebrated in mid-August, in which the Japanese people believe the ancestral spirits return home for a short time. The families go to the gravesites of their ancestors and light candles, lanterns, and bonfires to give the spirits light with which to see their way home. The highlight of this festival is the folk dances performed at temples or shrines.

Life Cycle

The eclecticism of Japanese religion is illustrated best in the Japanese life cycle. The newborn infant is taken to the local shrine between thirty and one hundred days after his or her birth and presented to the kami. The Japanese traditionally believe the kami watches over the child for the rest of his or her life.

Japanese weddings are traditionally held at shrines. However, an increasing number of weddings are taking place at Christian churches, even if the couple is not Christian. There are still some Shinto elements to the wedding, but more brides nowadays prefer to wear a white gown on their wedding day, rather than a traditional kimono.

Regarding death rituals, the Japanese people have great respect for their ancestors, so they visit the graves of deceased family members often during the year. Most cemeteries in Japan are Buddhist cemeteries. Generally, after the funeral, a series of memorial services is held over a period of months and years until the fiftieth year, when the deceased is considered to be truly an ancestor in the Japanese tradition.

A Woman's Place in Japan

There is some evidence that early Japan was politically matriarchal, and priestesses and shamanesses played an important role in early Shinto. All this changed when Japan came into contact with China and wholeheartedly adopt-ed Confucian ethics. By the eighth century, women were no longer permitted to rule, and by the fifteenth century, they had lost virtually all civil rights. Only during periods of severe crisis were some women politically influential, but only briefly.

Contact with the West during the nineteenth and twentieth centuries has done little to change the rights of women. Modern Japanese males have simply shifted their allegiance from feudal lords to the presidents of corporations and businesses. Husbands still consider their wives to be functional creatures essential to the fulfillment of family life: as mothers of their children and managers of their households. In traditional Confucian style, the ideal Japanese family consists of three generations living under one roof. Marriage provides a line of heirs for the "ancestral house." Marriages are still arranged by parents, and a barren woman is promptly returned to her home.[9]

■ Section 4 Summary

■ Matsuri is the name for Japanese festivals. Most matsuri are connected with Shinto, though all religious traditions play a part.

■ Because the social structure of Japan is based locally, there is a wide variety and number of festivals in Japanese religion.

■ New Year's Day is the greatest festival in Japan, though it is not strictly a religious festival.

■ Section 4 Review Questions

1. Why did Japan move to the Gregorian calendar?
2. Describe what takes place on the Girl's Day festival.
3. What happens on the fiftieth anniversary of a Japanese person's death?

● 5. Sacred Places and Sacred Spaces

There is no place that is not sacred on the land of Japan because all of Japan has a divine origin. Yet, the Japanese still do designate the sacred space from the profane space. Home, local, and national shrines, temples, mountains, rivers, trees, and boulders are all considered sacred places or spaces. Home shrines may be considered even more sacred because often both a kamidana and butsudan are in places of honor. While the kamidana recalls the presence of kami, the butsudan is a place for both Buddha and ancestor spirits to reside.

Shinto Shrines

As it lacks a formal scripture, doctrine, and ethical code, the Japanese religion places great emphasis on ritual. These rituals take place at home shrines, local shrines, or national shrines. Since there is no specific day of the week for worship, devotees generally perform their home ritual on any morning they wish, either as an individual or as a family. They can also go to the local shrine any day of the week to honor the local kami. There are thousands of Shinto shrines in Japan, though very few have priests.

Most Japanese homes, as well as many places of business or work, have both a kamidana and a butsudan. While the Shinto emphasize things of life such as birth, marriage, agriculture, or even a new job, the Buddhist emphasis is on the end of life and the afterlife. The head of the family makes offerings to the kami or Buddhist deity seeking blessings and protection for the family from evil.

The local Shinto shrine is a familiar piece of architecture in the Japanese landscape. Since it is believed that kami exist in nature, the Japanese find it important that flowers and foliage surround the shrines. Even in the most urban cities of Japan, the Shinto shrine is an oasis of tranquility and beauty, an

A tori is an entrance gate to a shinto shrine.

environment fit for a kami. Also, since Shinto and Buddhism are so closely connected in Japan, a Shinto shrine is generally located near a Buddhist temple.

The most distinctive element of the Shinto shrine is the torii, an entrance gate made of two timber posts and two timber cross beams. Symbolically, the torii separates the profane world outside from the sacred residence of the kami inside. Those shrines with a strong Buddhist influence tend to have the torii painted red or black, while the toriis that are decidedly Japanese are left unpainted.

The format for worship at the shrine is simple both for individual and communal worship. Devotees first perform a purification rite where they wash their hands and face and rinse their

kami body

An object in which it is believed the kami descends during a Shinto worship service. Often, the object is a mirror or sword.

mouths. They then enter a hall where the offering is made. Today the offering is usually money, but when Japan was more agricultural, the offerings were the fruits of the harvest. Next, there is a small chamber where the **kami body** is kept. Even though the kami body is normally something quite simple like a mirror or a pebble, it is considered so sacred and emits so much spiritual power that a priest rarely looks inside the chamber. Even if the door to the chamber is opened, a screen blocks the kami body. The occasion for opening the chamber is usually a festival in which the kami is invited to participate.

Whether the worship at a shrine is done individually or communally at a festival, the elements are similar. There is the rite of purification, the offering, and the prayer. Offerings at the national shrines bring spiritual benefits to all of Japan.

The Grand Shrine at Ise

bronze mirror

When the Japanese sun goddess Amaterasu fled to a cave because of the violent attacks of her brother Susanoo, and while the world was plunged into darkness, it was only when a bronze mirror was hung outside the cave that Amaterasu was a ray of light able to escape the cave and light the world.

Ise was the location of the shrine for the imperial family in ancient Japan. Since the imperial family believed they were direct descendants of the sun goddess Amaterasu, they dedicated this shrine to her and placed a **bronze mirror** as a kami body in its inner chamber. Hence, Amaterasu was the kami of the imperial family. Eventually the shrine of the imperial family became the national shrine of Japan. The emperor acted as the priest of that shrine, making offerings on behalf of his country. Today the Grand Shrine of Ise still has many pilgrims and visitors. It is one of the major symbols of Japanese religious, political, and cultural heritage.

■ Section 5 Summary

- ■ It is common for a home to have both a kamidana and a butsudan.

- ■ The local shrine is where much of Shinto individual and communal worship takes place.

- ■ The kami body is an object—often a mirror or sword—into which it is believed a kami descends during a Shinto worship service.

- ■ The greatest shrine in all of Japan is the Grand Shrine at Ise, originally dedicated to the sun goddess Amaterasu by the imperial family.

■ Section 5 Review Questions

1. Why do many Japanese homes have both Shinto and Buddhist shrines?

2. What is the significance of a torii at a shrine or temple?

3. Name the typical elements in a Shinto worship service.

4. Why is the Grand Shrine at Ise significant for Japanese religion?

6. Japanese Religions through a Catholic Lens

A point of comparison between Japanese religions and Catholicism is sacred time. Sacred time is defined as "the extraordinary within the ordinary," that is, a taste of the infinite in the finite. Sacred time is marked in a regular, periodic fashion such as weeks, months, and years. Individual and communal observances as well as feast days and religious festivals also mark sacred time.

Every religious tradition has its own calendar, and sometimes various groups within a tradition use different calendars. In any case, sacred time is oriented around the core beliefs of a faith community and usually essential to the practice of the faith.

Sacred Time in Japanese Religions

Those practicing Japanese religions use three different calendars to mark sacred time. They use the lunar calendar of 354 days in a year, the Gregorian solar calendar with 365 days in a year, and the complex Chinese calendar. It is the four seasons of the year rather than human construct that helps determine the day or days of a religious festival. The calendar of Japanese religions is thus filled with numerous festivals throughout the year. When local and regional festivals are included, the calendar seems overwhelming. With the intertwining of Shinto and Buddhism, it is clear that what people do and how they celebrate rituals is more important in Japanese religions than what they believe.

The gate to Kiyomizu Temple in Kyoto, Japan.

In Japanese religions, the core beliefs revolve around the kami and ancestor veneration. To be able to approach the deities, they must purify themselves, their dwelling places, and their places of worship before the first day of the new year. New Year's Day is a special time to welcome kami and buddhas. People attend their local Shinto shrine or Buddhist temple where they ask blessings for a prosperous new year. In attending these sacred places, the people are not only welcoming the deities into a new year and asking for their blessing, but they are also seeking harmony with kami and with all nature. There is newness seen in the purification rites prior to the New Year. The theme of purity continues in the Girl's Day festival in which a paper doll traditionally took on the impurities of the family so that they could stand before the deity in a state of purity. In the Buddhist Obon festival, one not only remembers and honors one's ancestors, but he or she also asks the ancestors for their blessings and protection.

Sacred Time in Catholicism

Catholics use calendars in a very different manner than as practiced in Japanese religions. Rather than using the four seasons of nature to help designate sacred time, Christians use the "Feast of Feasts," Easter, as the preeminent and central event of the Christian year. The core belief of Christianity is that through his death and Resurrection, Jesus Christ is the Savior of the world. This saving event took place not only on the first Easter over two thousand years ago, but that same saving event is present today (CCC, 1165). Jesus still saves. Though discrepancies in dating occurred between Eastern and Western Christianity when Western Christianity moved to the Gregorian calendar in 1582 (CCC, 1170), the sequence of the liturgical seasons within the liturgical year remains the same. The liturgical year is based on significant events in the life of Christ and his Church rather than the four seasons of nature.

With Easter as the preeminent, central feast of the Christian year (CCC, 1169), the Paschal Mystery unfolds and is celebrated throughout the year (CCC, 1171). The liturgical year begins with the season of Advent, a preparation for the coming of Jesus as a historical person, in our hearts, and at the Second Coming. The Christmas season celebrates the Incarnation, God becoming one of us. Winter Ordinary Time marks the initial ministry of Jesus. Lent is a period of repentance in preparation for the Church's greatest feast, Easter. The season of Easter celebrates the resurrection of Jesus as well as honors the beginning of the Church and the coming of the Holy Spirit at Pentecost. The period of Ordinary Time resumes for the rest of the liturgical year, celebrating the ministry of Jesus while sharing Gospel readings from one of the Gospels—primarily Matthew, Mark, or Luke.

Throughout the Church Year, special feast days are commemorated to honor the lives of Christian saints. Mary, the Mother of God, is the preeminent saint. Mary played an essential role in the saving work of her son, Jesus (CCC, 1172). The Church deems it right and proper to designate certain days of the year to honor Mary and memorialize the other women and

feast days men who lived exemplary lives (CCC,

Days that are celebrated with special liturgies in commemoration of the sacred mysteries and events tied to our redemption, or to honor Mary, the Apostles, martyrs, or saints.

1173). Besides the designation of Mary and the saints on the Church's universal calendar, there are regional or diocesan calendars created for just such a purpose.

Whatever the celebration, **feast days** are opportunities to give individuals a sense of belonging and to help build community in a world beset by secularism.

How do Christian celebrations of special seasons and feast days help to counterbalance secularism?

■ Section 6 Summary

■ Though designated in very different ways, sacred time is a dimension of all the religious traditions of the world.

■ Sacred time is more a communal observance than an individual observance.

■ Sacred time is oriented around the core beliefs of a religious tradition.

■ For the Japanese religions, sacred time is influenced by nature's four seasons, while for Christians, sacred time is oriented around Easter and the Paschal Mystery.

■ Section 6 Review Questions

1. How many calendars do Japanese religions typically use to designate their sacred time?

2. Why do Eastern and Western Christians use slightly different calendars?

3. Why are Mary and the saints honored and memorialized on the Catholic calendar?

● Conclusion

Shinto is the name given to the indigenous religion of Japan. One cannot speak of "pure Shinto" after the coming of Chinese religions to Japan. Once Chinese religions were introduced to Japan, Buddhism, Confucianism, and Taoism influenced Japanese religion forevermore. Yet the adherents of all the religious traditions were considered, at least until the end of World War II, part of a national clan with the emperor as the head. With the military collapse and economic growth of Japan, a number of "new religions" have emerged, predominantly influenced by Shinto or Buddhism.

Though few Japanese respond in public polls that they are religious, most Japanese also respond that they perform religious rituals at home, at the workplace, at shrines, or at temples. Traditionally, the Japanese do not separate religion from politics or nature, and it seems today that they do not separate religion from any part of their everyday lives.

■ Chapter 8 Summary

■ Japanese religious history begins with the Japanese creation myth.

■ Indigenous Japanese religion is heavily influenced by Chinese religions.

■ Many sects of Buddhism flourished in Japan and intermingled with Japanese Shinto.

■ The emperor was the sacred monarch of Japan until the end of World War II.

■ Shinto believes that the world is overflowing with kami, and thus, the world and human nature are intrinsically good.

■ The *Kojiki* and the *Nishongi* are closest to Japanese sacred writings, though neither is considered to be revealed by God.

- Most Japanese homes have both a kamidana and a butsudan.

- Though kami were originally worshipped in natural settings, they are now worshipped in shrines that are set in natural surroundings.

- Most Japanese worship is individual or family based. Communal worship is in the form of religious festivals.

- Buddhism, Shinto, and Christianity are all part of Japanese life cycle rites.

- Three types of calendars are used to mark sacred time in Japanese religions.

- The Grand Shrine at Ise is the most sacred of places in Shinto.

- Sacred time is oriented around the core beliefs of a religious tradition.

■ Chapter 8 Review Questions

1. Define the term *Shinto*.

2. Why is kami difficult to define?

3. What is the significance of the *Kojiki* and the *Nihongi*?

4. Define and give one example of *kami*.

5. What is the role of the kami body in Shinto shrine worship?

6. What is at the heart of Zen Buddhism?

7. Give an example of a koan.

8. What was the overall theme of Tokugawa reformers?

9. What is the purpose of a kamidana and a butsudan?

10. Explain why harmony is an apt word to describe Japanese living.

11. What is the most important festival celebrated by adherents of Japanese religions? What is the significance of this festival?

12. Why is the Grand Shrine of Ise so important to Shinto?

13. What is the purpose of the torii?

14. Why is ancestor veneration so important to the Japanese people?

15. What are the core beliefs of Japanese calendars?

16. What is at the center of the Catholic calendar?

■ Research & Activities

1. Write an essay on one of the following topics:

   the popular appeal of Japanese religions in America

   the various methods and symbols of ritual purification

   the influence of Chinese culture on Japan

   the state of religion in Japan today

   Japanese art, architecture, or literature and its relationship to religion

   the martial arts and Japanese religion

2. Read one of the following three books and write an essay on the author's portrayal of some aspect of Japanese religion:

   Silence by Shusaku Endo

   Shogun by James Clavell

   Zen and the Art of Motorcycle Maintenance by Robert Pirsig.

3. Create your own koan.

■ Prayer

This Shinto Prayer for Peace *was one of twelve prayers prayed at a recent World Peace Day in Assisi, Italy.*

> Although the people living across the ocean surrounding us, I believe, are all our brothers and sisters—why are there constant troubles in this world? Why do winds and waves rise in the ocean surrounding us?
>
> I only earnestly wish that the wind will soon puff away all the clouds which are hanging over the tops of the mountains.

Afterword

Blessed Mother Teresa may have believed fervently in only one faith, but her deeds made her beloved by many outside it.

"She is regarded as an angel, and not only that, but she is called Mother," said a former president of the Hindu Cultural Society in New York. "Mother in India, in our faith, is as a god. She has the highest honors you could ever give her."

"We consider her a great humanitarian," said Robin Schwarz-Kreger, a Jew. "I don't think Jews have too much pull when it comes to who gets to be a saint, but if anybody is a good candidate, I think it's Mother Teresa."

A lifetime of caring for others, especially the world's poorest people, rendered Mother Teresa like a "bodhisattva" according to a Buddhist minister in San Francisco.

"In our teachings, the ultimate human goal is to become a bodhisattva, someone who cares for people who are in need, poor, sick, and weak," he said.

From her years of tireless work in the slums, Mother Teresa has already profited, said Darui Fazad, a spokesperson for the Islamic Center in Washington, D.C.

"She was a very decent, good person who dedicated her life to the poor," he said. "The concept of Islamic charity is that there is no better reward in this life than what she did."

Mother Teresa died on September 5, 1997. Now that she has passed away, different religions have different ideas of what her final resting place might be. Catholics, Muslims, and Jews say "heaven." Buddhists say "reincarnated." Their strong opinions acknowledged how Mother Teresa's commitment transcended the boundaries of conventional religions.

Mother Teresa's own sisters in the Missionaries of Charity may have captured it best: "Mother Teresa's spirit is in the work, and the work will go on."[10]

If you recall, one of the tools deemed necessary for a study of the world's religions was empathy. Certainly this is a quality exhibited by and recognized in Mother Teresa of Calcutta.

Empathy is the ability to identify with and understand another's situation—for the purpose of this book, the situation is religion.

How have you done?

Certainly there are many checkpoints for you to gauge your success.

Whereas the early nineteenth century was influenced strongly by Protestant Christianity, and the later nineteenth century and early twentieth century marked by an influx of Roman Catholic and Jewish immigrants to North America, truly the most recent times have expanded our awareness of religions beyond those that are from the Judeo-Christian traditions.

Since the reform of immigration laws in the mid-1960s, many new immigrants from places other than Europe have graced the English-speaking world. American, Islam, Hinduism, Buddhism, and other Japanese and Chinese religions have become part of our consciousness. Today, the media reports not only on Christian festivals, the lives of Christian leaders, and Christian conflicts around the world, but also on these same events and people from a Muslim, Jewish, Buddhist, or Hindu perspective. Ecumenical councils in various regions that were until very recently the places of dialogue between various Christian denominations have now expanded to find commonalties among many of the world's religions.

Just the fact that you attend school on a daily basis provides the opportunity for you to encounter people of various ethnicities, cultures, and religions.

What might be the results of your survey of the world's religions? Perhaps you will report, like other teenagers in Catholic youth programs that emphasize cultural sensitivity, that the study has, among other things, helped you to be a more religious person, proud to be a Catholic, and to know and live your faith better.[11]

With knowledge and understanding of the world's religions and empathy toward people who profess beliefs other than your own, you can, in the words of Blessed Mother Teresa of Calcutta, confidently walk anywhere as a citizen of the world.

Religions
with
Christian &
American
Roots

appendix

Close to Home

Hopefully this course has helped you broaden your understanding of some of the world's religions, beginning with a study of those religions more familiar to you (Judaism, Christianity, Islam) before widening the circle to include religions with roots far away in both time and location (Hinduism, Buddhism, Chinese religions, and Japanese religions). In our increasingly close-knit world, even these religions have likely entered your consciousness previous to this class.

In this appendix, the circle will be drawn more tightly to your own experience as we examine five other religious traditions that have their roots mostly in nineteenth century America and in Protestant Christianity, though they advocate some beliefs that fall outside traditional Protestant Christianity. They are religions that your neighbors, friends, relatives, or perhaps even you subscribe to. They are also American religious traditions that are often misunderstood. For each of these we will briefly look at some historical background, beliefs, and practices. We will also briefly examine some of the ways these religions differ from Catholicism.

Church of Jesus Christ of Latter-day Saints

A Brief History

Mormon

The name for an ancient prophet believed to have compiled a sacred history of the Americas, which was then translated by Joseph Smith in 1830 as the Book of Mormon.

The Church of Jesus Christ of Latter-day Saints (commonly called the **Mormon** church) traces its origins to Joseph Smith, Jr. (1805–1844). At age fourteen, Smith was praying in a grove near his family's farm in upstate New York, seeking guidance after attending a church revival. There God the Father and Jesus Christ appeared to him and directed him not to claim membership in any church because they had become corrupted. Rather, Smith was told, the church founded by Jesus would be restored to its original purity in teachings and priesthood. Four years later, a heavenly being named Moroni appeared to Smith and directed him to a hill where metal plates containing ancient hieroglyphics were buried. Over the next four years, Smith translated the plates into what is known as the *Book of Mormon*. This sacred scripture contains religious writings of an ancient American civilization, including an appearance of Jesus on American soil after his resurrection. The Church of Jesus Christ of Latter-day Saints was established in 1830, the same year the *Book of Mormon* was published.

Followers of Smith were persecuted. Finding it necessary to move several times, the new community settled in Nauvoo, Illinois, in 1839, became prosperous, and built their first temple. However, even there the community found opposition. One reason for the persecution was that the Latter-day Saints, or Mormons, practiced **polygamy**, arising from a revelation of Smith's. A more practical reason for opposition was that the Mormons had established a powerful voting bloc in Nauvoo, thereby wiping away

polygamy

The taking of more than one spouse in marriage, a practice originally permitted by Mormons.

the political control of the locals. In 1844, Smith and his brother, Hyrum, were killed by an angry mob after being imprisoned in nearby Carthage.

Brigham Young succeeded Joseph Smith as leader of the Mormons. (Some members of the church believed that only a descendant of Joseph Smith—in this case, Joseph Smith III—should head the church. A splinter group of those followers formed the Reorganized Church of Jesus Christ of Latter-day Saints with headquarters to this day in Independence, Missouri.) Because of continuing persecution, Brigham Young led the Mormons on a 1300-mile journey across the Great Plains and into Utah and the Salt Lake basin. Salt Lake City, Utah, continues to be the center of the Mormon church.

Today, the Church of Jesus Christ of Latter-day Saints is one of the fastest-growing religions in the world. There are about ten million members world-wide, with approximately half living in the United States.

Joseph Smith

➤ If members of a new religion descended on a rural town today, what do you think would be the reaction of the local people?

Beliefs and Practices

Mormons hold that primitive Christianity as founded by Jesus was corrupted through **apostasy** in about the second century. Hence, to restore the church of Jesus Christ, Mormons believe there is a need for new revelation, new scripture, and a new priesthood, all of which are found in the church restored by Joseph Smith. Though Mormons accept that elements of truth are found in all religions, they also believe that they alone are the true Christians. Mormons do not consider themselves Protestants, but Christians in the most pure form as founded by Jesus. Some of the beliefs of Mormonism are:

apostasy

The abandonment of one's religion.

- Mormons believe that salvation is only possible within their church. In order to save ancestors, Mormons hold a type of baptism service that allows for the baptism of dead relatives of those already within the church.

- Mormons believe that Native Americans are one of the ten Lost Tribes of Israel.

- Though Mormons name the traditional Trinity, they do not believe that Jesus is God.

- As other **millenialists** do, the Church of Jesus Christ of Latter-day Saints teaches that Jesus will return to earth and set up a new Jerusalem in America and a 1000-year reign.

millenialists

People who believe that at his Second Coming, Jesus and his followers will rule on earth for one thousand years.

As Mormons hold that God's revelations did not stop with the last page of the Bible, neither do they cease with the Book of Mormon. The President (the name for the foremost Mormon leader) is seen as a prophet, no different from the biblical prophets. Mormon presidents succeeding Joseph Smith have received new revelations in the years since. For example, President Wilford Woodruff called for the end of the practice of polygamy at the end of the nineteenth century after receiving a revelation. In 1978, President Spencer Kimball received a revelation to allow males of African descent to be accepted to the Mormon priesthood. (Blacks had been denied priesthood because the church had claimed they were descendants of Cain, the murderer of his brother Abel.)

Besides the Book of Mormon, the *Pearl of Great Price* (writings and revelations of Joseph Smith) and *Doctrine and Covenants* (writings and revelations since the restoration in 1830) are considered sacred writings of the Mormon church.

The Mormon worship service is simple in nature. There are prayers, singing of hymns, listening to sermons delivered by lay people, and a celebration of the Lord's Supper using bread and water. Water is used instead of wine as Mormons are forbidden to use all drugs, including alcohol, tobacco, and caffeine.

Baptism by immersion happens at the age of eight or older. Proxies are baptized on behalf of dead ancestors. Mormons spend a great deal of time investigating and maintaining family genealogies in order to include relatives in this type of baptism.

The church is very involved in missionary work. It is common for young people around the age of twenty to participate in two years of missionary work, often in another country. About 50,000 people annually are engaged in missionary work.

> ➤ **Why do you think the Church of Jesus Christ of Latter-day Saints is one of the world's fastest-growing religions?**

The baptismal font at the St. Louis, Missouri, Church of Latter-day Saints. The font rests on the backs of twelve oxen representing the twelve tribes of Israel.

A Brief Look at Mormonism through a Catholic Lens

There is little common belief between Catholicism and the Church of Jesus Christ of Latter-day Saints. Most essentially, Catholics and other Christians believe that Jesus Christ is the Son of God, the Second Person of the Blessed Trinity. Mormons believe that Jesus was the first spirit born to heavenly parents. By not believing in the divinity of Christ, Mormons are essentially not Christians, but rather Mormons.

Catholics believe in one God who is a unity of Three Persons—Father, Son, and Holy Spirit. Mormons believe in three separate Gods in one Godhead and that Elohim and Jehovah are separate Gods.

Catholics do not believe in a baptism of the dead. While the Lord himself affirms Baptism is necessary for salvation, God "himself is not bound by his sacraments" (*CCC*, 1257).

Mormons believe that their church is the only true and living church. Rather, Catholics hold that the Church was founded by Christ and made manifest on the day of Pentecost.

While there are many differences between the two faiths, both Catholics and Mormons see evangelization as very important. Both are quite involved in missionary activities throughout the world. Both are also active in caring for the poor and disadvantaged. It is not unusual for Mormon communities to use the Catholic Relief Services to get food, money, and other material needs for people in need.

Finally, both Catholics and Mormons (and all people) are dependent on the grace and mercy of God for their life and salvation.

■ Church of Jesus Christ of Latter-day Saints Summary

- ■ The founder of the Church of Jesus Christ of Latter-day Saints is Joseph Smith, Jr. Members of the church are commonly called Mormons.

- ■ The church encountered much opposition and persecution and eventually settled in Salt Lake City, Utah.

- ■ The beliefs of the Church of Jesus Christ of Latter-day Saints both agree with and deviate from traditional Christian teachings.

- ■ Practices of the church include a simple worship service, baptism, baptism by proxy, and extensive missionary work.

- ■ Though Catholics and Mormons have little in common doctrinally, both take an active part in evangelization and missionary activities.

■ Church of Jesus Christ of Latter-Day Saints Review Questions

1. Where does the term "Mormon" come from?

2. Why is the Church of Jesus Christ of Latter-day Saints not considered a Protestant church?

3. Why were Mormons persecuted in Illinois?

4. Why do Mormons allow baptism by proxy of the dead?

5. What is one essential difference between Catholicism and Mormonism?

● Seventh-day Adventists

A Brief History

Adventist is the name for Christians who believe the Second Coming, or advent, of Jesus is imminent. The Seventh-day Adventist Church emerged from a nineteenth-century millennialist movement. Millennialism is the belief that at Jesus' Second Coming he would reign on earth for one thousand years.

William Miller (1782–1849) believed the Bible was very specific about when and how the Second Coming of Jesus would take place. Miller calculated that Jesus would return to earth in a physical form, and he also calculated a specific date. Miller gained a number of followers, calling themselves Adventists, who waited expectantly with him. When Jesus did not come, Miller recalculated the date for seven months later. When the Second Coming did not occur as expected for a second time, it was called the **Great Disappointment**, and many of his original followers left Miller. Some Adventists modified their teaching. They said that the Second Coming was to be preceded by an

Great Disappointment

The occasion when many Adventists left William Miller when Jesus failed to return after the second predicted time.

Investigative Judgment in which God would judge the living and the dead, pronounce the findings, and then execute judgment. Only after the Investigative Judgment was complete could Jesus return to earth and begin his 1,000 year reign. They did not set a date for the completion of the Investigative Judgment, but believed it was imminent.

Investigative Judgment

According to the Adventists, the time prior to the Second Coming when judgment will take place on the living and the dead.

The Seventh-day Adventist Church came from this movement and was officially formed in 1863. Ellen White, a follower of Miller, was considered a prophetess among the Seventh-day Adventists. She wrote a number of books and gave lectures throughout much of the nineteenth-century English-speaking world. The members of this church strictly followed the Bible for Sabbath and dietary laws, besides looking to the Bible for information about the Second Coming. As the Jewish Sabbath had been Saturday and early Christians also observed it, Saturday, the seventh day, was restored as the Sabbath. Seventh-day Adventists prohibited alcohol, nicotine, and caffeine use because of their harmful effects on the body, the temple of the Holy Spirit.

Beliefs and Practices

The Seventh-day Adventists believe the Bible is the sole source of authority for their members. However, their interpretation of the Bible deviates in many areas from most other Christians. For example, Seventh-day Adventists believe that Jesus' act of redemption was potentially for everyone, but was effective only for those who *truly* believe. They also hold that the righteous will be resurrected to heaven with the Second Coming of Jesus, but that the unrighteous will be annihilated in hell. Hence, they do not believe all souls are immortal.

Seventh-day Adventists are initiated through instruction and baptism by immersion. Saturday, the seventh day, is the day of worship. With regard to creation, Seventh-day Adventists deny the theory of evolution and take a literal approach to understanding the creation stories of the Bible.

Besides abstaining from alcohol, smoking, and caffeine, many Seventh-day Adventists are vegetarians. Some also abstain from dancing, theater-going, and any other activity deemed harmful to the soul. Ironically, though Ellen White played a significant role in the foundation of the Seventh-day Adventists, the church does not sanction the ordination of women.

➤ **Why do you think some Christians wish to forecast the exact date of Jesus' Second Coming?**

A Brief Look at Seventh-day Adventists through a Catholic Lens

Seventh-day Adventists agree with many Catholic doctrines and teachings, including belief in the Trinity, the divinity of Christ, the Virgin birth, the resurrection of the dead, and Christ's Second Coming. Also, their Baptism is valid. Seventh-day Adventists believe in the doctrine of Original Sin and also that a person's salvation is merited by both faith and good works.

However, Seventh-day Adventists hold many false teachings that are in opposition to Church teaching. For example, Catholics (and other Christians) disagree with Adventists who say that in not keeping Saturday as the Lord's Day, most Christians are breaking the covenant God made on Mount Sinai. Christians celebrate Sunday as the fulfillment of the Sabbath, for that is the day that Christ rose from the dead. St. Justin the Martyr wrote:

> We all gather on the day of the sun, for it is the first day [after the Jewish Sabbath, but also the first day] when God, separating matter from darkness, made the world; and on the same day Jesus Christ our Savior rose from the dead.[12]

All Christians believe in the Second Coming of Jesus and Catholics are no exception. At every Mass Catholics proclaim that "Christ will come again." As part of the Adventist belief in the Second Coming, they hold that the unrighteous will be completely destroyed in the fires of hell. In advocating this destruction, they are saying that not all souls are immortal. Catholics believe that every human possesses an immortal soul (see CCC, 366) and that each person "receives his eternal recompense in his immortal soul from the moment of his death" (CCC, 1022).

■ Seventh-day Adventist Summary

- The Seventh-day Adventist Church is an outgrowth of the Adventist movement of the nineteenth century in the United States.

- The Seventh-day Adventists believe the Second Coming will be preceded by an Investigative Judgment.

- Saturday is the Sabbath for Seventh-day Adventists.

- Seventh-day Adventists agree with Catholic teaching on several important doctrines, including belief in the Trinity and the divinity of Christ.

■ Seventh-day Adventist Review Questions

1. Summarize the origins of the Adventist movement.

2. What was the Great Disappointment?

3. Why do Seventh-day Adventists worship on Saturday rather than Sunday?

4. Why does the Catholic Church hold that Sunday is the proper day of worship?

● Watchtower Bible and Tract Society

A Brief History

Charles Russell (1852–1916) officially founded the Jehovah's Witnesses, then known as Zion's Watchtower Bible and Tract Society, in Pennsylvania in 1884. Russell had been studying with other Bible students attempting to pinpoint the Second

Coming of Jesus. He named the fall of 1914 as the time when Jesus would establish his invisible reign in heaven and expel Satan to earth. Then the battle of Armageddon between Satan and Jesus would begin on earth. When the battle did not begin, other dates were set, but no battle of Armageddon has taken place.

Russell was succeeded by Joseph Rutherford (1869–1942). Rutherford gave further shape to the Society by centralizing it, moving the headquarters to Brooklyn, New York, and refining the missionary work of the followers. Russell had been more democratic in his leadership, but Rutherford believed that the establishment of Jesus' invisible reign was a **theocracy**, and the Society must be ready for Jesus' rule. Rutherford adopted the name Jehovah's Witnesses to emphasize Jehovah (another name for Yahweh), the God of the Hebrew Scriptures, as the one true God. Those who witnessed in the name of Jehovah were the true followers of the one God. Nathan Knorr (1905–1977), the next president, expanded the publication of Jehovah's Witnesses materials, translated a Bible used by all Jehovah's Witnesses (known as the *New World Translation of Holy Scriptures*), and established the Watchtower Bible School of Gilead in New York for the training of leaders.

theocracy
A government that is ruled by God or by one who is divinely inspired.

Presently Jehovah's Witnesses can be found throughout the world. However, they do not always find a welcome, for their allegiance is not to any government but only to God's theocracy. Their various forms of publications are translated into numerous languages for worldwide distribution. In Europe, their affiliated group is known as the International Bible Students Association.

Beliefs and Practices

Many of the beliefs of Jehovah's Witnesses are not unlike traditional Christian beliefs. Jehovah's Witnesses believe the Bible is the word of God and the sole source of religious and moral authority. They believe that Jesus is the Son of God, born of a virgin, and the reconciler of humankind to God.

However, there are interpretations of the Bible and even translations that traditional Christians cannot accept as orthodox Christian beliefs. Christian biblical scholars reject the *New World Translation of the Holy Scriptures* as defective, citing that the sources of the translation are not the original Hebrew and Greek biblical texts and that the translation is bent to reflect the teachings of the Society.

Jehovah's Witnesses believe that they are the true Christians in the image of the primitive church and that salvation only comes through the beliefs and works of the Society. Jehovah's Witnesses hold that all others who claim to be Christians are false Christians, and all others are pagans.

Jehovah's Witnesses do not acknowledge the Holy Trinity. Though they hold that Jesus is the Son of God, they believe he is not God, but subject to God. Before his earthly birth, Jesus is believed to have been the Archangel Michael. Nor do the Jehovah's Witnesses believe that the Holy Spirit is God, but instead is merely a way to explain how Jehovah is present to and connects with creation.

Jesus' crucifixion and resurrection are explained in a spiritual sense. Jehovah's Witnesses do not believe Jesus was crucified on a cross. Neither do they believe in Jesus' bodily resurrection. They understand the Greek word for cross to mean one piece of timber, like a stake or a pole. There was no crossbeam. Since the cross or crucifix was not used as a symbol by the earliest Christians, Jehovah's Witnesses think of them as pagan symbols.

At Armageddon, Jesus will be victorious over Satan, the earth will be purified, and Jesus will set up a theocracy. In the meantime, Satan is on earth using everything at his disposal to win the battle. In particular, secular governments and all the world's religions are instruments of Satan. Hence, Jehovah's Witnesses pledge no allegiance to any government but Jehovah's. They do not salute a flag, serve in public office or military service, nor do they vote in public elections. In fact, children of Jehovah's Witnesses who attend public schools are not allowed to celebrate Halloween, Christmas, or any other holiday. In time of war, Jehovah's Witnesses are conscientious objectors.

Jehovah's Witnesses do not believe in a hell that is eternal damnation. When a person dies, the soul dies. At the time of the resurrection of the righteous, Jehovah will create a new, perfect body and reinstate the soul of the person.

Jehovah's Witnesses have great reverence for the Bible. They read and study it on a regular basis. Bible study generally takes place in people's homes.

Besides the Bible, the *Watchtower* and *Awake* are two semi-monthly periodicals that are very important to Society members. A common practice is to distribute these and other literature door-to-door and on street corners.

The place of worship for Jehovah's Witnesses is a Kingdom Hall, where the congregation is known as the "company." There is no day of rest, for every day is holy. Rather than times of worship, Jehovah's Witnesses have various kinds of meetings each week where there are talks on topics found in a recent Watchtower or training for various ministries, especially witnessing door to door.

Hundreds of Jehovah's Witnesses from Michigan, Ohio, and Indiana to take part in a "Quick-Build Kingdom Hall Project," where a new Kingdom Hall is built by volunteers in three days. Since 1983, thousands of new kingdom halls have been built this way nationwide.

The average member of the Society, who attends meetings during the week and goes door to door as much as possible, usually on Saturdays, is known as a publisher. Each person has a neighborhood for which he or she is responsible while each Kingdom Hall is responsible for a geographical area containing several neighborhoods.

The only day celebrated by Jehovah's Witnesses is the Memorial of Christ's Death, because Christ's command to do so is in the Bible. Neither Christmas nor Easter are celebrated because Jehovah did not command it: the first Christians did not celebrate those days, and since they *are* celebrated by other "false" Christians and pagans, they must be pagan feasts. Jehovah's Witnesses do not celebrate individual birthdays for the same reasons.

A controversial belief of Jehovah's Witnesses is the prohibition of blood transfusions, as blood transfusions are interpreted as "eating blood," something forbidden by Jehovah. The controversy often becomes heated when a child is in need of a blood transfusion and the parents refuse. The Child Protection Agency sometimes attempts to override the parents' decision through legal means.

All the Jehovah's Witnesses' teaching and practice is with one goal in mind: to establish a theocracy on earth. Jehovah's Witnesses hope to purify the earth of all evil before Christ sets up his earthly kingdom.

➤ In your opinion, have Christian holidays become too secularized?

A Brief Look at Jehovah's Witnesses through a Catholic Lens

As outlined above, there are many clear differences between the beliefs of Jehovah's Witnesses and Catholic belief.

One of the most central differences is the Jehovah's Witnesses' understanding of Christ's divinity. Witnesses believe that though Christ is God's Son, he is inferior to God the Father and created by him. Witnesses think that the title of Christ as "first born" of God's creation implies that he succeeded from God and is inferior to him. Rather, there was no time that the Son did not exist (see John 1:1–3). Jesus Christ is begotten, not made. He is equal to the Father. He is both God and man.

Jehovah's Witnesses use the Bible to support their beliefs. There are two problems with their approach. First, like some other Christians, they are apt to quote passages out of context, using only those passages that support their beliefs while ignoring other passages that contradict their beliefs. Also, the Jehovah's Witnesses use their own translation of the Bible, the *New World Translation*, which is regarded by many impartial theologians as a translation without scholarly care and thus highly inaccurate.

■ Watchtower Bible and Tract Society Summary

■ Charles Russell began the Watchtower Bible and Tract Society with the purpose of informing people about the Second Coming of Jesus, which he said would occur in 1914.

■ Joseph Rutherford succeeded Russell and coined the term "Jehovah's Witnesses."

■ Jehovah's Witnesses believe that Satan rules the present age on earth.

■ The Jehovah's Witnesses have no special day for worship and do not celebrate holidays such as Christmas and Easter, nor do they celebrate birthdays.

■ Jehovah's Witnesses use their own translation of the Bible as authoritative. Impartial biblical scholars find the translation problematic.

■ Watchtower Bible and Tract Society Review Questions

1. What is the significance of the name "Jehovah's Witness"?

2. What is the goal of Jehovah's Witnesses' teaching and practice?

3. Why do Jehovah's Witnesses not celebrate holidays and birthdays?

The Church of Christ, Scientist

A Brief History

Mary Baker Eddy (1821–1910) of Massachusetts founded the Church of Christ, Scientist in 1879. It is commonly known as Christian Science.

A historic display at the opening celebration of The Mary Baker Eddy Library in Boston.

Eddy was raised in a strict Congregationalist home where she grew to love the Christian Bible. She was ill much of her childhood and early adulthood and sought various methods of healing, both conventional and non-conventional. When she was in her forties, she fell on an icy sidewalk and severely injured herself. On reading one of Jesus' miracles from the Bible, she suddenly realized that sickness and suffering are merely illusions and can be overcome by right thinking. She believed that the discovery of this right mind, the mind of God, allowed her to be instantly healed. She spent several years intensely studying the Bible to learn precisely what her discovery meant. Her book, *Science and Health*, which she revised several times, forms the doctrine of the Christian Science religion.

Eddy settled the first Church of Christ, Scientist in Boston where it still exists today. The church expanded rather rapidly during the first half of the twentieth century before membership leveled off. Though self-governing, the *Manual of the Mother Church*, written by Mary Baker Eddy, sets guidelines for the individual churches. There are also Christian Science churches throughout the world, mostly in predominantly Protestant countries.

Beliefs and Practices

Through her vigorous study of the Bible, Mary Baker Eddy came to believe that the teachings of Jesus, especially those with regard to healing, had been lost over the centuries. It was her intention to recapture such teachings for her generation. Eddy considered both the Bible and Science and Health equally authoritative texts.

God is not a masculine God to Christian Science, but a Father-Mother who is both strong and compassionate. Christian Scientists deny Jesus as God, though they do believe Jesus is the Son of God. What is distinctive about Christian Scientists is their belief that physical healing is through spiritual means alone. By discovering the truth, that is, God, Christian Scientists believe that people can be both healthy and happy. Though the effects of evil—suffering and death—may seem to exist, they are actually illusions a person can rid himself or herself of as he or she forms a union with God. Prayer is the form of treatment for physical ills. Christian Scientists pray to possess the Mind of Christ so that through the healing of the mind and heart, the physical is also healed.

When a person needs healing, he or she turns to a registered practitioner. The church authorizes and pays these practitioners to devote their full time employment to assisting the healing of other church members through prayer. These practitioners are not intercessors. Only God heals through God's laws, so the practitioner prays with the member for guidance. They are paid for their services.

Contrary to popular belief, Christian Scientists do not excommunicate members of their church for seeking medical advice. They encourage their members to adhere to public health laws, including immunization requirements. They also seek medical help for baby deliveries. They visit dentists and eye doctors as well.

Though Christian Science does not have a creed *per se*, there are six tenets outlined in *Science and Health*:

1. As adherents of Truth, we take the inspired Word of the Bible as our sufficient guide to eternal Life.

2. We acknowledge and adore one supreme and infinite God. We acknowledge his Son, one Christ; the Holy Ghost or divine Comforter; and man in God's image and likeness.

3. We acknowledge God's forgiveness of sin in the destruction of sin and the spiritual understanding that casts out evil as unreal. But the belief in sin is punished so long as the belief lasts.

4. We acknowledge Jesus' atonement as the evidence of divine, efficacious Love, unfolding man's unity with God through Christ Jesus the Way-shower; and we acknowledge that man is saved through Christ, through Truth, Life, and Love as demonstrated by the Galilean Prophet in healing the sick and overcoming sin and death.

5. We acknowledge that the crucifixion of Jesus and his resurrection served to uplift faith to understand eternal Life, even the allness of Soul and Spirit and the nothingness of matter.

6. And we solemnly promise to watch and pray for that Mind to be in us which was also in Christ Jesus; to do unto others as we would have them do unto us; and to be merciful, just, and pure.

The presence of Christian Science Reading Rooms near every Christian Science church highlights the importance placed on study. The public is welcomed into Christian Science Reading Rooms to find out more about the religion. Always available there is the Lesson-Sermon from the Mother Church for the week taken from the "pastor of the church," that is, the combination of the Bible and *Science and Health*. The lessons comprise the sermon that will be read at every Christian Science Church worldwide on Sundays. There are twenty-six rotating subjects. The two readers for a particular Sunday are chosen from the congregation. Sunday service is quite simple. The chosen readers read from the Bible, *Science and Health*, and the Lesson-Sermon from the Mother Church. There may also be testimonials on healing.

A Brief Look at Christian Science through a Catholic Lens

Christian Science denies most essential Catholic dogma and doctrine, including the existence of a Creator God, the divinity of Christ, the Redemption, free will, Original Sin and Actual Sin, the existence of Magisterial teaching, the sacraments, and the necessity of faith, grace, prayer, the resurrection of the body, angels, demons, and both eternal rewards and punishments.

As to the healings taught and claimed by Christian Science, they are to be separated from the gift of miracles that was given to the Apostles (see Mark 16:17–18). The gift of healing is not intended to be a regular part of Christ's gift of priesthood, for physical healing is not essential to a person's salvation. Rather, the Church believes that God himself heals physically and spiritually at his pleasure and often through the **Sacrament of the Anointing of the Sick**. While Christian Scientists find suffering illusive, Catholics find it redemptive. It is through suffering that we share in the suffering of Christ. As we share in Christ's suffering, we also share in his resurrection.

Sacrament of the Anointing of the Sick

A sacrament of healing in which the healing and loving touch of Christ is extended through the Church to those who are seriously ill or dying.

➤ **What do you think is the connection between physical health and spiritual health?**

■ Church of Christ, Scientist Summary

- ■ Mary Baker Eddy founded the Church of Christ, Scientist, commonly known as Christian Science, in 1879.

- ■ Mary Baker Eddy believed physical healing took place through spiritual laws, not natural laws.

- ■ The two main scriptures of the Christian Scientists—the Bible and Eddy's book *Science and Health*—are known as the "pastor of the church."

- ■ Though the various branches of Christian Science churches are autonomous, they are still to abide by the guidelines stated in the *Manual of the Mother Church* written by Mary Baker Eddy.

- ■ Catholics hold that physical healing is not essential to one's salvation; on the contrary, as Jesus demonstrates, suffering can be redemptive.

■ Church of Christ, Scientist Review Questions

- ■ What did Mary Baker Eddy discover about healing?

- ■ Why is it incorrect to say Christian Scientists are hostile to the medical profession?

- ■ What is the role of registered practitioners?

- ■ Name a Christian Scientist belief that contradicts Catholic doctrine.

Unitarian Universalists

A Brief History

The Unitarian Universalist Association is a consolidation of the Universalist Church of America and the American Unitarian Association. These groups merged in 1961. Groups associated with these movements are commonly called the Unitarian Church.

Unitarians do not consider themselves a Christian church. They believe that spiritual wisdom can be found in all the religions of the world. In its origins, the Universalist movement advocated a belief that all will be saved and no one will suffer eternal damnation.

Some very famous Americans have been a part of the Unitarian Universalists, including John Adams, Ralph Waldo Emerson, Clara Barton, and Susan B. Anthony (at right, top to bottom).

Headquarters for the Unitarian Church in the United States are in Boston, but there is no central governmental control over many congregations. Each congregation is autonomous in all matters of government, finance, and communal religious practices. On the international level, the Unitarian Universalist Association is connected with religious groups through the International Association for Religious Freedom.

The Unitarian Universalist Association has no formal creed, though it does address a statement of principles (see pages 382–383). Unitarians are encouraged to form their own beliefs and moral judgments based on experience, science, and reason. Ultimate authority is within the individual. Unitarians believe that wisdom can be found in all the religions of the world, and they themselves have no sacred text, for they believe that the various sacred texts of the world contain much wisdom and guidance.

➤ **What would it be like being a part of a religion with no formal creed?**

Unitarian Universalist Statement of Principles and Purposes

We, the member congregations of the Unitarian Universalist Association, covenant to affirm and promote:

- The inherent worth and dignity of every person.

- Justice, equity, and compassion in human relations.

- Acceptance of one another and encouragement to spiritual growth in our congregations.

- A free and responsible search for truth and meaning.

- The right of conscience and the use of the democratic process within our congregations and in society at large.

- The goal of world community with peace, liberty, and justice for all.

- Respect for the interdependent web of all existence of which we are a part.

The living tradition which we share draws from many sources:

- Direct experience of that transcending mystery and wonder, affirmed in all cultures, which moves us to a renewal of the spirit and an openness to the forces that create and uphold life.

- Words and deeds of prophetic women and men which challenge us to confront powers and structures of evil with justice, compassion, and the transforming power of love.

- Wisdom from the world's religions which inspire us in our ethical and spiritual life.

- Jewish and Christian teachings which call us to respond to God's love by loving our neighbors as ourselves.

- Humanist teachings which counsel us to heed the guidance of reason and the results of science, and warn us against idolatries of the mind and spirit.

- Spiritual teachings of earth-centered traditions which celebrate the sacred circle of life and instruct us to live in harmony with the rhythms of nature.

Grateful for the religious pluralism which enriches and ennobles our faith, we are inspired to deepen our understanding and expand our vision. As free congregations we enter into this covenant, promising to one another our mutual trust and support.

The religious practices of Unitarian Universalists vary from congregation to congregation, though most have regular weekly worship. Some call themselves a society or fellowship rather than a congregation. Unitarian Universalists draw from various sources for their communal worship: the Judeo-Christian heritage, other major world religions, earth-centered religions such as Native American, humanism, prophetic men and women, and direct experience.

Unitarian Universalists through a Catholic Lens

Unitarians typically do not believe in the divinity of Christ or the doctrine of the Holy Trinity. Unitarians put into practice the message of love and service to the poor expressed in their principles and purposes and by Jesus, especially in the **Beatitudes**.

However, there are few other doctrinal agreements between Unitarians and Catholics. One reason for this, is that Unitarians have no formal doctrine of beliefs.

Beatitudes

Meaning "supreme happiness," the eight Beatitudes preached by Jesus in the Sermon on the Mount respond to our natural desire for happiness.

384

Exploring the Religions of Our World

■ Unitarian Universalist Summary

■ The Unitarian church began in the nineteenth century. It is not a Christian church.

■ Unitarians believe religious and moral authority come from the individual.

■ Unitarians draw inspiration and teaching from various traditions.

■ Several social principles of Unitarians are in agreement with Catholic Christianity.

■ Unitarian Church Review Questions

1. Why are Unitarians not considered a Christian church?
2. What are some sources Unitarians draw on for worship?

Research & Activities

1. Research the life of one of the following and write an essay on the influence of Unitarianism on his or her life: John Adams, Ralph Waldo Emerson, Clara Barton, or Susan B. Anthony.

2. Research the effects the Seventh-day Adventist Church had on the work of John Kellogg.

3. Investigate the connection between the Branch Davidians and the Seventh-Day Adventists.

4. Listen to some music of the Mormon Tabernacle Choir. Research the choir's history and mission.

5. Interview a member of one of the religions discussed in this appendix and write a report based on the interview.

Catholic Handbook for Faith

The information in this Catholic Handbook for Faith provides a further Catholic portrait of the main sections of the text: History, Scripture, Beliefs and Practices, Sacred Time, and Sacred Places and Spaces.

● A. History

Timeline of Church History

ca. 6–4 BC	Jesus is born
ca. 30–33 AD	Pentecost
ca. 50	The Council of Jerusalem (Gentiles can be admitted to the Church)
ca. 64	Persecutions of Christians begin under Roman emperor Nero
ca. 64 or 67	Peter and Paul are martyred in Rome
ca. 70	Temple destroyed
ca. 100	Death of St. John the Evangelist; apostolic era ends
311	Emperor Constantine ends persecution of Christians
313	Edict of Milan
325	Council of Nicaea (Arian heresy refuted; Nicene Creed composed)
381	First Council of Constantinople (Nicene Creed expanded; divine nature of Holy Spirit defined)
410	Rome invaded by Visigoths
431	Council of Ephesus (refutes Nestorianism; states that Mary is the Mother of God)
432	St. Patrick begins missionary work in Ireland
451	Council of Chalcedon defends the two natures of Christ
476	Roman Empire in West collapses
529	St. Benedict founds order of monks, the Benedictines
590	St. Gregory the Great becomes Pope
722	St. Boniface evangelizes the Germanic people
800	Pope Leo III crowns Charlemagne Roman emperor
1054	Final schism between the Eastern and Western churches which remains to today
1073	Pope St. Gregory VII begins reforms of the Church

1095	Pope Urban III calls First Crusade to free Holy Land from Muslims
1170	St. Thomas Becket murdered in Canterbury Cathedral
1209	St. Francis of Assisi founds Franciscan order
1215	St. Dominic founds Dominican order of preachers
1378	The Great Schism in the Church begins (lasts until 1417) with the Pope residing in France and two or three men claiming to be Pope
1431	St. Joan of Arc is executed
1517	Martin Luther posts ninety-five theses beginning the Protestant Reformation
1533	King Henry VIII is excommunicated, leading to the start of the Anglican Church
1540	St. Ignatius of Loyola founds Society of Jesus (Jesuits) to assist in reform of the church
1545	Council of Trent begins (lasts until 1563) that advances the Catholic Reformation
1642	Jesuits evangelizing the Native Americans are martyred (through 1647)
1769	The first of twenty-one California missions are founded (most by Junipero Serra)
1789	John Carroll is appointed first bishop of the United States
1820	Beginning of swell of nine million Catholic immigrants to the United States (through 1920s)

1869	The First Vatican Council convenes (through 1870)
1891	Pope Leo XII writes the encyclical *Rerum Novarum*, the first of the Church's body of social teaching doctrine
1903	Beginning of pontificate of St. Pius X (through 1914)
1917	Apparitions of Our Lady of Fatima
1962	The Second Vatican Council convenes (through 1965)
1978	Beginning of pontificate of Pope John Paul II
1994	Vatican and state of Israel establish formal relations
2005	Pope John Paul II dies; Joseph Ratzinger elected Pope Benedict XVI

● B. Sacred Scripture

Canon of the Bible

There are seventy-three books in the canon of the Bible, that is, the official list of books the Church accepts as divinely inspired writings: forty-six Old Testament books and twenty-seven New Testament books. "Protestant Bibles" do not include seven Old Testament books (1 and 2 Maccabees, Judith, Tobit, Baruch, Sirach, and the Wisdom of Solomon). Why the difference? Catholics rely on the version of the Bible that the earliest Christians used, the *Septuagint*. This was the first Greek translation of the Hebrew scriptures begun in the third century BC. Protestants, on the other hand, rely on an official list of Hebrew scriptures compiled in the Holy Land by Jewish scholars at the end of the first century AD. Today, most Protestant Bibles print the disputed books in a separate section at the back of the Bible BC, called the *Apocrypha*.

There are forty-six books in the Old Testament canon. The Old Testament is the foundation for God's self-revelation in Christ. Christians honor the Old Testament as God's word. It contains the writings of prophets and other inspired authors who recorded God's teaching to the Chosen People and his interaction in their history. For example, the Old Testament recounts how God delivered the Jews from Egypt (the Exodus), led them to the Promised Land, formed them into a nation under his care, and taught them in knowledge and worship.

The stories, prayers, sacred histories, and other writings of the Old Testament reveal what God is like and tell much about human nature, too. In brief, the Chosen People sinned repeatedly by turning their backs on their loving God; they were weak and easily tempted away from God. Yahweh, on the other hand, *always* remained faithful. He promised to send a Messiah to humanity.

Listed below are the categories and books of the Old Testament:

The Old Testament

The Pentateuch

Genesis	Gn
Exodus	Ex
Leviticus	Lv
Numbers	Nm
Deuteronomy	Dt

The Historical Books

Joshua	Jos
Judges	Jgs
Ruth	Ru
1 Samuel	1 Sm
2 Samuel	2 Sm
1 Kings	1 Kgs
2 Kings	2 Kgs
1 Chronicles	1 Chr
2 Chronicles	2 Chr
Ezra	Ezr
Nehemiah	Neh
Tobit	Tb
Judith	Jdt
Esther	Est
1 Maccabees	1 Mc
2 Maccabees	2 Mc

The Wisdom Books

Job	Jb
Psalms	Ps(s)
Proverbs	Prv
Ecclesiastes	Eccl
Song of Songs	Sg
Wisdom	Wis
Sirach	Sir

The Prophetic Books

Isaiah	Is
Jeremiah	Jer
Lamentations	Lam
Baruch	Bar
Ezekiel	Ez
Daniel	Dn
Hosea	Hos
Joel	Jl
Amos	Am
Obadiah	Ob
Jonah	Jon
Micah	Mi
Nahum	Na
Habakkuk	Hb
Zephaniah	Zep
Haggai	Hg
Zechariah	Zec
Malachi	Mal

The New Testament

The Gospels

Matthew	Mt
Mark	Mk
Luke	Lk
John	Jn

Acts of the Apostles	Acts

The New Testament Letters

Romans	Rom
1 Corinthians	1 Cor
2 Corinthians	2 Cor
Galatians	Gal
Ephesians	Eph
Philippians	Phil
Colossians	Col
1 Thessalonians	1 Thes
2 Thessalonians	2 Thes
1 Timothy	1 Tm
2 Timothy	2 Tm
Titus	Ti
Philemon	Phlm
Hebrews	Heb

The Catholic Letters

James	Jas
1 Peter	1 Pt
2 Peter	2 Pt
1 John	1 Jn
2 John	2 Jn
3 John	3 Jn
Jude	Jude

Revelation	Rv

● C. Beliefs and Practices

Apostles' Creed

I believe in God, the Father almighty,
Creator of heaven and earth.

I believe in Jesus Christ, his only son,
    our Lord.
He was conceived by the power of the
    Holy Spirit,
and born of the Virgin Mary.
He suffered under Pontius Pilate,
was crucified, died, and was buried.
He descended into hell.
On the third day he rose again.
He ascended into heaven,
and is seated at the right hand of the Father.
He will come again to judge the living and
    the dead.

I believe in the Holy Spirit,
the holy catholic Church,
the communion of saints,
the forgiveness of sins,
the resurrection of the body,
and the life everlasting. Amen.

The Ten Commandments

The Ten Commandments are a main source for Christian morality. The Ten Commandments were revealed by God to Moses. Jesus, himself, acknowledged them. He told the rich young man, "If you wish to enter into life, keep the commandments" (Mt 19:17). Since the time of St. Augustine (fourth century) the Ten Commandments have been used as a source for teaching baptismal candidates.

I.   I, the Lord am your God: you shall not have other gods besides me.

II.   You shall not take the name of the Lord, your God, in vain.

III.   Remember to keep holy the sabbath day.

IV.   Honor your father and your mother.

V.   You shall not kill.

VI.   You shall not commit adultery.

VII.   You shall not steal.

VIII.   You shall not bear false witness against your neighbor.

IX.   You shall not covet your neighbor's wife.

X.   You shall not covet your neighbor's goods.

The Beatitudes

The word *beatitude* means "happiness". Jesus preached the Beatitudes in his Sermon on the Mount. They are:

Blessed are the poor in spirit, for theirs is the kingdom of God.

Blessed are they who mourn, for they will be comforted.

Blessed are the meek, for they will inherit the land.

Blessed are they who hunger and thirst for righteousness, for they will be satisfied.

Blessed are the merciful, for they will be shown mercy.

Blessed are the clean of heart, for they will see God.

Blessed are the peacemakers, for they will be called children of God.

Blessed are they who are persecuted for the sake of righteousness, for theirs is the kingdom of heaven.

Cardinal Virtues

Habits that help in leading a moral life that are acquired by human effort are known as moral or human virtues. Four of these are the *cardinal virtues* as they form the hinge that connect all the others. They are:

Prudence	Justice
Fortitude	Temperance

Theological Virtues

The theological virtues are the foundation for moral life. They are related directly to God.

Faith   Hope   Love

Corporal (Bodily) Works of Mercy

1. Feed the hungry.
2. Give drink to the thirsty.
3. Clothe the naked.
4. Visit the imprisoned.
5. Shelter the homeless.
6. Visit the sick.
7. Bury the dead.

Spiritual Works of Mercy

1. Counsel the doubtful.
2. Instruct the ignorant.
3. Admonish sinners.
4. Comfort the afflicted.
5. Forgive offenses.
6. Bear wrongs patiently.
7. Pray for the living and the dead.

Precepts of the Church

1. You shall attend Mass on Sundays and on holy days of obligation and rest from servile labor.
2. You shall confess your sins at least once a year.
3. You shall receive the sacrament of Eucharist at least during the Easter season.
4. You shall observe the days of fasting and abstinence established by the Church.
5. You shall help to provide for the needs of the Church.

D. Sacred Time

Church Year

The cycle of seasons and feasts that Catholics celebrate is called the Church Year or Liturgical Year. The Church Year is divided into five main parts: Advent, Christmas, Lent, Easter, and Ordinary Time.

Holy Days of Obligation in the United States

1. Immaculate Conception of Mary
   December 8
2. Christmas
   December 25
3. Solemnity of Mary, Mother of God
   January 1
4. Ascension of the Lord
   Forty days after Easter
5. Assumption of Mary
   August 15
6. All Saints Day
   November 1

The Seven Sacraments

1. Baptism
2. Confirmation
3. Eucharist
4. Penance and Reconciliation
5. Anointing of the Sick
6. Holy Orders
7. Matrimony

E. Sacred Places and Spaces

Patron Saints

A patron is a saint who is designated for places (nations, regions, dioceses) or organizations. Many saints have also become patrons of jobs, professional groups, and intercessors for special needs. Listed below are patron saints for several nations:

Americas	Our Lady of Guadalupe, St. Rose of Lima
Argentina	Our Lady of Lujan
Australia	Our Lady Help of Christians
Canada	St. Joseph, St. Anne
China	St. Joseph
England	St. George
Finland	St. Henry
France	Our Lady of the Assumption, St. Joan of Arc, St. Thérèse of Lisieux
Germany	St. Boniface
India	Our Lady of the Assumption
Ireland	St. Patrick, St. Brigid, St. Columba
Italy	St. Francis of Assisi, St. Catherine of Siena
Japan	St. Peter
Mexico	Our Lady of Guadalupe
New Zealand	Our Lady of Help Christians
Poland	St. Casmir, St. Stanislaus, Our Lady of Czestochowa
Russia	St. Andrew, St. Nicholas of Myra, St. Thérèse of Lisieux
Scotland	St. Andrew, St. Columba
Spain	St. James, St. Teresa of Ávila
United States	Immaculate Conception of Mary

Glossary

adan—In Islam, the "call to prayer."

Allah—The Arabic word for God.

anatma—The Buddhist doctrine of "no soul" or "not self" that means a permanent, unchanging, independent self does not exist, though people act as if it does. Ignorance of anatma causes suffering.

ancestor veneration—A religious practice based on the belief that deceased family members are still living and that they have an interest in family affairs and can influence the fates of family members. Ancestor veneration refers to various ways of showing respect and reverence for family ancestors after their deaths. Family members bring offerings to their ancestors in order to obtain protection and guidance.

apocalyptic—A prophetic or symbolic revelation of the end of the world. These were written in a number of Jewish and Christian texts from around the second century BC to the second century AD.

apostasy—The abandonment of one's religion.

Apostles—The word Apostle means "one who has been sent." Originally it referred to the Twelve whom Jesus chose to help him in his earthly ministry. The successors of the twelve Apostles are the bishops of the Catholic Church.

arhat—From the Sanskrit for "worthy one," it is a concept of Theravada Buddhism which refers to one who has attained Nirvana in their present lifetime and is thus liberated from the cycle of rebirth.

Ark—A repository traditionally in or against the wall of a synagogue for the scrolls of the Torah.

ascetic—A person who renounces material comforts to live a self-disciplined life, especially in the area of religious devotion.

atman—In Hinduism, the individual soul or essence.

avatar—The incarnation of a Hindu god, especially Vishnu, in human or animal form. According to Hindu belief, Vishnu has been incarnated nine times. The tenth time will usher in the end of the world.

Beatitudes—Meaning "supreme happiness," the eight Beatitudes preached by Jesus in the Sermon on the Mount respond to our natural desire for happiness.

bhakti—In Hinduism, the devotional way of achieving moksha, emphasizing the loving faith of a devotee for the gods. It is open to all persons regardless of gender or caste.

bimah—The elevated platform in a Jewish synagogue where the person reading aloud from the Torah stands during the service.

blasphemy—Any word or deed that defames that which is considered sacred by a group of people. In Christianity, it is any thought, word, or act that expresses hatred for God, Christ, the Church, saints, or other holy things.

bodhi tree—The large, sacred fig tree at the Mahabodhi Temple at Bodh Gaya where Siddhartha the Buddha arrived at enlightenment.

bodhisattva—A being that compassionately refrains from entering Nirvana in order to save others and is worshipped as a deity in Mahayana Buddhism.

Brahman—In Hinduism, Ultimate Reality or Absolute Reality.

Brahmins—Hindu priests. The term is also used to describe the highest social class in the Hindu caste system.

bronze mirror—When the Japanese sun goddess Amaterasu fled to a cave because of the violent attacks of her brother Susanoo, and while the world was plunged into darkness, it was only when a bronze mirror was hung outside the cave that Amaterasu was a ray of light able to escape the cave and light the world.

butsudan—In Japanese households, the Buddhist family altar; historically, it was maintained in addition to the kamidana. It generally contains memorial tablets for dead ancestors.

caliphs—Islamic leaders regarded as successors of Muhammad for Sunni Muslims.

canon—For Catholics, the twenty-seven New Testament books and forty-six Old Testament books that are accepted as inspired books by the Church.

caste system—The social class system that is prevalent in Hindu India.

Chinese Rites Controversy—A dispute within the Church about whether or not Chinese folk religion rites and offerings to their ancestors constituted idolatry. The Jesuits believed the rites were compatible with Catholicism; the Dominicans did not. Pope Clement XI decided in favor of the Dominicans, but his teaching was relaxed in the twentieth century to allow for some participation by Catholics in those rites.

chun-tzu—According to Confucius, a person who lives by the ideal of jen and is neither petty, arrogant, mean-spirited, nor vengeful.

Church Fathers—Church teachers and writers of the early centuries whose teachings are a witness to the Tradition of the Church.

communion of saints—The term refers to the unity of all those living on earth (the pilgrim Church), those being purified in purgatory (the Church suffering), and those enjoying the blessings of heaven (the Church in glory).

council—The gathering of all bishops in the world in their exercise of authority over the universal Church. A council is usually called by the pope.

covenant—A binding and solemn agreement between human beings or between God and his people, holding each to a particular course of action.

Crusades—A series of military expeditions by Western Christians in the eleventh through thirteenth centuries designed to take the Holy Land back from the Muslims.

cult—Any external religious practice, observance, or devotion surrounding a deity, holy person, or religious object of a particular religious tradition.

Dalai Lama—The head lama of Tibetan Buddhism. He was the spiritual and political leader of Tibet until its takeover by Chinese communist leaders and a forced exile to India.

Dead Sea Scrolls—Between 1947 and 1956 thousands of fragments of biblical and early Jewish documents were discovered in eleven caves near the site of Khirbet Qumran on the shores of the Dead Sea. These important texts have revolutionized our understanding of the way the Bible was trasmitted and have illuminated the gerneral cultural and religious background of ancient Palestine, out of which both Rabbinic Judaism and Chritianity arose.

denominations—A religious organization whose congregations are united in their adherence to its beliefs and practices.

devas—From the Sanskrit for "sitting one." they are celestial beings in the Hindu tradition.

Dharma—From the Sanskrit, meaning "uphold," in Hinduism it is that which is in accordance with the laws of the cosmos and of nature such as righteous acts. In Buddhism it is the teachings of the Buddha.

divination—The attempt to ascertain knowledge by the interpretation of omens or supernatural events such as the use of spiritual practices like Tarot card reading or the casting of bones.

doctrines—Principles, beliefs, and teachings of a religion.

ecumenism—The movement, inspired and led by the Holy Spirit, that seeks the union of all Christian faiths and eventually the unity of all peoples throughout the world.

evangelization—From the root word for Gospel, the "sharing of the Good News."

feast days—Days that are celebrated with special liturgies in commemoration of the sacred mysteries and events tied to our redemption, or to honor Mary, the Apostles, martyrs, or saints.

feng-shui—The practice of positioning objects—especially gravesites, buildings, and furniture—to achieve positive effects based on belief in yin and yang and the flow of chi.

Five Classics—The collection of five ancient Chinese books used by Confucianism for study. They were written or edited by Confucius.

Five Pillars—The foundational principles and practices of Islam that were set forth by Muhammad and are practiced by all Muslims.

Four Books—During the Ming and Qing Dynasties, the accepted curriculum to be studied and passed in order to hold civil office.

Four Sights—The inspiration to become a monk for Siddhartha the Buddha, the four sights were an old crippled man (old age), a diseased man (illness), a decaying corpse (death), and finally an ascetic that Siddhartha encountered on an unannounced journey outside of the palace.

Gentile—A person who is not of Jewish origin.

Great Disappointment—The occasion when many Adventists left William Miller when Jesus failed to return after the second predicted time.

Gupta dynasty—240–550 CE, when the Gupta Empire ruled India with political peace and prosperity.

gurus—From the Sanskrit for "teacher," Hindu teachers and guides in philosophical and spiritual matters.

Hadith—A word meaning "story," the sayings and stories of Muhammad that are meant to form guidance for living out religion.

hafiz—A Muslim who has memorized the *Qur'an*.

halakhic—From the Hebrew meaning "way," Jewish law that covers all aspects of the life of an individual and of the community.

harakiri—Ritual suicide by disembowelment practiced by the Japanese samurai or formally decreed by a court in lieu of the death penalty.

Hasidism—From the Hebrew meaning "pious," a movement within Judaism founded in eighteenth-century Poland where pious devotion to God is as important as study of Torah.

Havdalah—A religious ceremony that symbolically ends the Shabbat, usually recited over kosher wine or kosher grape juice.

Hellenization—The adoption of Greek ways and speech as happened in the case of Jews living in the Diaspora.

heresy—For Christians, an obstinate denial after Baptism to believe a truth that must be believed with divine and Catholic faith, or an obstinate doubt about such truth.

Hijrah—A term meaning "migration," it recalls the escape of Muhammad from his enemies in 622 CE and the beginning of the establishment of Islam. The Hijra marks the start of the Islamic calendar.

Holy of Holies—The sanctuary inside the tabernacle in the Temple of Jerusalem where the Ark of the Covenant was kept.

hsien—Means "immortal." It refers to a Taoist who has reached his or her ultimate goal—physical immortality.

iconoclasm—The "breaking of icons," the belief that there should be no human depiction of the sacred for it places the icon as a source of worship rather than what the image represents.

icons—Religious images or paintings that are traditional among many Eastern Christians.

idolatry—Giving worship to something or someone other than the one, true God.

Imam—The leader for prayer at a mosque who is chosen for his knowledge of Islam and his personal holiness.

Incarnation—Meaning "enfleshed," for Christians it is the taking on of human nature by God's Son.

inculturation—Defined Pope John Paul II as "the incarnation of the Gospel in native cultures and also the introduction of these cultures into the life of the Church."

intercession—Making an offering or saying a prayer or petition to God on behalf of another.

Investigative Judgment—According to the Adventists, the time prior to the Second Coming when judgment will take place on the living and the dead.

Ka'bah—The first Islamic shrine, which Muslims believe was built by Abraham. Destroyed by pagans, it was reclaimed by Muhammad when he captured Mecca in the seventh century.

kami—The Japanese name for any kind of spiritual force or power.

kami body—An object in which it is believed the kami descends during a Shinto worship service. Often, the object is a mirror or sword.

kamidana—From the Japanese for "kami shelf," a place for a home shrine dedicated to kami.

karma—Based on the belief in reincarnation, the Hindu and Buddhist belief that the form the soul will take in the next life is determined by its behavior in this life.

kimono—A long robe with wide sleeves traditionally worn with a broad sash as an outer garment by the Japanese.

koan—A paradox that is to be meditated upon that is used to train Zen Buddhist monks to abandon ultimate dependence on reason and to force them into gaining sudden intuitive enlightenment.

kosher—From the Hebrew word *kaser*, meaning "proper." Commonly, it refers to food permitted by Jewish dietary laws. Jews observe kosher laws to remind themselves that they are to be a holy and separate people.

lamas—In Tibetan Buddhism, teachers and often heads of monasteries.

li—From the Chinese meaning "proper" or "rites," it is the practice of proper behavior specific to one's relationship to another as well as the rituals that must be properly performed in order for one to be called a chun-tzu.

liturgy—A definite set of forms for public religious worship, the official public worship of the Church. The Seven Sacraments, especially the Eucharist, are the primary forms of liturgical celebrations.

Lotus Sutra—A Mahayana Buddhist text where Enlightenment is made available not only to monastics, but to all because of the great compassion of bodhisattvas.

Magisterium—The official teaching authority of the Church. The Magisterium is the bishops in communion with the successor of Peter, the Bishop of Rome (pope).

Mahayana Buddhism—Literally the "Great Ox Cart." This branch of Buddhism differs from Theravada Buddhism because it accommodates a greater number of people from all walks of life.

Mandate of Heaven—The Chinese concept of legitimacy used to support the rule of the kings of the Chou dynasty and later the emperors of China, in which Heaven would bless the authority of a just ruler, but would give the Mandate to another if the ruler proved unjust.

mantra—A sacred verbal formula that is repeated in prayer or meditation.

martyr—A witness to the truth of faith, who endures even death to be faithful to his or her beliefs.

maya—Sanskrit for "illusion." A teaching of the Upanishads that says that only Brahman is permanent; everything else is only an illusion.

menorah—A candelabra with seven or nine lights that is used in Jewish worship.

mezuzah—Meaning "doorpost," a small parchment containing Jewish scripture, usually the Sh'ma, that is placed in a case on or near the right doorframe at the home of an observant Jew.

Middle Way—The Buddhist teaching that liberation from samsura comes neither through severe ascetical practices nor through wild indulgences, but in the middle of the spectrum between those two opposites.

Midrash—The type of biblical interpretation found in rabbinic literature, especially the Talmuds. Midrash assumes that the Scriptures provide answers for every situation and every question in life.

millenialists—People who believe that at his Second Coming, Jesus and his followers will rule on earth for one thousand years.

mitzvot—A commandment of the Jewish law.

monotheistic—Subscribing to the doctrine or belief that there is only one God.

Mormon—The name for an ancient prophet believed to have compiled a sacred history of the Americans, which was then translated by Joseph Smith in 1830 as the *Book of Mormon.*

myths—Traditional or ancient stories that help to provide a worldview of a people by explaining their creation, customs, or ideals.

Neo-Confucianism—A movement in the eleventh century CE that promulgated the resurgence of Confucianism while reinterpreting it in the light of Taoist and Buddhist influences.

Nirvana—Meaning "to extinguish" or "to blow out," it refers to the extinction of suffering, impermanence, delusion, and all that keeps the life cycle (samsara) going. Nirvana is the spiritual goal for all Buddhists.

Original Sin—The condition of sinfulness that all humans share, resulting from Adam's first sin of disobedience.

Pagoda—A tower in eastern Asia, usually with roofs curving upward at the division of each of several stories and erected as a temple or memorial.

Pala dynasty—The empire that controlled the Indian subcontinent from the eighth to twelfth centuries. The word *pala* means "protector."

Pali Canon—The authoritative Buddhism scripture of Theravada Buddhists written in the Pali language, and important, but not definitive, for Mahayana Buddhists. Another name for the *Tripitaka.*

patriarchates—Any of the bishops of the ancient or Eastern Orthodox seas of Constantonople, Alexandria, Antioch, and Jerusalem or the ancient and Western see of Rome with authority over the bishops.

polygamy—The taking of more than one spouse in marriage, a practice originally permitted by Mormons.

pope—From the Latin word for "papa," the pope is the Bishop of Rome and has primacy over the other bishops in the Catholic Church.

Qur'an—In Muslim belief, God's final revelation, superceding both the Jewish and Christian Bibles. The word means "recite" or "recitation."

rabbi—Hebrew for "my master" or "my teacher." A rabbi became known as someone who was authorized to teach and judge in matters of Jewish law.

Ramadan—The Fourth Pillar of Islam, which is a month of prayer and fasting that commemorates the Night of Power, the first revelation to Muhammad by God.

relics—Items of religious devotion, especially a piece of the body or personal items of an important religious figure.

Sacrament of the Anointing of the Sick—A sacrament of healing in which the healing and loving touch of Christ is extended through the Church to those who are seriously ill or dying.

samsara—The experience of birth, life, and death over and over again until one has achieved oneness with Brahman.

samurai warriors—From the Japanese word for "to serve," a hereditary feudal warrior class who cultivated virtues such as loyalty, honor, and courage, and served Japanese rulers.

sangha—At first just the Buddhist monastic community, later it came to describe the entire community of monks, nuns, and lay people.

Sanskrit—An ancient language of India that is the language of Hinduism and the *Vedas.* It is derived from a word that means "perfected."

satyagraha—The policy of non-violent resistance initiated by Gandhi as a means for pressing political reform.

sect—A religious group that separates from the larger religious denomination.

Shinto—Meaning "the way of the gods," from the Chinese *shin tao.* It has its roots in *animism,* a belief that says there is a spirit, or god, in all things. Japanese are especially in tune to the presence of gods and spirits in nature.

Shoah—Hebrew for "calamity," it refers to the mass murder of Jews by the Nazis during World War II.

shogunate—A form of military government that ruled Japan until the nineteenth century.

shruti—A canon of Hindu scripture, it is from a word that means "what is heard."

Soka Gakkai—Founded in 1930, it emphasized the power of the *Lotus Sutra* and advocated non-violence. Today it is not only the largest of Japan's "new religions," but it is also an international organization.

soma—A hallucinogenic beverage that was used as an offering to Hindu gods and used in Vedic ritual sacrifices.

spirit tablet—A household shrine set up to honor ancestors.

surahs—Chapters or sections in the *Qur'an*. Each surah is a separate revelation received by Muhammad.

Talmud—Two long collections of Jewish religious literature that are commentaries on the Mishnah, the Hebrew code of laws that emerged about 200 CE.

tantric—A word to describe Hindu literature written in Sanskrit and concerned with rituals acts of body, speech, and mind.

Taoism—From the root word *Tao*, meaning "the way." Tao is considered to be the driving force of the universe.

theocracy—A government that is ruled by God or by one who is divinely inspired.

transcendent—A term that means "lying beyond the ordinary range of perception."

Transcendental Meditation—A technique derived from Hinduism that promotes deep relaxation through reciting a mantra.

transubstantiation—The term used to express how the reality (substance) of bread and wine changes into the reality of Jesus' risen and glorified body and blood in the Eucharist.

Tripitaka—From the Sanskrit meaning "Three Baskets," and also known as the *Pali Canon* in Theravada Buddhism, the compilation of three collections of early Buddhist texts.

ulama—A Muslim scholar trained in Islam and Islamic law.

Vajrayana Buddhism—Literally "Diamond Vehicle," it is the prominent branch of Buddhism in Tibet.

Vedas—Ancient scriptures that are the foundation of Hinduism. They were composed in Sanskrit. The most important part of the *Vedas* is the Rig Veda, which consists of 1,028 hymns praising the gods of the Aryan tribes who invaded India from the northwest around 2,000 BCE.

witnessing—Giving testimony of one's religious faith to another.

wudu—The ritual washing of the face, hands, arms, top of head, and feet that a Muslim must perform before salah, the second pillar of Islam.

wu-wei—Meaning "action without action," it centers on allowing nature to evolve without human interference.

yin and yang—Meaning "shaded and sunny," they are opposite but complementary extremes in Chinese culture.

yoga—A Hindu discipline aimed at training the consciousness for a state of perfect spiritual insight and tranquility.

zazen—In Zen Buddhism, seated meditation. The instructions for zazen direct the disciple to sit in a quiet room breathing rhythmically and easily, with legs fully or half crossed, spine and head erect.

Zionism—From the name Zion (the historic land of Israel), it is a movement with origins in the nineteenth century that sought to restore a Jewish homeland in Palestine in response to anti-Semitism.

Notes

1. Both quotations are taken from Declaration on the Relationship of the Church to Non-Christian Religions, Vatican Council II: *The Conciliar and Post Conciliar Documents, Austin Flannery, O.P.*, editor. 1975. Northport, New York: *Costello Publishing Company.*

2. The *Vedas* are a collection of revelations believed to have been given to the ancient sages by the gods. Meaning "knowledge," the *Vedas* contained the knowledge the religious leaders needed to perform religious duties. The *Vedas* were memorized and orally transmitted. To this day, there are Hindu religious leaders who have memorized the *Vedas*.

3. Quoted from *My Journey, My Prayer*, by Sr. Bernadette Vetter H.M. Villa Maria, PA: The Center for Learning, 1991

4. Reported from Mike Lynch at www.heraldnet.com/ stories/06/07/15/100out_f1star-watch001.cfm.

5. Quoted from an article by Alan Watts (www.alanwatts.com/Taoism.html).

6. Quoted from *Reading About the World, Volume 1*, edited by Paul Brians, Mary Gallwey, Douglas Hughes, Michael Myers Michael Neville, Roger Schlesinger, Alice Spitzer, and Susan Swan. American Heritage Custom Publishing.

7. The excerpts on Mount Fuji are taken from *Sacred Mountains of the World* by Edwin Baldwin. University of California Press, 1997 www.karl-loren.com/ogc/research/r4.htm#6.

8. Quoted from *The World's Religions,* by Whilst/ Smart. Englewood Cliffs, NJ: Prentice-Hall, Inc., 1989.

9. Quoted from *World Faiths, second edition*, by S.A. Nigosian. New York: St. Martin's Press, 1994).

10. Adapted from an article by Jan M. Faust (ABC News.com, September 12, 1997 © 1997 ABC News and Starwave).

11. *CARA Report.* "New Directions in Youth Ministry: A National Study of Youth Ministry Participants," 1996.

12. Quoted from 1 *Apologiae* 67: PG 6, 429 and 432.

Index

287; in Islam, 145–47; of Japanese religion, 332–33
Reform Judaism, 42
Reincarnation. *See* Cycle of rebirth
Relics of Buddha, 238
Religion and state, 146. *See also* Church, and state
Religious diversity. *See* Diversity
Religious freedom, 14

Religious practices. *See* Practices of religion
Religious tradition: aspects of, 17; moral code of, 20; practices of, 19. *See also* Religious practices
Repentance, 54
Resurrection: doctrine of, 33; of Jesus, 85
Revelation: in Islam, 151–52; in Judaism, 49
Ricci, Mateo, 244
Rig Veda, 194
Rinzai Zen, 330
Rishis, 186
Rites of passage, 21
Rituals: and sacred stories, 18; and sacred times, 20; in Shinto, 345
Roman Empire, 34, 36; and Christianity, 84–90
Rome, 86
Rosh Hashanah, 52, 53–54
Russell, Charles, 370–71
Russia: and Buddhism, 245; Christianity in, 96; persecution of Jews in, 41–42
Rutherford, Joseph, 371

■ S
Sabbath, 57–59; and Seventh-day Adventists, 368, 369
Sacrament of the Anointing of the Sick, 379
Sacraments, 113–14; Protestants on, 94. *See also particular sacraments*
Sacred meals, 19
Sacred places, 21; in Buddhism, 265–68; in Chinese religion, 309–11; in Christianity, 116–18; in Hinduism, 214–19; in Islam, 168–71; in Japanese religion, 344–47; in Judaism, 61–65
Sacred stories and sacred scriptures, 17–18, 20; in Buddhism, 246–51; in Chinese religions, 293–96; in Christianity, 99–103; of

Hinduism, 193–97; in Islam, 151–54; in Japanese religions, 335–36; of Judaism, 45–47; of Sikhism, 212–13
Sacred times: in Buddhism, 257–64; in Catholicism, 349–50; in Chinese religions, 304–9; in Christianity, 109–16; in Hinduism, 207–14; in Islam, 166–68; in Japanese religions, 341–42, 348; in Judaism, 52–61; in religious tradition, 20–21
Sacrifice: in Chinese folk religion, 283; in Hinduism, 187, 194; in Islam, 167; as religious practice, 19
Sadducees, 33
Saints: feast days to, 350; images of, 222; veneration of, 223, 313–14
Saladin, 38
Salah. *See* Prayer, in Islam
Salt Lake City, 363
Salvation: Catholics on, 95; Christianity on, 105; and Church, 108, 119; Jehovah's Witnesses on, 372; and Jesus, 173; of Jews, 71; of Muslims, 172; Protestants on, 94; and world religions, 15–16. *See also* Moksha
Samsara, 188, 201, 253; and Nirvana, 233; Sikhism on, 213; and suffering, 270. *See also* Cycle of rebirth
Samuel, 31
Samuri warriors, 339
Sangha, 237, 255–57, 263; purification of, 239
Sannyasin, 206
Sanskrit, 188, 194; and Buddhist scriptures, 247
Sarah: in Islam, 160; and Judaism, 30
Saraswati, 200
Sarnath, 267
Satan: in Islam, 161; Jehovah's Witnesses on, 371, 372
Satyagraha, 191, 202
Saudi Arabia: and Islamic fundamentalism, 146; and Muhammad, 136
Saul, 31
Sawm. See Fasting, in Islam
Science and Health, 376, 377–78
Scripture. *See titles of particular texts*
Seal of the Prophets. *See* Muhammad

Christian Scripture INDEX

Catechism of the Catholic Church INDEX

Photo Credits

Agnus Images 110

Associated Press 175 © Michael Conroy, 212 © Aman Sharma, 363 © Toby Talbot, 365 © Mormon Church, 366, 369, 373 © Linda Radin/Stringer, 376 © Adam Hunger/Stringer.

Corbis Images 28, 40 © Julia Donoso/Corbis Sygma, 44 © Bettmann/Corbis, 58 © Najlah Feanny/Corbis, 60 bottom © Reuters/Corbis, 71 © Bettmann/Corbis, 94 (4 photos) © The Gallery Collection/Corbis, © Bettmann/Corbis, © The Gallery Collection/Corbis, © Archivo Iconografico, S.A./Corbis, 97 © Alan Levenson/Corbis, 112 © Con Tanasiuk/Design Pics/Corbis, 123 © Pascal Deloche/Godong/Corbis, 140 © Stefano Bianchetti/Corbis, 147 © Bettmann/Corbis, 148 © Hulton-Deutsch Collection/Corbis, 149 © Michael Ochs Archives/Corbis bottom © Ralf-Finn Hestoft/Corbis, 155 © Reuters/Corbis, 161 © Money Sharma/epa/Corbis, 166 © Ali Jarekji/Reuters/Corbis, 190 © Bettmann/Corbis, 200 © Brooklyn Museum/Corbis (top), 200 © Rafiqur Rahman/Reuters/Corbis (bottom), 243 © Reuters/Corbis, 264 © John W. Gertz/zefa/Corbis, 281 © Pascal Deloche/Godong/Corbis, 286 © Archivo Iconografico, S.A./Corbis, 291 © Michael Maslan Historic Photographs/Corbis, 305 © Franklin Lau/Corbis (top),305 © Michael S. Yamashita/Corbis (bottom) 306 © Buddy Mays/Corbis (top), 306 © Kin Cheung/Reuters/Corbis (bottom), 307 © Gareth Brown/Corbis, 326 © Asia Art & Archeology, Inc./Corbis, 332 © Archivo Iconografico, S.A./Corbis, 358 © Polak Matthew/Corbis Sygma, 381(4 images) © Bettmann/Corbis, © Bettmann/Corbis, © Charles E. Smith/Corbis, © Frances Benjamin Johnston/Corbis.

Jupiter Images 136, 192, 217 © Rajat Ghosh/OnAsia/Jupiter Images

Thomas Merton Center 269 © Photograph of Thomas Merton by Sibylle Akers. Used with permission of the Merton Legacy Trust and the Thomas Merton Center at Bellarmine University.

Northwind Picture Archive 136

Wolfgang Schmidt 256 (2), 260

Superstock 30, 84.